Encountering Jesus in the New Testament

Teacher's Manual

Michael Pennock

ave maria press   **Notre Dame, IN**

Text Introduction, Bibliography, Resources, and Tests by Michael Pennock

Lesson Plan contributions by Kenneth Ogorek

Project Editor: Michael Amodei

© 2003 by Ave Maria Press, Inc.

International Standard Book Number: 0-87793-953-5

Cover and text design by Katherine Robinson Coleman

Cover photos by Rubberball Productions and Photodisc, interior photos by Photodisc

Printed and bound in the United States of America.

Contents

Introduction to the Teacher Manual

Thank you for choosing *Encountering Jesus in the New Testament* to use with your students. May the Holy Spirit be with you and your students and enflame you with the love of the Lord and his holy word. May we all, catechists and students alike, draw close to the Light of the Word so we can be beacons of the Way, the Truth, and the Life. May we be instruments that our Lord and Savior uses to promote his reign of peace and justice.

The Second Vatican Council's *Constitution on Divine Revelation* tells us of the importance of Sacred Scripture in the life of the church. Along with Tradition, it is the "supreme rule of faith," transmitting God's word and filled with the voice of the Holy Spirit. Along with the *Catechism of the Catholic Church*, scripture is a fundamental source of our catechetical activity (see the *General Directory for Catechesis*, #127-128).

We believe the inspired scriptures impart God's word. In them we meet the Word, and the Holy Spirit opens our hearts to the love of the Father. What a serious duty we have to break open the scriptures in a way that the students might listen to God's word intelligently. As ministers of God's holy word, may the Lord bless us in our vocation. May we teach our students with wisdom, witness to them with conviction, and love them patiently as the Lord does us, his co-workers in the vineyard.

This Introduction to the Teacher's Manual will cover:

- catechetical dimensions for a course on Jesus and the New Testament
- several thoughts and applications for teaching Jesus in the New Testament
- an overview of the key features of each chapter of the Student Text
- the curriculum model used in both the Student Text and this Teacher's Manual
- the format of this Manual
- mailing addresses for films and videos
- a weekly planning chart

Catechetical Dimensions

Christocentrism of Catechesis

The *General Directory for Catechesis* reminds us of some important truths about catechesis that can be singularly realized in a course on Jesus and the New Testament. Important quotes from this document are given with some discussion following.

- Jesus Christ not only transmits the word of God: he *is* the Word of God. . . . Thus what must characterize the message transmitted by catechesis is, above all, its "christocentricity."

- The fundamental task of catechesis is to present Christ and everything in relation to him. . . .

- Christocentricity means that Christ is the "center of salvation history," presented by catechesis. . . .

- The gospel message does not come from man, but is the Word of God. The Church, and in her name, every catechist, can say with truth: "my teaching is not from myself: it comes from the one who sent me" (Jn 7:16). Thus all that is transmitted by catechesis is "the teaching of Jesus Christ, the truth that he communicates, or more precisely, the Truth that he is."

- The gospels, which narrate the life of Jesus, are central to the catechetical message. . . .

- Every mode of presentation must always be christocentric-trinitarian: "Through Christ to the Father in the Holy Spirit."[1]

It is clear from these citations that:

Jesus is the center of our teaching endeavors. In the words of Pope John Paul II's *Catechesi Tradendae*, "Everything else is taught in reference to him—and it is Christ alone who teaches" (# 6).[2] In a course devoted to Jesus, especially as he reveals himself to us in the New Testament, we will have little difficulty fulfilling the requirement of "Christocentrism in catechesis." The points highlighted above also remind us that we are teaching Jesus himself, not ourselves. To do this effectively and authentically we must draw on Church teaching and scripture. However, no teaching about Jesus will "ring true" with students unless we too have a deep love for the Lord who has called us to proclaim his message. Our commission is to share our faith to help enliven and strengthen the faith of our students. We have been invited into a personal relationship with a living Lord. As catechists, we have accepted this gift and—in the name of the church—are sharing with our students Jesus' invitation to a fuller life. We must keep in mind that we really have two goals: *knowledge about* and *knowledge of* Jesus Christ, our Lord and Savior.

The focus of our teaching is not a body of abstract truths but communication of the living God as revealed to us in Christ Jesus. A course on Jesus in the New Testament is really good news for our students. In it students can hear the good news that they are loved. Everyone, but especially teenagers who live in a world that treats them mainly as consumers to be exploited, needs to be reassured of God's unconditional love for them in Jesus. The gospel of Jesus is a true counterpoint to a culture of death and isolation. Jesus reaffirms our dignity and worth, inviting us into a personal relationship with him, one that can transform our lives, giving us meaning and direction. Pope John Paul II stated it well in writing of a genuine faith education for adolescents:

> The revelation of Jesus Christ as friend, guide and model, capable of being admired but also imitated; the revelation of his message which provides an answer to fundamental questions; the revelation of the loving plan of Christ the Savior as the Incarnation of the only authentic love and as the possibility of uniting the human race. . . .(*Catechesi Tradendae*, #38)

Our students need to know that the Lord calls them personally. High school religious education presumes some pre-evangelization and even more evangelization. However, many of our students have not heard (or were not ready to hear) the gospel of the Lord. So we need to take time to review the basics, to proclaim Jesus to them (through media, faith testimonials, Bible reading, enthusiastic lecturing, etc.), to correct mistaken notions about Jesus and Church teaching on him. But we reach a point where some genuine catechesis can take place, that is, an enriching and deepening reflection on that which is proclaimed.

Catechesis on Jesus must "draw its content from the living source of the word of God transmitted in Tradition and Scriptures" (*Catechesi Tradendae,* **#27).** Central to this catechetical effort is Jesus' call to faith. Jesus comforts those who are upset, but he also upsets the comfortable. Jesus' message of love and salvation demands response, that is, faith and action. As sharers of the gospel, we must also challenge our students to be and do more. Jesus reminded us that faith without action is empty and does not guarantee salvation.

Students need to learn something about Jesus: his teachings, his miracles, the passion narrative, how the gospels were written, the various gospel portraits of him, how the early Church spread his message, dogmatic formulae developed through the ages, how the media present him today, and so forth. A real challenge, though, is to help our students see that a growing knowledge of friendship with Jesus is a lifelong task worth pursuing above any other. In teaching the content, we want to leave students with the impression that there is so much more to know and learn about Jesus. In showing them ways to pray to the Lord, we want them to sense that ending a course on Jesus is just the beginning of a lifelong journey with him.

In teaching about Jesus and the New Testament, however, we must also appeal to the affective and behavioral dimensions of our students. Jesus' message about the kingdom requires *metanoia*, repentance. To encourage this basic change of mind and heart, the Student Text includes various exercises, prayer reflections, activities, and discussions to involve the whole learner. Students need "to know," but also to discover, develop, respond, compare and contrast, pursue, identify, celebrate, feel, pray, live, proclaim, show concern, and discuss what they learn.

Finally, any course on Jesus recognizes that Christ wills the salvation of all people, that God's grace reaches all people. However, as Catholic teachers working in Catholic institutions, we need not apologize for presenting our belief that Jesus founded his Church and lives in it and works through it. The Student Text, though respecting the beliefs of non-Christians and non-Catholics, draws on the Catholic tradition to present Jesus: on its official teachings as summarized in the *Catechism of the Catholic Church,* on sound biblical scholarship primarily from Catholic scholars, and on the faith and sacramental life of Catholics through the centuries.

We catechists can be effective and authentic only if we are fully committed to Jesus Christ. In the words of *Sharing the Light of Faith,*

> Faith must be shared with conviction, joy, love, enthusiasm, and hope. "The summit and center of catechetical formation lies in an aptitude and ability to communicate the Gospel message." This is possible only when the catechist believes in the gospel and its power to transform lives. To give witness to the gospel, the catechist must establish a living, ever-deepening relationship with the Lord. He or she must be a person of prayer. (#207)[3]

Elements of Adolescent Catechesis

A course on Jesus, especially as the gospels present him, will note several critical elements in adolescent catechesis. *Catechesi Tradendae* (#21) stresses four elements of catechesis:

1. It must be systematic; that is, not improvised but programmed to a precise goal.
2. It must deal with essentials, not claiming to tackle all the disputed questions or make itself into theological research or scientific exegesis.
3. It must be sufficiently complete, not stopping short of initial proclamation.
4. It must be open to other factors of Christian life.

Systematic

Teaching scripture is a worthy end in itself. All "catechesis must be impregnated and penetrated by the thought, the spirit and the outlook of the Bible and the Gospels through assiduous contact with the texts themselves" (*Catechesi Tradendae*, #27). A basic introduction to Jesus in the New Testament and Church Tradition should have pride of place in a four-year high school religious education curriculum. In addition, students who achieve basic biblical literacy from their study of scripture will advance their knowledge in all religious education courses, serving well the laudable goal of a systematic catechesis.

Essentials

Sharing the Light of Faith (#60) highlights some essentials of a course on New Testament and Christology:

1. Students should have and use their own copies of the Bible. (This text quotes from *The New American Bible with Revised New Testament*.)

2. Catechesis should explain the number and structure of the biblical books, speak of them as God's inspired words, and treat their major themes, for example, creation, salvation, and final fulfillment.

3. Literary form, authorship, and history of the composition of the biblical books should be presented so students might grasp what the sacred writers really intended.

4. In the New Testament, the gospels enjoy a pre-eminent position as the principal witness of the life and teachings of Jesus.

5. According to their ability, students should have an acquaintance with the infancy narratives, miracles and parables of Jesus' public life, and the accounts of his passion, death, and resurrection.

6. Catechesis should also develop the principal themes found in the epistles, give some attention to the literary characteristics of all the New Testament books, and introduce critical exegesis.

7. Major Old Testament themes should be presented as preparing for Christ: creation and redemption, sin and grace, the covenant with Abraham and the Chosen people, the exodus from Egypt and the Sinai covenant, the Babylonian captivity and the return, the Emmanuel and suffering servant passages in Isaiah, and so forth.

8. Students should be encouraged to pray with and meditate on the meaning of the scriptures for their lives.

9. Memorization has a role to play in learning the Bible.

10. Furthermore, both Testaments should be used to show how Biblical faith and teaching are an important foundation for Catholic social teaching (*Sharing the Light of Faith*, #151-154).

In addition, to isolate the Church's essential teachings about Jesus, the Student Text draws from the relevant sections of the *Catechism of the Catholic Church* as its major reference source for teachings about divine revelation, God's word, and the Word and teachings about him. These sections of the *CCC* are treated in the Student Text as follows:

Description of section of the *Catechism*	*CCC* numbers	Text chapter(s)
Christ, the unique Word of Sacred Scripture	101-104; 134	1
Inspiration	105-108; 135-136	1
Holy Spirit: Interpreter of Scripture	109-119; 137	1
New Testament canon and stages in formation of the gospels	124-127; 138-139	1
Unity of the two Testaments	128-130; 140	1
Scripture and the life of the Church	131-133	10
Gospel: God sends his Son	422-425	Introduction
Christ: Heart of catechesis	426-429	Introduction
The name *Jesus*	430-435; 452	Introduction
The title *Christ*	436-440; 453	Introduction
Only Son of God	441-445; 454	Introduction
Lord	446-451; 455	Introduction
Centrality of the Incarnation	101-102	Introduction
	456-463	7
True God, true man	464-469	9
Early heresies about Jesus	465-467	9
Key dogmatic teachings about Jesus	468-483	9
Beliefs about Mary	484-511; 722-726; 963-975	6
Mysteries of Christ's life	512-570	3
➜ Christ living in each of us	519-521; 562	10
➜ Parables	541-546; 567	5
➜ Miracles	547-550	4
Paschal Mystery	571-573	4
Jesus and Israel	574-594	2, 4
Trial of Jesus	595-598	4
Christ's redemptive death	599-623	4
Jesus' death and burial	624-638	4
Resurrection of Jesus	639-658	7
Ascension of Jesus	659-667	7
Jesus the judge [discussed in relation to the Book of Revelation]	668-692	9
Christ lives in his Church by power of the Holy Spirit	737-747; 774-776; 779	10
Christ meets us in the sacraments	1113-1134	10
➜ Baptism	1279	
➜ Confirmation	1316	
➜ Matrimony	1660-1661; 1664	
➜ Holy orders	1592	
➜ Anointing of the sick	1527; 1532	
➜ Reconciliation	1486-1487; 1496	
➜ Eucharist	1406-1407; 1409; 1413; 1415-1416	
Jesus: Teacher of the New Law	1965-1970; 1983-1985	5
Meeting Jesus in prayer	2565; 2607-2615; 2620-2621	10
The Lord's Prayer	2759-2865	5, 6

Sufficiently Complete

The United States bishops' *Guidelines on Doctrine for Catechetical Materials* point out four essential dimensions of catechesis to be included in a student text:

1. Catechesis must proclaim Christ's message, a task that takes place within the Church community which is a believing community.
2. Catechesis must help develop Christian community by keeping traditions alive and recommending activities that build up the Church.
3. Catechesis should lead people to worship and prayer.
4. Catechesis should clearly explain the Church's moral teaching to help students strive for holiness and witness to Christian virtues, that is, to motivate them to Christian living and service, especially respect for life, service to others, and working to bring about peace and justice.[4]

The Student Text, assisted by this Teacher's Manual, strives to do all four. For example, it often reiterates the good news of Jesus' message. It fosters community through various exercises, for example, reflections that ask students to discuss with others. It includes suggestions on how to use the New Testament to pray, reviews Eucharistic themes, and underscores the value of reconciliation. Finally, the Student Text and the Teacher's Manual review Jesus' moral teaching and present several opportunities for students to engage in a service project.

The following statements from *Guidelines on Doctrine for Catechetical Materials* are especially noted in the focus of the content of the Student Text:

#4 Describe the many ways that God has spoken and continues to speak in the lives of human beings and how the fullness of revelation is made known in Christ. . . .

#5 Explain the inspired scriptures according to the mind of the Church, while not neglecting the contributions of modern biblical scholarship in the use of various methods of interpretation, including historical-critical and literary methods. . . .

#7 Reflect the wisdom and continuing relevance of the Church Fathers and incorporate a sense of history that recognizes doctrinal development and provides background for understanding change in Church policy practice.

#8 Explain the documents of the Second Vatican Council as an authoritative and valid expression of the deposit of faith as contained in Holy Scripture and the living tradition of the Church. . . .

#13 Focus on the heart of the Christian message: salvation from sin and death through the person and work of Jesus, with special emphasis on the Paschal mystery—his passion, death, and resurrection.

#14 Emphasize the work and person of Jesus Christ as the key and chief point of Christian reference in reading the scriptures. . . .

#15 Present Jesus as true God, who came into the world for us and for our salvation, and as true man who thinks with a human mind, acts with a human will, loves with a human heart . . . highlighting the uniqueness of his divine mission so that he appears as more than a great prophet and moral teacher.

#16 Describe how the Holy Spirit continues Christ's work in the world, in the Church, and in the lives of believers. . . .

#17 Maintain the traditional language, grounded in the scriptures, that speaks of the Holy Trinity as Father, Son, and Spirit, and apply, where appropriate, the principles of inclusive language as approved by the NCCB. . . .

#20   Emphasize the missionary nature of the Church and the call of the individual Christians to proclaim the gospel wherever there are people to be evangelized, at home and abroad. . . .

#21   Nourish and teach the faith and, because there is often a need for initial evangelization, aim at opening the heart and arousing the beginning of faith so that individuals will respond to the Word of God and Jesus' call to discipleship. . . .

#22   Emphasize that Jesus Christ gave the apostles a special mission to teach and that today this teaching authority is exercised by the pope and bishops, who are successors to St. Peter and the apostles.

#23   Highlight the history and distinctive tradition of the Church of Rome and the special charism of the pope as successor of St. Peter in guiding and teaching the universal Church and assuring the authentic teaching of the gospel.

#30   Integrate the history of the Jews in the work of salvation so that, on the one hand, Judaism does not appear marginal and unimportant and, on the other hand, the Church and Judaism do not appear as parallel ways of salvation. . . .

#35   Explain the biblical basis for the liturgical cult of Mary as mother of God and disciple *par excellence*; and describe her singular role in the life of Christ and the story of salvation (*Lumen Gentium*, 66, 67).

#36   Foster Marian devotions and explain the Church's particular beliefs about Mary (e.g., the Immaculate Conception, Virgin Birth, and Assumption). . . .

#39   Emphasize God's saving and transforming presence in the sacraments. In the Eucharist, Christ is present not only in the person of the priest but in the assembly and in the Word and, uniquely, in the eucharistic species of bread and wine that become the Body and Blood of Christ. . . .

#40   Link the Eucharist to Christ's sacrifice on the cross. . . .

#52   Introduce prayer as a way of deepening one's relationship with God and explain the ends of prayer so that a spirit of adoration, thanksgiving, petition, and contrition permeates the daily lives of Christians (NCD, 140).

#61   Present Catholic teaching on justice, peace, mercy, and social issues as integral to the gospel message and the Church's prophetic mission. . . .

#62   Explain that the Church's teaching on the "option for the poor" means that while Christians are called to respond to the needs of everyone, they must give their greatest attention to individuals and communities with the greatest needs.

#67   Teach that though sin abounds in the world, grace is even more abundant because of the salvific work of Christ (NCD, 98).

#73   Integrate biblical themes and scriptural references in the presentation of doctrine and moral teaching, and encourage a hands-on familiarity with the Bible (NCD, 60a).

#74   Challenge Catholics to critique and transform contemporary values and behaviors in light of the gospel and the Church's teaching.

#75   Maintain a judicious balance between personal expression and memorization, emphasizing that it is important both for the community and themselves that individuals commit to memory selected biblical passages. . . .

#76   Provide for a variety of shared prayer forms and experiences that lead to an active participation in the liturgical life of the Church and private prayer (NCD, 145, 264).

#77   Continually hold before their intended audience the ideal of living a life based on the teachings of the Gospel.

#78   Include suggestions for service to the community that is appropriate to the age and abilities of the persons who are being catechized.

Open

Knowledge of the New Testament, of course, will influence other aspects of Christian or Catholic living. Its whole purpose is to get to know the Lord better so that we can love him more deeply and serve him more faithfully, especially through others. The text constantly challenges students to apply their learning so they can experience for themselves the truth of God's word and see that it does make a difference in their lives. The text concludes by challenging students to be open to making scripture reading, study, and prayer a lifelong task. Their study of scripture is only a beginning, not an end.

Teaching Jesus in the New Testament

Several unique situations arise in teaching a high school course on Jesus and the New Testament. (I write from the experience of teaching such a course for over thirty years.) Several of these situations are addressed in this section.

First, reading the biblical text itself should have pride of place in a course on the New Testament and Christology. Consider the Student Text as a *guide* to help students read the New Testament, not an end in itself. Therefore, the key text for the course must be the Bible itself. Every student should own a copy of the Bible, one with some explanatory footnotes in it, and one in which you can encourage them to write marginal notes, underline, highlight, and the like. The Student Text quotes from *The New American Bible with Revised New Testament. The New Revised Standard Version* is a highly regarded translation and available in a Catholic edition. *The New Jerusalem Bible* is a perennial Catholic favorite. The American Bible Society provides inexpensive Bibles. Student copies of the ABS's New Testament in *Today's English Version* (with Imprimatur) continue to sell for approximately two dollars.

It is certainly handier for students to use only a copy of the New Testament for this course rather than to carry around a copy of the entire Bible. However, be sure to have enough classroom copies of both Old and New Testaments so students can complete various exercises that ask them to check references in the Old Testament.

Second, we should try to connect biblical themes to student lives. We face enormous odds in tearing today's students away from the world of the video, Internet, and computer games to open a book and carefully study the meaning of words. Religious educators face even greater obstacles asking students to read the Bible, a book that, to them, seems foreign, old-fashioned, and out of touch. As a result, we must constantly show the relevance of the New Testament to the lives of our students. The Student Text and this Teacher's Manual include exercises and reflections to help students make the connection between God's word and their lives. Use these as well as your own witnessing, discussions, and exercises to relate the biblical themes to your students' lives.

One way to actively involve students is to assign a major ongoing project to engage them for several weeks and to help assess deeper learning. Listed below are suggestions that may help sustain their interest. Be sure to allot enough class time to set the assignment up, allow for cooperative learning or individual research, and sufficient time for presentations to the class:

➠ A Jesus journal of key quotes and daily reflections

➠ A scriptural exegesis of a key passage using approved commentaries; seminar-type presentation to classmates

➠ A PowerPoint presentation on: the mysteries of Jesus' life; Stations of the Cross (traditional and updated); Jesus in art through the ages

- After viewing a feature film on Jesus, write one's own script for a film about Jesus
- Parable assignment: mime presentation of a traditional parable; enactment of a parable modernized; a rewrite of a parable using a kingdom theme; a PowerPoint presentation on a parable; an exegesis of a parable using multiple scholarly resources; creation of a modern allegory based on a parable
- Writing a Jesus catechism for a particular age group (25-50 questions)
- Drawing/painting a portrait of Jesus
- Internet project: annotate a bibliography of 25-50 good websites on Jesus; share a Bible tour of holy sites; develop a Jesus contest of questions that could be answered by visiting specific websites; reading and reporting on some scholarly articles on various gospel questions regarding Jesus
- Sound lecture/audiotape on Jesus in music through the ages
- Trip to art gallery to view works inspired by the New Testament
- Reading and reporting on a "Jesus allegory" in a fictional work (e.g., play *Man of La Mancha*)
- Group mini-action project of service based on Matthew 25:31-46
- Design and lead a prayer service utilizing themes on discipleship
- Creation of an illustrated Jesus prayer book
- Writing of a five-page Jesus biography
- Outline of a homily on the kerygma to be delivered to various age groups
- Cartoon panels on a gospel story
- Creation of a Jesus Monopoly-like game to quiz knowledge about Jesus
- Debate between Paul and the Athenians
- Creation of a magazine on one of the gospels—using pictures, ads, stories, sidebars
- Film interviews of people regarding their beliefs about Jesus
- Draw Jesus icons
- Design a coat of arms for gospel personages
- Collect illustrations from art on Jesus symbols (*Ixthus*, *Chi Rho*, etc.); prepare presentation
- Write term paper on some aspect of New Testament life
- Write an epistle to imaginary Christian community in the style of St. Paul
- Compose a musical composition illustrating a biblical theme
- Design a Christmas crèche
- Create a word puzzle on terms used in this course, New Testament personages, titles of Christ, etc.
- Create a travelogue of Jesus' itinerary in Luke or Paul's journeys in Acts

Third, use the New Testament to help teach prayer. We have a wonderful opportunity to help students meet the living Lord when we have them read the Bible. The Student Text includes prayer and reflection exercises that reference the biblical text.

Fourth, and most importantly, we must transmit to our students a love of the New Testament.

As we all know, our love of something flows from our knowledge of it. It is hard to love what one does not know. A recent study showed that

➥ 60% of Americans can't name all Ten Commandments

➥ only 40% of them knew that Jesus delivered the Sermon on the Mount

➥ 63% cannot name all four gospels![5]

A key catechetical goal for us is that our students master a certain minimum fund of biblical knowledge that will make them biblically literate. The text assigns many New Testament passages for student reading. You undoubtedly will not cover everything suggested. It is recommended that you focus on the gospels, at least one major letter of Paul, a "Catholic" epistle, and key sections in Acts.

We certainly do not wish to overwhelm our students with work. We want to give them enough to show them the riches to be mined and give them a thirst for more. We must help them develop the skills to find answers to questions they may have in the future. We want the Lord to meet them in those key passages that speak to their own lives: questions about friendship, love, sin, salvation, forgiveness, priorities in life, sacrifice, the person of Jesus and his immense love for them, the power of the Holy Spirit and the gifts the Spirit bestows on God's children.

We are confident that if the students approach the Bible with open minds and searching hearts, the Lord will speak to their condition. Our own enthusiasm and love for God's word will show the way. May the Lord bless you in your efforts.

Features Common to the Student Text

There are several features common to the chapters in the Student Text. These include:

Introduction

• • • • • • • • •

The chapter Introductions include several common features.

Each chapter opens with a quote from the New Testament that is related to one of the themes developed in the chapter. This is most appropriate because, as the *General Directory for Catechesis* teaches:

> [T]he Church desires that in the ministry of the word, Sacred Scripture should have a pre-eminent position. In concrete terms, catechesis should be "an authentic introduction to *lectio divina*." . . . (§127)

Next there is a story or short anecdote that introduces one of the main topics of the chapter. For example, Chapter 6 tells of a father who lost his son at Disney World to call to mind the parable of the Prodigal Son, a key story Jesus told in Luke's gospel, the subject of this particular chapter of the text. These short stories or anecdotes serve as attention "grabbers" and help relate some aspect of the chapter to everyday life.

A brief topic outline gives a short overview of what is to come in the chapter.

An exercise that may require values clarification, self-reflection, mini-research into one of the themes of the chapter, a pre-test to pique student interest in what is to follow, or a post-test in the last chapter to check student recall of some important New Testament persons is also included in the chapter Introductions.

Scripture Reading

• • • • • • • • • • • •

Most of the exercises assigned in the Student Text ask students to read either whole books or various chapters and verses in the New Testament. Occasionally, students are also asked to read some Old Testament passages that link dramatically to the New Testament passages under consideration. The Student Text occasionally offers certain New Testament readings for the students to summarize for their classmates. You may, however, want all students to read all the assigned reading.

Journal Entries

• • • • • • • • • • •

Sprinkled throughout the chapters are suggestions for topical journal entries that ask the students to apply the learned material to their lives. These can be assigned for homework or in-class exercises. Journal-writing:

➳ encourages self-reflection

➳ provides a meaningful way to pray

➳ helps students apply, analyze, synthesize, and evaluate chapter learnings

➳ develops and hones writing skills

➳ organizes and helps in the retention of key ideas presented in the course

➳ gives students a sense of pride and ownership in the course.

Journal-keeping in a New Testament/Christology course also encourages lifelong reflection on one's own friendship with Jesus. Several journal exercises help students do this kind of reflection. For example, some suggested journal assignments include starters like:

➳ Jesus asks: "Do you love me?"

➳ Which person most reminds you of Jesus? Why?

➳ If Jesus were your age and attending your school, what would he be like?

➳ What are your three favorite titles of Jesus? Why?

Students are also instructed to record in their journals information they learned from several of the "mini-reading" assignments. The journal becomes, then, a handy log that helps students keep track of their assignments throughout the course.

Personal Reflections and Discussions

• •

All chapters of the Student Text include various personal reflection and discussion exercises. As previously indicated, students are sometimes directed to write their reflections in their journals, but you may wish them to record all their reflections there and use them as a prelude to class discussion.

Research Projects

• • • • • • • • • • •

Various chapters suggest students do further research beyond just reading the biblical word. For example, students are asked to consult a biblical dictionary (Chapters 1, 4, and 7) and Bible atlas (Chapter 1), consult some Internet sites to read more about the Dead Sea scrolls (Chapter 2), and analyze TV commercials for consumerism contrary to Jesus' message (Chapter 6).

Summary, Review Questions, and Terms to Know

Each chapter includes a list of Summary points followed by Review Questions which students could complete as homework assignments or journal entries. The review questions help students master the cognitive content of the chapter. After the review questions, students will find the definitions of important terms that they should know. Mastery of these will help students develop "religious literacy" and a common vocabulary of essential terms. The Chapter Tests provided with this Teacher's Manual were mostly composed from the Review Questions and Selected Terms sections of the chapters. The terms set aside for mastery include the following. You may wish to add to this list:

Allegory	Logos
Apocalypse	Lord
Ascension	Martyr
Assumption	Midrash
Canon of the Bible	Mystery
Catechesis	Parable
Christ	Paschal mystery
Christology	Pentateuch
Deuteropauline	Q
Dogma	Qumran
Eschatalogical	Paraclete
Evangelist	Pentecost
Glory of God	Priest
Gnosticism	Pseudonymous
Gospel	Sanhedrin
Hellenists	Scandal
Hierarchy	Septuagint
Kerygma	Synoptic gospels
Kingdom of God	Testament
Immaculate Conception	Torah
Incarnation	Transfiguration
Inspiration (biblical)	

Prayer Reflection

Each chapter has a concluding prayer reflection. Almost all of these reflections are drawn from some aspect of the scriptural word. A reflection is provided and an activity suggested as a follow-up to extend the prayer for the following days. In addition,

➬ throughout the text, prayer is presented as a constant theme stressed by Jesus and the New Testament

➬ a major catechesis on prayer is given in Chapter 3 as students are asked to study Jesus' didaches on prayer in Luke and Matthew

➬ Chapter 5 provides an extended personal meditation on the Lord's Prayer

- ➦ Chapter 6 asks students to do a self-check on personal prayer as a follow-up to a discussion of the need for persistence in prayer

- ➦ Chapter 10 discusses the role of prayer and scripture-reading as essential means to grow in holiness and friendship with Jesus. Various types of prayer are introduced as part of this discussion

- ➦ a number of journal entries require meditation, prayerful dialogue, or reflection

- ➦ some traditional prayers other than the Lord's Prayer are included in the Student Text, notably the *shema* (Dt 6:4-9) and Paul's hymn on Jesus' self-emptying in Philippians (*kenosis*)

- ➦ detailed directions on how to pray imaginatively with the Bible are included in Chapter 4. You might wish to spend a class going over this technique with your students, perhaps guiding them through the meditation on the Passion Narrative as provided at the end of Chapter 4.

Christian Lifestyle—Service

The Student Text integrates the important theme of Christian service in the following ways:

- ➦ Jesus is presented as a model of service. So is his mother Mary. Students are challenged to reflect on the meaning of Jesus' washing the feet of his disciples and to describe how this happens in their own lives.

- ➦ Several key exercises ask students to examine their gifts and commit themselves to use them in the service of others. Students are asked to analyze their future career choices in light of Jesus' call to serve.

- ➦ A major project on the theme of serving the hungry is introduced in Chapter 5 of the text.

- ➦ Chapter 7 includes a reflection on qualities of leadership, ingredients that are essential to living a life of service.

- ➦ Chapter 10 stresses that a key way to meet Jesus is by loving and serving other people, especially poor and marginalized people.

Curriculum Plan of the Text

A major source of a course's curriculum is the objectives of a school's religious education program. Ideally each religious education department develops and publishes its objectives for the four-year program, incorporating the following elements of a systematic catechesis:

1. the teaching of the Christian *message* as it is handed down in the Catholic tradition;
2. the fostering of *Christian community*;
3. the development of student skills in *serving* others;
4. the celebration of Christian identity through *liturgy.*

High-school catechists draw on a variety of sources to develop the objectives of our four-year programs, including the *Catechism of the Catholic Church*, the *General Directory for Catechesis*, the National Catechetical Directory (*Sharing the Light of Faith*), *Catechesi Tradendae*, *To Teach as Jesus Did*, directives from the local bishop and diocesan religious education office, national catechetical guidelines, and other pertinent documents.

In addition, research findings on adolescent growth and development, needs analyses of students, practical classroom experience, the charism and spirituality of the religious orders that staff the schools, and parent surveys all help religious educators put together a solid, relevant, integral, and interesting program for students.

A key to improving the curriculum is the periodic evaluation of program and course objectives. Objectives adopted for certain courses dictate the specific content to be taught, its scope, sequence, and organization. They guide us in selecting the specific day-to-day methods and media we employ to teach our classes. They help us resist fads and control the overall direction of our course and programs.

The curriculum model suggested for this course encourages periodic evaluation to help verify how effectively goals are being met. Evaluation can help religion departments to judge the suitability of the scope of coverage of key concepts, to adjust sequencing of the material, and to check the reliability of methods and choice of media to accomplish goals. Another benefit of evaluation might be to reveal that some goals are unrealistic and not worth the time and energy expended on them.

Evaluation can take many forms. For example, quizzes and tests can help in determining the effectiveness of both teaching and learning. Professional colleagues from other institutions can help reveal lacunae in programs. Parent and student surveys can suggest ways needs are being met or not being met.

The text subscribes to a "closed-loop" model of curriculum. In schematic form it looks like this:

OBJECTIVES	Content
	Scope
	Sequence and Content Organization
	Method
	Media
	Evaluation

Objectives

The Teacher's Manual lists several objectives for the various sections of the Student Text chapters. Objectives gleaned from *Guidelines for Doctrinally Sound Catechetic Materials* were discussed under "Sufficiently Complete" catechesis above. Other objectives are that students:

•◆ reflect on and respond to Jesus' timeless question: "Who do you say that I am?"

•◆ know some of the proofs for the existence of the historical Jesus and explain the continuity between "the Jesus of history" and the "Christ of faith"

•◆ reflect on and discuss the meaning of Jesus through his titles (e.g., Lord, Christ, Son of Man, Son of God, Word of God) and roles (e.g., teacher, model of prayer, savior, brother, friend)

- ➻ personally reflect on their growing relationship with the Lord, especially through journal-writing and meeting him in others
- ➻ explain the growth of the New Testament
- ➻ understand some of the social, political, and religious features of the New Testament world and how they influenced the creation of the New Testament
- ➻ identify and use with facility the following tools of New Testament study: concordance, atlas, dictionary, synopsis, commentary
- ➻ distinguish among some of the different styles of writing in the New Testament
- ➻ identify the "synoptic problem" and explain how the various gospels differ as to theology, audience, and authorship
- ➻ identify the author, date, intended audience, and major themes of each book of the New Testament
- ➻ understand the major events and mysteries associated with Jesus' life (for example, the infancy narratives, genealogy, Paschal mystery, key moral teachings, etc.)
- ➻ hear, understand, and discuss the message of Jesus, especially the components of unconditional love, forgiveness, conversion, faith, and response in service
- ➻ explain the various meanings of New Testament miracles
- ➻ know the meaning of the key parables of Jesus
- ➻ outline the growth of the early Church as described in the Acts of the Apostles
- ➻ comprehend and explain key passages of the New Testament
- ➻ recognize and discuss major themes in Pauline theology and where they can be found in the epistles attributed to St. Paul
- ➻ come to a richer understanding and appreciation of the Christian vocation that challenges them in the pages of the New Testament (e.g., read scripture on their own; commit themselves to the good news of God's love; pray with the scripture; apply biblical teaching, especially in the area of conscience formation, to their own lives; examine and evaluate personal beliefs in light of the biblical word; respond to Jesus' example and invitation to be a "person for others")
- ➻ confidently read many New Testament passages and know some of the key questions answered by the text
- ➻ develop "religious literacy" by learning certain key terms associated with the Bible
- ➻ know and explain the various dogmatic teachings concerning Jesus
- ➻ reflect on and respond to Jesus' call to personal friendship with him

Content and Scope

• • • • • • • • • • • • •

The content of the course includes an introduction to all the books of the New Testament, with special emphasis on the gospels; the historical Jesus; the Church's dogmatic teaching about Jesus as presented in the *Catechism of the Catholic Church*; the meaning of discipleship, and how Jesus can be met in today's world. (The major content themes treated in *CCC*, and consequently in the Student Text, are outlined on page 10.) The content focuses on knowledge about the biblical texts and the intelligent reading of the texts themselves.

Like all textbooks, the *Encountering the Jesus of the New Testament* Student Text stresses the cognitive domain of learning. Students will become familiar with the gospels, Acts of the Apostles, key Pauline epistles, and other New Testament texts, as well as the Church's classic statements about Jesus. A goal of the textbook is that students will be able to recall, recognize, and comprehend what they are learning. Moreover, students will gain enough background to begin to read the New Testament with appreciation and understanding.

In exposing students to the biblical texts, and by asking key questions about it, students should be able to exercise higher levels of cognitive learning, including application, analysis, synthesis, and evaluation.

The text does not neglect either the affective or behavioral domains of learning. Many of the journal entries and most of the values exercises appeal to acquiring "heart knowledge." Questioning, reflecting, imagining, internalizing, appreciating, responding to, examining, deciding—these are the outcomes that help students to read the Bible not as a dead letter, but a living word from the Lord.

The suggestions for service projects, prayer exercises, role-playing situations, researching, interviewing, celebrating the sacraments, reading the biblical word, applying values exercises to one's personal life—all these appeal to the behavioral domain.

The scope of the text is broad and survey-like in that it provides an introduction to the entire New Testament and the basic dogmatic teachings about Jesus. Touched on in a non-technical way is basic background information on the development of the New Testament, its historical context, methods of exegesis, and the like. However, students are asked to apply the information they learn to the biblical texts themselves.

Concerning the New Testament books, the Student Text briefly comments on authorship of each and gives a probable date of composition. In some cases, an outline of the book in question is provided. Major theological themes are offered with much greater emphasis given to the gospels, Acts, Paul's letter to the Philippians, and the book of Revelation. Interpretations given reflect the opinions of major Catholic commentators, especially Fr. Raymond Brown and commentators in the *New Jerome Biblical Commentary* and *Catholic Study Bible*. Controversial and novel ideas are avoided as is technical jargon.

Sequence

The Introduction of the Student Text distinguishes between the Jesus of history and the Christ of faith, introduces some key titles of Jesus, and discusses the meaning of the "real" Jesus.

Chapters 1 to 3 give basic background to both the historical Jesus and the New Testament. Chapter 1 looks at extra-biblical sources, discusses the canon of the New Testament, and shows how the gospels were formed and are studied by scholars. Chapter 2 examines the New Testament world of Jesus, while Chapter 3 summarizes the life of Jesus along the lines treated in the *Catechism of the Catholic Church*, that is, the "mysteries" of Christ's life.

Chapters 4 to 7 treat the gospels in this order: Mark, Matthew, Luke-Acts, and John. This is the order recommended for study, but a teacher may choose to address John after studying Mark and Matthew, allowing for Luke/Acts to serve as a transition between the gospels and the epistles.

Chapter 8 treats the Pauline corpus, extracting from each book a special teaching about Jesus. A similar approach is taken for the rest of the New Testament canon, treated in Chapter 9.

Chapter 9 also presents the key dogmatic teachings about Jesus. The concluding chapter discusses where Jesus can be found in the world today, recommends prayer and regular scripture reading, and critiques certain Jesus films. It is recommended that all these chapters be taught in the order presented in the Student Text.

Chapter outlines for *Encountering the Jesus of the New Testament* follow:

●✧ Introduction: "Who Do You Say That I Am?"

▸ Examine personal and scriptural beliefs about who is Jesus

▸ Meaning of the Incarnation

▸ Distinction between Jesus of history and Christ of faith: the historical Jesus (his dates, his surnames); B.C./A.D.

▸ The "real" Jesus

▸ Jesus Prayer and the titles of Jesus: Christ, Son of God, Lord

●✧ Chapter 1: The Historical Jesus

▸ Evidence for his existence: Roman sources (Tacitus, Suetonius, Pliny the Younger); Jewish sources (Josephus); Babylonian Talmud

▸ The Bible: Old Testament preparation; Jesus as the New Covenant; inspired writings; evangelist; canon of the New Testament (criteria used)

▸ Formation of the gospel: historical Jesus; oral tradition (*kerygma*, *didache*, liturgy); New Testament writings (why finally committed to writing)

▸ Reading the Bible with the Church—senses of scripture

▸ Methods of studying the gospels: source criticism (the synoptic problem); historical criticism (linguistic analysis, criterion of originality, convergence, consistency, form criticism, sample forms in the gospels: miracle stories, parable, riddle, pronouncement story, hyperbole, controversy story, hymn, prayer, revelation discourse); redaction criticism (e.g., genealogy of Jesus); textual criticism

▸ Translations

●✧ Chapter 2: The New Testament World of Jesus

▸ Map of the Holy Land in Jesus' day: geography, regions (Galilee, Samaria, Judea, Idumea); cities; Jerusalem in the time of Jesus

▸ Languages spoken (Aramaic, Hebrew, Greek, Latin); parallelisms; comparisons; exaggeration

▸ Synagogue vs. Temple

▸ Key Jewish feasts: Passover, Pentecost, Tabernacles

▸ Political Scene: *Pax Romana*; Maccabean dynasty; Herod the Great and his sons (Herod Antipas, Archelaus, Philip); Roman rule (Pontius Pilate)

▸ Slavery in New Testament times: Philemon

▸ Important Jewish beliefs: the Messiah and Messianic expectations; covenant and Torah; judgment and resurrection; spirit world

▸ Jewish sects in Jesus' day: Sadducees; Pharisees; Essenes; Zealots.

▸ Other New Testament notables: tax collectors; common people; Gentiles; women

●✧ Chapter 3: The Essential Jesus

▸ Mysteries of Christ's life

▸ Jesus' infancy and hidden life: compare/contrast the infancy narratives of Matthew and Luke

▸ Jesus' public life: baptism (synoptic comparison; Jesus and John the Baptist; historical context of the event—criterion of embarrassment); temptations of Jesus (Matthew and Luke compared)

▸ Jesus the teacher: proclaimer of the kingdom; characteristics of Jesus the teacher; Jesus and parables; Jesus' proclamation (reign of God is present; God is loving and merciful; God's love is universal; repent, believe the good news, and serve; the Lord is present in the Church; the Lord sends the Holy Spirit; pick up the cross)

▸ Jesus the miracle worker: types of (physical healings, nature miracles, exorcisms, raisings from the dead miracles and faith); New Testament concepts of *miracle*; miracles revelatory of God's power (*dynamis*); miracles as signs (*semeia*) of the coming kingdom

- Jesus' authenticity leads to Paschal mystery
- Jesus teaches how to pray; exercise in redaction criticism (Mt 6:5-15/Lk 11:1-13)

Chapter 4: The Gospel of Mark: Jesus the Suffering Servant

- Authorship, audience, date, purpose, and method of Mark
- Prologue to Mark's gospel
- Jesus the teacher
- Jesus the miracle worker and healer
- The human Jesus
- Messianic secret: Son of Man; Suffering Servant; Christ
- Suffering—the way of discipleship: rich young man in Mk 10:17-31
- The Paschal mystery: historical background to the passion narrative; theological background to the passion narrative; why Jesus died; meditation on the passion narrative
- How to use the gospels to pray meditatively

Chapter 5: The Gospel of Matthew: Jesus the Teacher

- Authorship, audience, date, purpose, and themes of Matthew's gospel
- Matthew's Jesus fulfills Old Testament prophecies
- How Matthew uses Mark: Peter's confession of faith and resurrection appearances
- Jesus the Teacher discourses: Sermon on the Mount (5-7); Missionary instructions (10); kingdom parables (13)—Sower analyzed; Church instructions (18); judgment (24-25); call to service (25)
- Jesus challenger to Judaism (23); problem of anti-Semitism; historical context

Chapter 6: The Gospel of Luke and Acts of the Apostles: Jesus the Savior

- Authorship, audience, date, purpose, and method, and outline of Luke-Acts

- Theology by geography in Luke-Acts
- Jesus as prophet in Luke: Church continues Jesus' prophetic ministry in Acts
- The Holy Spirit in Luke-Acts: age of promise; time of Jesus; age of the Church
- Common themes in Luke-Acts: prayer; joy and peace; women in Luke (key Church teachings about Mary)
- Jesus the compassionate savior in Luke: friend of the poor and lonely; Lazarus and the rich man (16:19-31); Zacchaeus (19:1-10); Good Samaritan (10:25-37); Friend of sinners (15)
- Luke's Jesus: the martyred Lord
- Overview of Acts: awaiting the Messiah (1); mission in Jerusalem (2-8:1a); mission in Judea and Samaria (8:1b-12:25); Jerusalem Council (13:1-15:35); Paul's mission to the end of the earth (15:36-28:31)

Chapter 7: The Gospel of John: Jesus the Word of God

- Authorship, date, audience, and outline of John
- Prologue of John: Christology from above
- Titles of Jesus in John's gospel
- Signs in John's gospel and what they reveal about Jesus: water into wine (2:1-12); discourse with woman at well (4:1-26); cure of official's son (4:46-54); paralytic at pool (5:1-47); feeding of 5,000 and walking on water (6:1-14; 16-24); cure of blind man (9:1-41); raising of Lazarus (11:1-44)
- Book of Glory: supper discourses (service, 13; love, 14:1-16:4; unity, 17)
- Resurrection of Jesus: John's account (20-21); synoptic accounts; essentials agreed on; meaning of

Chapter 8: Paul's Letters: The Universal Lord

- Biographical highlights of Paul's life
- Paul's three missionary journeys outlined
- The Pauline corpus
- Style of a Pauline letter

▸ Key themes in Pauline letters

▸ Genuine Pauline letters summarized: 1 Thessalonians (Jesus hope of our salvation); Galatians (Jesus frees us from the law); Philippians *in depth* (Jesus perfect model of humility); Philemon (all brothers in Christ); 1 Corinthians (the risen Christ head of the Church); 2 Corinthians (Jesus as comfort, victory, freedom); Romans (Jesus as the second Adam)

▸ Deuteropauline letters summarized: 2 Thessalonians (Jesus the coming judge); Colossians (Jesus the Cosmic Christ); Ephesians (Jesus the head of the Church, cornerstone)

▸ Pastoral letters: 1 Timothy and Titus; 2 Timothy (Jesus is the one mediator)

☞ Chapter 9: The Early Church: Jesus, True God and True Man

▸ Jesus the high priest in Hebrews

▸ The "catholic" epistles: James (prove faith in action); 1 Peter (Jesus the suffering servant); Jude and 2 Peter (Christ will come again); 1, 2, 3 John (Jesus the Incarnate Love of God)

▸ The book of Revelation: context; theme (remain faithful, God will prevail); apocalyptic literature; symbols; Jesus in Revelation (Alpha and Omega, Almighty, Lamb of God, Messiah); meaning of Revelation today

▸ Christology of the early Church: heresies (Docetism, Arianism, Nestorianism, Monophysitism)

▸ Church Fathers and ecumenical councils

▸ Key dogmatic proclamations about Jesus (CCC 464-483): only Son of God, true God, Light from Light, begotten, not made; all things made through him; Mary is the Mother of Jesus and the Mother of God; one divine person with two natures; possessing a human intellect and human will; in him God shared humanity; Jesus is our savior

☞ Chapter 10: The Living Jesus Today: Constant Friend and Companion

▸ Jesus lives in each of us

▸ Jesus is present in the Church: Church as body of Christ; Church as sacrament of Christ; tasks of the Church to proclaim the gospel, build community, serve, and worship

▸ Jesus present in others, especially the poor and suffering

▸ Jesus meets us in the sacraments: special opportunity to meet Jesus in the sacrament of Reconciliation; special gift of the Eucharist; Jesus is present in his scriptural word

▸ We can meet Jesus in prayer: types of prayer; why pray

▸ Images of Jesus in contemporary cinema: evaluating Jesus films; critique of selected films

Length of Course

Assuming *Encountering the Jesus of the New Testament* will provide the basic text for a semester course, here is a possible breakdown of the chapters and topics from the Student Text for an eighteen-week course:

Chapter	Weeks
Introduction	.5
Chapter 1	1
Chapter 2	1
Chapter 3	1
Chapter 4	2
Chapter 5	2
Chapter 6	2
Chapter 7	2
Chapter 8	1.5
Chapter 9	2
Chapter 10	1
Feature film	1
Student project	1
	Total: 18 weeks

Of course, this is just a suggestion. You may wish to have several student projects and presentations and more than one feature film. You will have to budget your time accordingly. You will also need to factor in time for review, quizzes, and tests.

If you have time, it would be appropriate to involve the students in a class service project, perhaps with the hunger project suggested in Chapter 5 of the Student Text. Factor in time to plan, execute, and evaluate.

Methods and Media

Each chapter of the Teacher's Manual annotates some videos you may want to use to enhance the content of that particular chapter. There are good background films on Jesus and his times and a number of very good feature films on Jesus.

It is highly recommended that you show and discuss at least one of the feature films listed. Chapter 10 of the text annotates some of the more popular ones.

Most of the feature-length videos annotated in this manual should be relatively easy to find in video stores or over the Internet. Over time, some of the shorter videos might be a bit more difficult to obtain or even be withdrawn from use. The works annotated in this manual were checked against recent catalogues of their producers. Your local diocesan film library might have some of these as well.

You can keep up with recent releases by checking the *Religion Teacher's Journal* and *Catechist*, both of which periodically annotate audiovisual resources.

Some suggestions for using audiovisuals:

↦ *Always preview with an eye toward their suitability for your own students.* In the case of films, although we recognize that students can sometimes benefit from some excellent R-rated films, it is prudent not to use anything but films rated G, PG, and possibly PG-13 with high school students. Parents are the prime religious educators, and we should not presume to use materials some parents would find objectionable. As far as can be determined, none of the films recommended in this manual are R-rated.

❧ *Order materials early to avoid disappointment.* Consider purchasing videos of feature films for your departmental library. You can find many of them at extremely reasonable costs from a source like Amazon.com or Critics Choice.

❧ *Follow up your use of an audiovisual with a discussion and some meaningful assignments.* We should not give our students the impression that viewing a film is an excuse to stop thinking. Provide study sheets on the film so they will be prepared for discussion. You might have selected questions (for example, incomplete quotes) for them to complete while watching the film. (Don't overdo!) A short quiz to check their attention might be in order at the end of a particular day's segment.

Following are some other methods that can be successful in a New Testament/Christology course:

Article reading. Consider assigning an article or two from a popular Catholic magazine or a more scholarly journal, depending on the ability of your group. *Bible Today* has excellent and readable articles. Each year, magazines like *U.S. Catholic* often have several interviews with leading biblical scholars on a topic of New Testament studies. Give your students a list of Catholic periodicals available in your school, departmental, parish, and local libraries. Teach students how to use *The Catholic Periodical and Literature Index.*

Creative parable assignment. You may want to have students enact, rewrite, update, or present in some other creative way one of the parables. This assignment lends itself to a small group project, for example, the videotaping of a student-written drama on one of the parables.

Discussion (both small and large-group). Discussion builds Christian community in the classroom and often leads to faith sharing among students. For example, the text sometimes asks students to read, analyze, and report on a given section of a New Testament book. This can help the class to get a bird's-eye view of a whole book in a relatively short period of time.

Faith sharing. Throughout the course you'll find several opportunities to give personal Christian witness. Testify openly about your own love of the Bible. Invite students to do the same.

Guest speakers. You might want to invite in a knowledgeable expert on the Bible to speak on some aspect of New Testament study.

Interviewing. Ask your students to discuss material with their parents or other adults. This can open up dialogue and help parents exercise their own ministry of religious education.

Jesus on the Internet. Students love doing research on the Internet. There are some excellent sites annotated in the bibliographies provided for each chapter. It is highly recommended that you assign a short project that familiarizes your students with the wealth of biblical resources on the World Wide Web.

Journal-keeping. Keeping of a journal is highly recommended in a Jesus/New Testament course. Explain its value to your students, especially as a method of prayer. In the New Testament course, many recommended journal-keeping exercises involve short reading and reflection assignments rooted in the biblical text itself. Here's an idea students have enjoyed doing over the years. As a journal exercise, have them transcribe ten to fifteen favorite quotes from or about Jesus from each of the gospels. You may even ask them to memorize some of them or prepare a short commentary on certain ones to present to their classmates. It is highly recommended that a significant part of students' grades for the New Testament course be derived from the careful keeping of a journal.

Lecture and note-taking. A great lecture on your part can stimulate student interest, introduce difficult material, organize units logically, and summarize key ideas. Requiring students to take notes on key points teaches an essential skill that will help them in all their courses. Perhaps you can spend a short session on how to take good notes in your class. You may wish to duplicate some key passages that you want to study more intently, allowing enough "white space" for marginal notes. Instruct students to keep these handouts in a separate section of a three-ring binder journal/notebook.

Prayer. Each chapter contains a prayer reflection. You can add to these by using the introductory scriptural quotes and other prayers provided. In addition, student meditations and reflections are suggested for journal entries. Also, consider celebrating the sacrament of reconciliation and at least one Eucharist during your semester together. Have students plan the readings for the Eucharist. If teaching the course during second semester, you might tie the Eucharist into the Triduum or the Holy Thursday celebration of the first Eucharist.

Reading and summary. Students are asked to read various New Testament passages and summarize their reading.

Service project. You may wish to assign the hunger project noted previously or devise a class project to be worked on throughout the semester.

Text reading and summarizing. You may simply wish students to write out all the answers to the Review Questions and include them in a separate section of their journal.

Values exercises. Most chapters in the Student Text have at least one key exercise designed to get students to think about their relationship to Jesus, their life in the Christian community, or their current beliefs about and practice of Catholicism. Be sure to allot time to discuss these.

Various creative assessments. Think more long-range by assigning one of the alternative, creative techniques from the list given above in the section of this chapter entitled "Some Thoughts about Teaching Jesus in the New Testament."

Evaluation

• • • • • • • •

Evaluation and grades are important in Catholic high school religious education. They help communicate to students the seriousness of the course. The *General Directory for Catechesis* reminds us that

> It is necessary . . . that religious instruction in schools appear as a scholastic discipline with the same systematic demands and the same rigor as other disciplines. It must present the Christian message and the Christian event with the same seriousness and the same depth with which other disciplines present their knowledge. It should not be an accessory alongside of these disciplines . . . (#73).

Without testing and other means of evaluation to hold both students and teachers accountable, students especially will get the message that religious education courses really do not count.

A major benefit of evaluation is to determine whether objectives are being met. If good teaching happens, then learning is taking place, too.

The chapter tests included in this manual, as well as ones that you will devise yourself, offer one means of evaluation. Other ways to judge the effectiveness of your teaching and student learning include observing student attention in class; participation in class discussions; the quality of student questions and responses; journal entries; fidelity to homework assignments; the gathering, reporting, and oral presentation of research; participation in service projects; cooperation with you and fellow students; participation in prayer; personal interviews with each student; and informal interaction.

Religious educational and catechetical courses teach to the cognitive ("head" knowledge), affective ("heart" knowledge), and the behavioral ("feet" or action knowledge) domains. Student performance in all these areas should be reflected in the grade you assign for the course.

Assigning grades is a key way to emphasize the importance of our classes. However, grades should never be used to manipulate, control, or intimidate students. In Christian charity and justice, many opportunities should be given for students to do well. Grasp of cognitive content should not be the exclusive criterion for grades. Rewarding students for effort, participation, and cooperation helps create a loving and just classroom.

Format of the Teacher's Manual

Each chapter of this Manual includes the following regular elements:

Introducing the Chapter is an overview of the content, approach, and rationale of the chapter.

Bibliography lists approximately ten books that provide further background reading for teachers.

Videos include feature-length motion films you may wish to use with your students.

Resources list some good Internet sites that you and your students can research.

Procedures suggest instructions for teaching each chapter. Veteran teachers might use very little of these procedures as they draw on their own repertoire of teaching techniques and years of experience. Novice teachers might depend more on the suggestions given.

Reproducible supplementary exercises and assignments not included in the Student Text. Some of these are reprinted at the end of this manual so that they can be easily duplicated for your students.

The procedures suggested divide each chapter of the Student Text into several "teachable" sections. Generally they are arranged to cover the text under one or two main headings in the Student Text. For each of these sections, the Teacher's Manual usually follows this format:

Objectives of the particular section.

Summary of the section being taught.

Background Information for teachers to help contextualixe the particular section of the chapter.

Warm-up Activity to help students get started in the class.

Using the Section offers approaches to cover the text's material.

Extending the Section includes project ideas, research topics, journal entries, and the like.

Creative Learning activities are offered for some of the sections of each chapter. These optional ideas, for example, the showing of a video, could considerably extend the time it takes to teach a particular chapter.

Correct Answers to Review Questions are provided for the questions included at the end of each chapter in the Student Text.

Chapter Test formats contain a sample test of 25 items. These tests use a variety of question types (true-false, matching, fill-ins, multiple-choice, short answers). Answers to these tests are also provided. It is highly recommended that teachers construct their own quizzes and tests to evaluate the specific learning outcomes of their courses.

Sources for Videos

Amazon.com: www.amazon.com

Christian Book Distributors
P.O. Box 7000
Peabody, MA 01961-7000
1-800-247-4784

Critics Choice Video:
www.ccvideo.com

Films for the Humanities and Sciences®
P.O. Box 2053
Princeton, NJ 08543-2053
www.films.com

Harcourt Religion Publishers
1665 Embassy West Drive, Suite 200
Dubuque, Iowa 52002-2259
1-800-922-7696
www.harcourtreligion.com

Ignatius Press
P.O. Box 1339
Ft. Collins, CO 80532
1-800-651-1531
www.ignatius.com

Insight Media: www.insight-media.com

Kultur: www.kultur.com

Pflaum Publishing Group
P.O. Box 49727
Dayton, OH 45449-9927
1-800-543-4383
www.pflaum.com

Reader's Digest
www.rd.com

Videos with Values
Oblate Media and Communication
1509 Washington, Ave., Suite 550
Saint Louis, MO 63103-1821
www.videoswithvalues.org

Vision Video/Gateway Films
Box 540
Worchester, PA 19490
Phone: (610) 584-3500
Fax: (610) 584-6643
www.visionvideo.com/vv/home.asp

Weekly Planning Chart

Day Pp. #	Objectives	Activities	Follow-up work
Mon.			
Tues.			
Wed.			
Thurs.			
Fri.			

Evaluation of Week:

Sample Weekly Planning Chart: New Testament World of Jesus

Day Pp. #	Objectives	Activities	Follow-up work
Mon. 9/15 pp. 0-0	Test knowledge of NT world of Jesus View RD *Jesus and His Times* video, pt. 1, and identify Palestine, cities, Magi, and theories about the star	**Warmup:** Read opening pages of Chapter 2. Focus on story 1. Assign exercise entitled "Test your knowledge of world of Jesus." Correct and discuss. 2. Show 25 min. segment from RD video, pt. 1. Students to take notes.	**Homework:** Read section of Chapter 2 entitled "Holy Land and Language." Assign relevant "Review Questions" at end of chapter to be worked on during the week.
Tues. 9/16 pp. 0-0	Review homework reading View rest of video and identify Herod the Great, Archelaus, Jewish feasts, etc.	**Warmup:** Review homework reading on characteristics of Aramaic. Give example of Mt 5:29 at end of this section. 1. Ask questions about videotape. 2. Show rest of RD video. Students to take notes on key points	**Homework:** Read section of chapter on synagogues, Temple, and Feasts. Have students complete enrichment section at end of this section.
Wed. 9/17 pp. 0-0	Review key points from the video Discuss the political scene in the time of Jesus Read Philemon	**Warmup:** Read Philemon for class prayer. 1. Ask questions re videotape. Focus on theories about star of Bethlehem and the three Jewish feasts. 2. List key political figures on the board/overhead. Review who they were. Point to map of Palestine to indicate their rule. 3. In small groups, have students answer questions re Philemon	**Homework:** Read sections on political scene and Jewish beliefs. Have students do the exercise on angels.
Thurs. 9/18 pp. 0-0	Differentiate between/among the major sects in Jesus' day Identify other groups in Jesus' day	**Warmup:** For prayer, read Lk 1:11-22. Petition guardian angels for special intentions. 1. Divide students into groups to read and then report on each of the four sects and other groups mentioned in chapter. 2. Create chart on board that contrasts/compares the four sects. Work through the "Reading Deeper" exercise on Pharisees/Sadducees.	**Homework:** Assign Review Questions for completion. Have them review for quiz.
Fri. 9/13	Review for quiz on week's material Administer the quiz	**Warmup:** : Use Prayer Reflection at end of chapter for opening prayer. 1. Go over and correct Review Questions. 2. Administer quiz on week's work.	**Homework:** Note from Sunday's gospel readings any interesting new fact they learn about Jesus and those who followed him.

Evaluation of Week:

Mon: Students have skimpy knowledge of the world of Jesus.

Tues: They enjoyed the RD video. In future, make up a question sheet for them to write answer to key points of the video as they watch. (Don't overdo.)

Wed: Philemon reading assignment went very well. They seemed interested in the mini-lecture on the political background.

Thurs: Lackluster class. Board work: dumb idea. In future, refer to the chart in the text under the chapter review.

Fri: Fantastic review. No time for the quiz. Will give on Monday.

On-Line Access

Access to specific material from the Student Text and Teacher's Manual of *Encountering the Jesus of the New Testament* is available on-line. To access the following material, address an e-mail to encounteringtheJesusofthenewtestament@avemariapress.com

You will automatically receive an e-mail response that includes attachment files saved in both Rich Text File (rtf) and DOS Text File (txt) format, sort of generic formats.

Both a Macintosh or Macintosh-compatible computer, and an IBM or IBM-compatible computer will be able to open the attachments.

Material included in the files can be adjusted to fit the specific needs of your course. For example, resource and test questions can be added or subtracted.

Review Questions Short answer questions for each chapter are included. Answers to these questions are found in the Teacher's Manual with the particular chapter.

Testing Program One hundred point objective tests are included for each chapter. The test answers are included in the Teacher's Manual.

Resource Pages The Teacher's Manual includes several other reproducible assignments to facilitate and extend the various lessons within the chapters. These pages are also included in the email. When applicable, answers for these handout activities are found in the Teacher's Manual with the particular chapter.

Introduction

"Who Do You Say That I Am?"

Introducing the Introduction

The Introduction opens with the essential question of Christianity: Who is Jesus of Nazareth? While the subsequent chapters will attempt to answer the question, especially related to the faith stories described in the pages of the New Testament, the book opens by sharing several thoughts about Jesus from believers and non-believers alike down through the ages.

The fundamental doctrine of Christianity is introduced: belief in the Incarnation, the essential dogma that holds that Jesus Christ "assumed a human nature in order to accomplish our salvation in it" (CCC, 461).

The Introduction also points to several ways we can learn about Jesus, his life on earth, and doctrines the Church teaches about him.

Also, the Introduction sets up an important challenge of this course and for life beyond any specific study of Jesus and the New Testament: ways for Christians today to meet the living Jesus. Three specific ways are mentioned: reading of scriptures, prayer, and meeting Jesus in other people.

Finally, understanding the names and titles used for Jesus can help us to know him better. The Introduction offers explanation for *Jesus*, *Christ*, *Son of God*, and *Lord*.

Bibliography

Abbott, Walter, S.J., ed. *The Documents of Vatican II.* Revised edition. New York: America Press, 1967.
   The *Dogmatic Constitution on Divine Revelation* is essential background reading.

Achtemeier, Paul J., ed. *Harper's Bible Dictionary*, rev. ed. San Francisco: HarperCollins, 1996.
  An outstanding, readable reference work from an ecumenical perspective. Get this one for your library.

Drane, John William. *Introducing the New Testament*, rev. ed. Minneapolis: Fortress Press, 2001.
  Lavishly illustrated and delightfully written. A wonderful introduction by a balanced Protestant scholar.

Harrington, Daniel, S.J. *How to Read the Gospels: Answers to Common Questions*. New York: New City Press, 1996.
  Wonderful, simple overview on Jesus and the gospels, how to read the gospels intelligently, and a discussion of how to understand some vexing gospel passages. Highly recommended.

Johnson, Luke Timothy. *The Real Jesus: The Misguided Quest for the Historical Jesus and the Truth of the Traditional Gospels*. San Francisco: HarperSanFrancisco, 1996.
  A penetrating critique of the Jesus Seminar's approach to recreating Jesus in the image and likeness of skeptical scholars. Highlights the Risen Jesus as the "real" Jesus.

Karris, R. J. and D. Bergant, eds. *Collegeville Bible Commentary*. Collegeville, MN: Liturgical Press, 1989.
  Belongs in every teacher's library. Good simple introductions to each book of the Bible.

Kee, Howard Clark. *Understanding the New Testament*, 5th edition. Englewood Cliffs, NJ: Prentice-Hall, 1993.
  Magisterial in scope.

Miller, Stephen M. *Get into the Bible: Journey through the Greatest Story of All Time*. Nashville, TN: 1998.
  Great teacher reference. Nice overviews of each book of the Bible.

Perkins, Pheme. *Reading the New Testament*. Second Edition. New York: Paulist Press, 1988.
  An outstanding one-volume introduction to the New Testament. Excellent supplementary reading for your more advanced students.

Rohr, Richard and Joseph Martos. *The Great Themes of Scripture: New Testament*. Cincinnati: St. Anthony Messenger Press, 1988.
  A delightful overview of some key themes of the New Testament.

Senior, Donald, ed. *The Catholic Study Bible*. New York: Oxford University Press, 1990.
  Includes the text of *The New American Bible* which has excellent notes. The articles and commentary on each book of the Bible are well written. A good resource for your students.

Stott, J. R. W. Men with a Message: *An Introduction to the New Testament*, rev. ed. Grand Rapids: Eerdmans, 1995.

Videos
• • • • •

Face of Jesus in Art

  A stunning documentary on how Jesus has been portrayed in art through the ages. Very well done (two hour video or DVD, Kultur; Vision Video).

The Jesus File: Tracking the Messiah

  Four-part series (26 minutes each) which portrays the security apparatus of a hypothetical first-century secret service equipped with modern technology to study the life of Jesus of

Nazareth. Titles include: "Preparing the Way," "Jesus: From Carpenter to Preacher," "Jesus Gathers a Following," and "The Last and First Days of Jesus" (Films for the Humanities and Sciences®).

Resources

The Bible Gateway
Allows searches of various translations of the Bible, by passage or search words.
http://bible.gospelcom.net/bible

The Bible and Interpretation
Interesting articles from an evangelical point of view.
http://www.bibleinterp.com/

Bible quizzes
Lots of fun quizzes on biblical information.
http://www.biblequizzes.com/

Bible Research CyberCenter
Some good hints on how to write a paper on a biblical theme.
http://www.tagnet.org/brc/

Electronic New Testament Resources
Fantastic website by Fr. Felix Just of Claremont University. Put this one at the top of your "must-sees." Your students could really profit from this website.
http://clawww.lmu.edu/faculty/fjust/Bible.htm

From Jesus to Christ
A graphically rich website based on the PBS Frontline series of the same name. Good articles, though slanted in favor of the Jesus Seminar approach. Definitely worth your investigation for articles and images you can recommend for your students.
http://www.pbs.org/wgbh/pages/frontline/shows/religion/

General Information on the Bible
Wonderful links from a Catholic educator's website.
http://www.silk.net/RelEd/bible.htm

Internet Theology Resources: Scripture
Great source for good sites for Bible studies.
http://www.csbsju.edu/library/internet/theosson.html

Jesus: The Complete Story
A good website that accompanies the BBC videos by the same name.
http://dsc.discovery.com/convergence/jesus/jesus.html

Jesus Christ—Images, Art, and Photos
Great place to get pictures of Jesus.
http://www.virtualchurch.org/images.htm

Narrow Gate
Great website for high-school teachers by a religion teacher at Christian Brothers High School, Memphis, TN. Be sure to check this one out.
http://www.cbhs.org/rmartin/index.htm

New American Bible
At the United States Conference of Catholic Bishops' website.
http://www.nccbuscc.org/nab/bible/index.htm

New Testament Gateway

Maintained by Dr. Mark Goodacre, this is truly one of the outstanding websites on the entire WWW. Highly recommended.

http://www.ntgateway.com/

Jesus Archive

A site "dedicated to the study of the historical Jesus, early Christianity and Second Temple Judaism." Many links to research resources, a scholars' database, forums, and book reviews. Worth checking out.

http://www.jesusarchive.com/

Meier, John P. "The Present State of the 'Third Quest' for the Historical Jesus: Loss and Gain." *Biblica* **80; 1999.**

http://www.bsw.org/?l=71801&a=Comm11.htm

Resource Pages for Biblical Studies

Great website for links on early Christian writings and their social context. Highly recommended.

http://www.torreys.org/bible/

The Scripture Course

Good notes by an Irish priest, Fr. Tommy Lane, who teaches scripture to adults.

http://www.frtommylane.com/scripturecourse.htm

Symbols in Christian Art and Architecture

http://home.att.net/~wegast/symbols/symbols.htm

Theology Library: Sacred Scripture

This site gives many good links to Church documents on scripture. Check out the other links associated with the Theology Library. Kids love this site. They should. It is maintained by a Catholic high school teacher.

http://www.shc.edu/theolibrary/

Theology/Religion/Catholic Education Resources

Lesson plans for world religions, Church history, famous people, prayer, and the *Catechism*.

http://www.cloudnet.com/~edrbsass/edthe.htm

University of St. Mary of the Lakes Sacred Scripture web links

Annotated lists of biblical and related resources, from Rev. Jim McIlhone, the librarian at Archdiocese of Chicago's seminary. Highly recommended, especially for its scholarly sites.

http://www.vocations.org/library/linkss.htm

World Wide Study Bible

http://www.ccel.org/wwsb/

Yale Divinity School's Image Database for Biblical Studies

Great source for images and pictures related to biblical books and scenes. Check it out.

http://eikon.divinity.yale.edu/eikon.taf

SECTION 1: Saving Life and The Fundamental Doctrine: The Incarnation (pages 14-15)

Objectives

• • • • • • • •

The goals of this section are to enable the students to:
➥ begin to ponder the fundamental question: "Who is Jesus Christ?"
➥ examine a variety of statements and beliefs about Jesus;
➥ define Incarnation and discuss its benefits for us.

Summary and Background Information

Ask a person "Who do you say I am?" and you'll get a variety of answers—often from the very same person! All of us have many facets and dimensions. This Introduction and entire course helps explain how answering Jesus' question "Who do you say that I am?" can help us to know him and ourselves—created in God's image and redeemed by Christ.

In this section, the students will preview the text outline and briefly examine their own beliefs about Jesus. They will then read about the doctrine of the Incarnation, setting the stage for a deepening of knowledge and faith that will take place throughout the rest of the course.

Warm Up

a) Ask the students to write a brief definition of themselves—who they say they are. Invite them to share their definition with a partner. Then facilitate a brief discussion bringing out the points that (1) it's important to know ourselves and (2) that we can be somewhat complex, deep, and multifaceted. Share with the students that knowing Jesus ultimately helps us know our true selves and the beautiful things that God has planned for us.

b) Assign the exercise under "Examining Your Belief about Jesus" (page 12). Allow opportunity for discussion.

Using the Section

a) Assign the text under "Saving Life" up to and including the exercise "Learning More About Peter" (page 13 and page 202 of this text). Point out that Peter reminds us of the Church through whom much of what we know about Jesus comes to us, and in whom we encounter Jesus.

Answers: **Matthew 4:18-22** What was Peter's profession? (fisherman) Who was his brother? (Andrew) Who else were among Jesus' first apostles? (James and John, sons of Zebedee) **Matthew 8:5; 14** Where was Peter's home? (Capernaum) **Luke 9:28-36** Which other apostles were at Jesus' Transfiguration? (John and James) Who did the apostles see with Jesus? (Moses and Elijah) What did Peter propose to do? (make three tents to honor Jesus, Moses, and Elijah) **Mark 14:27-31; 66-72** What did Peter say he would do rather than deny Christ? (die with Jesus) Why did the woman think Peter was Jesus' companion? (she saw him with Jesus) What did Peter do when he realized he had betrayed Christ? (broke down and wept) **John 21:1-19** What did Peter do once he saw Jesus? (he jumped into the sea) How many times did Jesus ask Peter to profess his love? (three) How will Peter die? (with hands stretched out, as on a cross)

b) Regarding the journal activity (page 13) that accompanies the exercise, you might mention to the students that you hope that not only their knowledge, but love for Jesus will grow throughout this course.

c) Write the following on the board:

> ## INCARNATION
> God became one of us in order to save us from sin and death.

Point out that "Incarnation" is another way of saying God became one of us; that he took on human flesh. Though this mystery is beyond our comprehension, the person of Jesus has been revealed to us by God the Father so that we can know the Way to eternal happiness. Refer to the text section "The Fundamental Doctrine: The Incarnation" (page 14).

d) Summarize "The Purpose of the Incarnation" (see page 15).

e) Assign the feature "A Human 'Incarnation'" (page 15).

Extending the Section

Share the following story with the students. Ask them to tell how the story relates to the Incarnation:

The Man and the Birds
BY PAUL HARVEY

Unable to trace its proper parentage, I have designated this as my Christmas Story of the Man and the Birds. You know, *the* Christmas Story, the God born a man in a manger and all that escapes some moderns, mostly, I think, because they seek complex answers to their questions and this one is so utterly simple. So for the cynics and the skeptics and the unconvinced I submit a modern parable.

Now the man to whom I'm going to introduce you was not a scrooge, he was a kind, decent, mostly good man. Generous to his family, upright in his dealings with other men. But he just didn't believe all that Incarnation stuff which the churches proclaim at Christmas time. It just didn't make sense and he was too honest to pretend otherwise. He just couldn't swallow the Jesus Story, about God coming to Earth as a man. "I'm truly sorry to distress you," he told his wife, "but I'm not going with you to church this Christmas Eve." He said he'd feel like a hypocrite.

That he'd much rather just stay at home, but that he would wait up for them. And so he stayed and they went to the midnight service.

Shortly after the family drove away in the car, snow began to fall. He went to the window to watch the flurries getting heavier and heavier and then went back to his fireside chair and began to read his newspaper. Minutes later he was startled by a thudding sound. Then another, and then another. Sort of a thump or a thud. At first he thought someone must be throwing snowballs against his living room window. But when he went to the front door to investigate he found a flock of birds huddled miserably in the snow. They'd been caught in the storm and, in a desperate search for shelter, had tried to fly through his large landscape window.

Well, he couldn't let the poor creatures lie there and freeze, so he remembered the barn where his children stabled their pony. That would provide a warm shelter, if he could direct the birds to it. Quickly he put on a coat, galoshes, and tramped through the deepening snow to the barn. He opened the doors wide and turned on a light, but the birds did not come in. He figured food would entice them in. So he hurried back to the house, fetched bread crumbs, sprinkled them on the snow, making a trail to the yellow-lighted wide open doorway of the stable. But to his dismay, the birds ignored the bread crumbs, and continued to flap around helplessly in the snow. He tried catching them. He tried shooing them into the barn by walking around them waving his arms. Instead, they scattered in every direction, except into the warm, lighted barn.

And then, he realized that they were afraid of him. To them, he reasoned, I am a strange and terrifying creature. If only I could think of some way to let them know that they can trust me. That I am not trying to hurt them, but to help them. But how? Because any move he made tended to frighten them, confuse them. They just would not follow. They would not be led or shooed because they feared him. "If only I could be a bird," he thought to himself, "and mingle with them and speak their language. Then I could tell them not to be afraid. Then I could show them the way to safe, warm . . . to the safe warm barn. But I would have to be one of them so they could see, and hear and understand."

At that moment the church bells began to ring. The sound reached his ears above the sounds of the wind. And he stood there listening to the bells—*Adeste Fidelis*—listening to the bells pealing the glad tidings of Christmas. And he sank to his knees in the snow.

SECTION 2: Learning About Jesus (pages 16-20)

Objectives

The goals of this section are to enable the students to:

➥ examine their current knowledge and beliefs about Jesus;

➥ understand more about the historical Jesus;

➥ discuss several ways for "meeting" Jesus today.

Summary and Background Information

This section is intended to allow the students to examine their current knowledge and beliefs about Jesus. The students are asked to consider the origin of this original knowledge about Jesus. The material points out that if we trace the source all the way back to Jesus' time, the conclusion is that the information about Jesus comes from the apostles.

The phrase, "Jesus of history, Christ of faith" is examined briefly with an eye toward understanding the importance of uncovering the real Jesus. The "real Jesus" of Christian faith is the resurrected Jesus, a living person, that God has revealed as both Lord and Christ (Acts 2:36).

Finally, ways a person can "meet Jesus today" are discussed. Four ways—scriptures, sacraments, prayer, and through others—are introduced in order to be fleshed out in more detail later in the book.

Warm Up

a) Call on volunteers to respond to the questions listed on page 16. Who is the real Jesus? How do you learn about him? Where do you find him? Summarize responses on the board.

b) Wrap up the discussion by summarizing the text under the heading "Learning About Jesus" (page 16).

Using the Section

a) Assign the text section "The Jesus of History" (pages 16-18).

b) To accompany the reading, have the students write a bare bones outline of Jesus' life. Another option is for the students to write a one paragraph obituary style article on Jesus' life and death.

c) Read or have the students read paragraphs 422-423 of the *Catechism of the Catholic Church* which also provides a brief summary of the life of Jesus.

d) Assign the text under "Belief in Jesus Christ" (pages 18-19). Print the following sentence on the board: **The "real Jesus" of Christian faith is the resurrected Jesus, a living person, that God has revealed as both Lord and Christ (Acts 2:36).** Ask the students to comment: "Who is the 'real Jesus' for you?"

e) Related to the text section "Meeting Jesus Today" (pages 19-20), summarize by printing the following on the board:

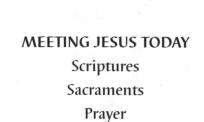

MEETING JESUS TODAY

Scriptures

Sacraments

Prayer

In Others

Point out to the students that in addition to learning historical facts and detailed Church teachings about Jesus, this course will encourage them to know Jesus better by spending time with him in these ways.

Extending the Section

a) Write the following biographical facts about Jesus on the board. Ask the students to look up and read the accompanying gospel passage that verifies the fact.

> ✓ Jesus lived in Nazareth (Mt 2:23).
> ✓ Jesus had a large extended family (Mk 3:31-32).
> ✓ Jesus was a carpenter (Mk 6:3).
> ✓ Jesus could read (Lk 4:16b-17).
> ✓ Jesus spoke Aramaic (Mk 5:41).

b) Assign the exercise on page 20. Check the answers as follows: John the Baptist (Jn 1:29)/Lamb of God; Jesus' relatives (Mk 3:21)/"out of his mind"; The People (Mt 21:10-11)/prophet; Herod Antipas (Mk 6:14-16)/John the Baptist.

Creative Learning

Assign the margin questions on page 20 as an individual writing assignment. When completed, call on one person to be "on the spot." Ask the person to share his or her response to the first question with the entire class. Then call on one or two other students to be "on the spot" with the same question. Continue using different people and the other questions.

SECTION 3: Names and Titles for Jesus (pages 20-24)

Objectives

The goals of this section are to enable the students to:

➡ learn and recite the Jesus Prayer;

➡ analyze the titles for Jesus contained within the Jesus Prayer;

➡ consider names and titles they personally feel comfortable addressing Jesus.

Summary and Background Information

After introducing the Jesus Prayer—"Lord Jesus Christ, Son of God, have mercy on me, a sinner"—the texts analyzes in more depth each name or title for Jesus contained in the prayer.

This notion of titles, names, and prayers is a fitting conclusion to the Introduction. Jesus has many titles. We, too, have many facets that make up our individual selves. Knowing Jesus, cultivating a relationship with Jesus through prayer, the scriptures, the sacraments, and interaction with other people, we come to know ourselves as loved, nurtured, and saved.

Using the Section

a) Introduce the section, "Names and Titles for Jesus" (pages 20-21). Then name small groups with four students each. Assign one person in each small group to be responsible for reading and reporting on the name "Jesus" (pages 21-22), a second person to read and report on "Christ" (page 23), a third on "Son of God" (pages 23-24), and the fourth on "Lord" (page 24). Each student is responsible for sharing information on his or her section with others in the small group.

b) Encourage the use of the margin questions on page 22 and page 24 to help the students facilitate discussion in their small groups.

c) Do the exercise "More New Testament Titles of Jesus" (page 24) with the entire class. Write the titles and scripture references on the board. Have the students look up the passages and share responses (samples given).

> ✓ Good Shepherd (Jn 10:11)/he lays down his life
> ✓ Living Water (Jn 4:14)/eternal life
> ✓ Bread of Life (Jn 6:35)/we will never be hungry
> ✓ Light of the World (Jn 1:4-5, 9)/life-giving
> ✓ Divine Physician (Mt 9:12-13)/calls all sinners to healing
> ✓ Judge (Acts 17:31)/judges in justice

Extending the Section

a) Assign the exercise "New Testament Names" (page 22; also on page 203 of this Manual). *Answers*: 1) f; 2) c; 3) e; 4) i; 5) a; 6) j; 7) h; 8) b; 9) d; 10) g.

b) Invite the students to see what famous people other than those quoted on page 11 have had to say about Jesus. Brief reports can summarize their results.

Creative Learning

• • • • • • • • • • • • •

a) Assign a short essay or journal entry, "Why It's Okay to Say 'B.C.' and 'A.D.' in a Pluralistic Culture."

b) Ask the students to report on references to Jesus in popular music lyrics. Also, have them report on the following: What is the context of "Jesus" in the lyrics? Is the use of "Jesus" respectful and uplifting or disparaging?

Conclusion

a) View all or part of one of the videos suggested on pages 34-35 of this Manual.

b) Introduce the students to some of the several websites available on the New Testament and Jesus (pages 35-36 of the Manual).

c) Assign the Summary points and Review Questions (pages 25-26). Grade them and review them as the students prepare for the Test on the Introduction (page 204 of this Manual).

d) Ask the students to memorize and/or record the Selected Vocabulary terms in their notebooks or journals. Quiz the students on the spelling and definitions.

Answers to Review Questions

1. What were some common views concerning Jesus in his own day?

   Some saw Jesus as a threat or an enemy, the agent of the devil. Others saw him as God's agent who would throw off the Roman yoke. Still others, including the apostles, continually misunderstood him. Jesus' interpretation of messiahship either went over their heads or frightened them.

2. What did Peter profess about Jesus?

   Peter professed, "You are the Christ, Son of God."

3. List three interesting facts about the apostle Peter.

   Answers will vary. For example, 1) He was a fisherman. 2) He witnessed the Transfiguration. 3) He denied that he knew Jesus.

4. Discuss one view from outside of Christianity that people have had about Jesus through the ages.

   Answers will vary. Look for the students to reference one or more of the quotations about Jesus from page 11.

5. What is the meaning of the term *Incarnation*?

   Jesus Christ, the Son of God, "assumed a human nature in order to accomplish our salvation in it" (CCC, 461). The Word of God took on human flesh from his mother Mary by power of the Holy Spirit. Thus, Christians believe that Jesus Christ is both fully God and fully human.

6. Define the term *dogma*.

   A dogma *is a doctrine or teaching of the highest authority.*

7. What scriptural passage highlights Catholic belief in the dogma of the Incarnation?

   The scriptural basis for the Incarnation comes from John 1:1-4; 14 ("In the beginning was the Word," etc.).

8. Who were the Docetists? What follows from their false concepts about Jesus?

   Docetists believed falsely that Jesus only "seemed to be a man." If this is true, than Jesus would have only "seemed" to die for our sins and rise from the dead.

9. Discuss one benefit of the Incarnation for mankind.

   Answers will vary. For example, the Word became flesh to save us by reconciling us with God. As God's Son, Jesus reveals God's love to us. Also, as God-made-man, Jesus serves as the perfect model of holiness.

10. List five significant facts from Jesus' life.

    Answers will vary. For example, he was born a Palestinian Jew, he worked as a carpenter, he lived in Nazareth, he was a wandering preacher, he was turned over to Pontius Pilate.

11. What might Jesus' surname have been?

    His surname would have been Jesus bar Joseph (son of Joseph). He might also have been known by his trade or place of residence.

12. What are the probable birth and death dates for Jesus?

    His birth year was probably between 4 and 6 B.C. He likely died in either A.D. 30 or 33.

13. Identify Dionysius Exiguus.

    Dionysisus Exiguus was the Roman monk who attempted to calculate a chronology of the Christian faith. His error led to the assumption that Jesus was born approximately 4 to 6 B.C.

14. Why do Catholics believe Jesus is more than just a famous person from the past?

    Catholics believe God raised this man Jesus from the dead.

15. Who is the "real Jesus"?

    The "real Jesus" is the resurrected Jesus, a living person, that God has revealed as both Lord and Christ.

16. Name four different ways you can meet Jesus Christ today.

    Jesus can be met today through reading scriptures, participating in the sacraments, prayer, and through the lives of others.

17. Write the Jesus Prayer.

    "Lord Jesus Christ, Son of God, have mercy on me, a sinner."

18. What is the meaning of the name *Jesus*?

    Jesus means "God saves" or "Yahweh is salvation."

19. What is the meaning of the term *Christ*?

    Christ translates the Hebrew word, Messiah. It means "anointed."

20. What does it mean to call Jesus the Son of God? the Lord?
    The title "Son of God" expresses Jesus' divinity. The title "Lord" is likewise associated with the name of God. To call Jesus "Lord" is to state that he is God.

Assign and grade the Test on the Introduction (page 204 of this Manual). The answers follow below:

Test on the Introduction   Name:_____

Part 1: True or False. Mark **+** if the item is true and **0** if the item is false. (4 points each)

__0__ 1. A.D. stands for "in the year of the Lord."

__0__ 2. There is little or no connection between the historical Jesus and the living Christ of faith.

__+__ 3. God becoming human makes it possible for humans to share in the divine nature.

__+__ 4. Christian faith in Jesus as God's Son depends on apostolic testimony about him.

__0__ 5. Caesar Tiberius was the Roman Emperor at the time of Jesus' birth.

__+__ 6. The "real Jesus" of Christian faith is the resurrected Jesus.

__+__ 7. The name Jesus means "savior."

__0__ 8. By the end of the first century, the name *Jesus* was used often by Jewish fathers to name their boys.

__+__ 9. When Christians proclaim that Jesus is the "Son of God," they are professing that Jesus has the same divine nature as God the Father.

__+__ 10. *Adonai=Yahweh=Kyrios=*Lord!

Part 2: Multiple Choice. Write the letter of the best choice in the space provided. (4 points each)

__C__ 11. Which title of Jesus means "anointed one"?

  A. Lord

  B. Good Shepherd

  C. Christ

  D. Son of God

__A__ 12. Which title definitively proclaims the divinity of Jesus?

  A. Lord

  B. Christ

  C. Judge

  D. Prophet

__B__ 13. The essential teaching about salvation accomplished in the life, death, and resurrection of Jesus is known as:

  A. *diakonia*

  B. *kerygma*

  C. *leitourgeia*

  D. *koinonia*

__D___ 14. This heresy held that Jesus only "seemed" to be human:
- A. Arianism
- B. Nestorianism
- C. Fideism
- D. Docetism

__A___ 15. The title that translates the Hebrew word for *Messiah*:
- A. Christ
- B. Lord
- C. Jesus
- D. Alpha

Part 3: Short Fill-ins (4 points each)

__dogma___ 16. Term: "a doctrine taught with the highest authority"

__Incaration___ 17. Term: "the central teaching that God's Son became man in the person of Jesus Christ."

__Nazareth,___ 18. Give a possible "surname" for Jesus.
__Carpenter, Son of Joseph___

__4-6 B.C.___ 19. What year was Jesus born?

__Peter___ 20. This person proclaimed Jesus' true identity on the road to Caesarea Philippi.

Part 4: Short Answers (4 points each)

21. Write out the "Jesus Prayer."

Lord Jesus Christ, Son of God, have mercy on me, a sinner.

22-25. List and discuss four ways you can meet the living Lord today.

There are many acceptable answers. For example, scripture, prayer, each of the sacraments, the Church, other people, the poor, etc. Assign two points for the listing and two points for cogent discussion.

Prayer Lesson

➥ Assign for personal prayer and reflection the material in the Prayer Lesson, pages 26-27.

➥ To extend the lesson, have the students write a profile of one or two people who represent the gifts of thanks and humility in their words and actions.

one
·····

The Historical Jesus

Introducing the Chapter

Learning about the historical life of Jesus is an important endeavor for an academic course in Christology. The exercise is also a benefit to our faith, as it provides the groundwork evidence that the One who Christians hold to be Messiah and Savior can be witnessed and acknowledged even by those without faith.

This chapter begins by examining evidence outside of the New Testament for Jesus' existence. These include references to Roman and Jewish historians.

The focus of the chapter then addresses evidence compiled in the primary source material about the historical Jesus, the scriptures themselves. The chapter provides background on the Messiah as called forth in the Old Testament, looks at the establishment of the New Testament canon, and traces the kinds of writing and dates of writing of the New Testament books.

Next, the formation of the gospels are explored; from the public life and teachings of Jesus, to the oral tradition, and finally the actual writing of the good news of Christ.

The final major section examines contemporary methods of scripture scholarship, including detailed explanation of five subcategories under the historical-literary method: source, historical, form, redaction, and textual criticism.

Bibliography
· · · · · · · · · ·

Borg, Marcus. *Meeting Jesus Again for the First Time: the Historical Jesus and the Heart of Contemporary Faith*. San Francisco: HarperCollins, 1994.

Another book by a leading Jesus Seminar scholar. Not as radical as Crossan, but controversial conclusions nonetheless.

Brown, Raymond E. *Responses to 101 Questions on the Bible*. New York: Paulist Press, 1990.

Collins, Raymond F. *Introduction to the New Testament*. Garden City, NY: Doubleday, 1983.
Contains a good discussion of various scholarly methods of studying the New Testament.

Crossan, John Dominic. *The Historical Jesus: The Life of a Mediterranean Jewish Peasant*. San Francisco: HarperCollins, 1992.
This is the much-discussed book by Crossan, one of the founders of the controversial Jesus Seminar. Most competent Catholic biblical scholars (for example, John Meier) take great issue with Crossan's approach, especially his use of non-canonical works to build his case.

Green, Joel B. *Hearing the New Testament: Strategies for Interpretation*. Grand Rapids, MI: Wm. B. Eerdmans, 1995.

Harrington, Daniel, S.J. *Interpreting the New Testament*, rev. ed. Collegeville, MN: Liturgical Press, 1988.
Good section on methods of biblical criticism.

Johnson, Luke Timothy. *The Writings of the New Testament: An Interpretation*, rev. ed. Minneapolis: Fortress Press, 1999.

Marsh, Clive and Steve Moyise. *Jesus and the Gospels: An Introduction*. The Cassell Biblical Studies Series. London, England: Cassell, 1999.
Most readable overview. Short overview of apocryphal writings included and some discussion of various interpretations of the historical Jesus in vogue today.

Meier, John P. *A Marginal Jew: Rethinking the Historical Jesus*. New York: Doubleday, 1991, 1994, 2001.
Simply the best work by a Catholic author on the historical Jesus. If you read only one scholar on the historical Jesus, please work through these volumes. Outstanding and highly regarded by all in the scholarly community. Volume 1 sets out the critical method Meier uses to pursue the historical Jesus and sketches his cultural, political, and familial background. Volume 2 contrasts Jesus with John the Baptist, establishes him as an eschatological prophet in the line of Elijah, and gives a lengthy treatment to Jesus' miracles. The most recent volume, *A Marginal Jew: Companions and Competitors*, studies the various groups around Jesus and profiles groups like the Pharisees, Sadducees, Essenes, Samaritans, and so forth. Add these books to your personal library.

Perrin, Norman. *What Is Redaction Criticism?* Philadelphia: Fortress Press, 1969.

Porter, J.R. *Jesus Christ: The Jesus of History, the Christ of Faith*. New York: Oxford University Press, 1999.
Lavishly illustrated and very readable. Good to put into student hands.

Powell, Mark Allan. *Fortress Introduction to the Gospels*. Minneapolis: Fortress Press, 1997.

_____. *What Is Narrative Criticism?* Minneapolis: Fortress Press, 1991.

Throckmorton, Burton, ed. *Gospel Parallels*, 5th edition. Nashville, TN: Nelson, 1992.
A classic synopsis of the gospels which prints them in parallel texts for detailed comparison.

Van Voorst, Robert E. *Jesus Outside the New Testament: An Introduction to the Ancient Evidence*. Grand Rapids, MI: William B. Eerdmans Publishing Company, 2000.
A most helpful collection of the various non-canonical texts that mention Jesus. Excellent resource for teachers and others interested in the historical Jesus.

Wright, N.T. *Jesus and the Victory of God.* Volume 2 of *Christian Origins and the Question of God.* Minneapolis: Fortress Press, 1997.
    A great critique of the Jesus Seminar which does a good job of reconstructing the person and message of the historical Jesus.

Videos

The Gospels: The Holy Scriptures in Art, Music, and Text

This interactive CD-ROM allows synoptic comparisons. Includes interactive maps, art works, and music index (Films for the Humanities and Sciences®).

Jesus: The Complete Story

Produced in 2001, this is a good series that focuses on many archaeological sites that figure in Jesus' ministry. The second segment on Jesus' mission tends to stress more a political motivation for Jesus' healings and teachings. Segment 3 tries to reconstruct Jesus' face and reveals the mechanics of crucifixion. However, this segment also unduly raises issues about the historicity of the resurrection. Use with care. The series might be good background for the teacher. Fr. Jerome Murphy-O'Connor was one of the consultants for the series (BBC/Discover Channel video production on three videos of approximately 50 minutes each, Critics Choice).

Jesus: The New Way

An excellent series produced by Dr. Tom Wright, noted British biblical scholar who accepts the basic gospel message about Jesus, unlike so many of those in the Jesus Seminar who have a particular ax to grind. Segments could be used successfully with students or purchase for teacher background. Segment 6 on the resurrection is probably the best segment of all. A good counteract to the previous citation (six half-hour programs on two videotapes with script, teacher's guide, and student worksheets, Vision Video/Gateway Films).

Yeshua: The Land, The Promise, The Messiah

Presented by Dr. Oswald Hoffmann, *Yeshua* reveals ancient customs and beliefs with exceptional clarity and detail. Starts with Abraham and moves through Old Testament history to the time of Jesus. Well done, and despite that it was produced in the mid 1980s, it is still useful (five programs approximately 50 minutes each, Vision Video).

Resources

Craig, William Lane. "Contemporary Scholarship and the Historical Evidence for the Resurrection of Jesus Christ"; Truth 1, 1985.
    http://www.leaderu.com/truth/1truth22.html

The Development of the Canon of the New Testament
    http://www.ntcanon.org/

Early Christian Writings
    This magnificent site gives links to primary sources along with detailed commentary on origins of each document.
    http://www.earlychristianwritings.com/

The Encyclopedia of New Testament Textual Criticism
    Conceived by Rich Elliott.
    http://www.skypoint.com/~waltzmn/

Executable Outlines
Outlines on various books of the Bible.
http://www.ccel.org/contrib/exec_outlines/

Flavius Josephus
A list of his writings on-line can be accessed from this source:
http://www.jesusarchive.com/rd_josephus.html

Flavius Josephus Home Page
Contains the life and works of Josephus and studies about him.
http://members.aol.com/FLJOSEPHUS/home.htm

Jesus of Nazareth in Early Christian Gospels
Provides the texts of many non-canonical, or apocryphal gospels, such as the infancy gospel of James.
http://www.earlygospels.net/

The Jesus Seminar Forum
"The Jesus Seminar Forum is an introduction to the research of the Jesus Seminar of the Westar Institute and a bridge to Jesus scholarship on-line. Convened in 1985 by Robert W. Funk, the Jesus Seminar has become a lightning rod for international debate about the "historical Jesus"—that is, the real facts about the person to whom various Christian gospels refer. The Seminar's on-going project has been to evaluate the historical significance of every shred of evidence about Jesus from antiquity (about 30-200 CE). Over the past seventeen years more than two hundred scholars from North America & beyond have participated in its semi-annual meetings."
http://religion.rutgers.edu/jseminar/

Symbols of the Four Evangelists
http://clawww.lmu.edu/faculty/fjust/Evangelists_Symbols.htm

A Synoptic Gospels Primer
By Mahlon H. Smith of Rutgers University. Very good introduction to issues surrounding the synoptics.
http://religion.rutgers.edu/nt/primer/

The Synoptic Problem Home Page
Great website. Highly recommended.
http://www.mindspring.com/~scarlson/synopt/index.html

SECTION 1: One of a Kind and Historical Evidence for the Existence of Jesus (pages 29-34)

Objectives

• • • • • • • •

The goals of this section are to enable the students to:

➡ understand the uniqueness of Jesus;

➡ recognize Tacitus, Suetonius, and Pliny the Younger;

➡ identify Josephus as the most important Jewish historian who verifies Jesus' existence;

➡ summarize what we know of Jesus and his followers from Josephus' *Jewish Antiquities*.

Summary and Background Information

A mistaken impression persists: "If it weren't for the Bible we wouldn't know anything about Jesus." This misperception implies that maybe Jesus never even really existed, or if he did live there's no reason to believe anything in the Bible about him because the Bible has no basis in fact (another misperception).

This section presents historical evidence from outside of the Bible that not only did Jesus live, but also much of what we know about him from scripture has a very firm basis for belief, for faith. The section, after an activity that encourages the students to explore their relationship with Jesus, treats several Roman and Jewish sources—each of whom has something to say about Jesus, thereby adding to our extra-Biblical knowledge about him.

The section closes by pointing out that such historical evidence should provide some reassurance to Christians when they come up against the mistaken mentality mentioned above. Students are asked to list reasons why Jesus' real existence is important as if to say that while his nonexistence is a theoretical possibility, our study of Christ will be based on firm, confident belief about his reality.

As an opener, the students read the famous soliloquy, "One Solitary Life," as they consider the uniqueness of Jesus.

Warm Up

a) Point out to your students that no matter how much they know, there's always more to learn. There are things that even the best students want to know more about. We all know things, and we all want to know more about something; encourage the students to keep this in mind as they study this section.

b) Read and discuss the opening text under "One of a Kind" (pages 29-30).

c) Assign the activity under "Rate Your Relationship" (page 30 and page 205 of this manual) facilitating a brief class discussion that includes answering the questions that follow.

Using the Section

a) Assign the text under "Historical Evidence for the Existence of Jesus" up to and including "Pliny the Younger" (pages 31-32). Print the following on the board:

Cornelius Tacitus
Claudius Suetonius
Pliny the Younger

Invite volunteers to summarize briefly who each is and what they tell us about Jesus, proceeding until satisfactory identifications are elicited. Then assign the reading and questions from Acts 18:1-4 (page 32), as well as the questions (page 32) and journal writing activity (page 33). For follow up, allow for discussion to occur in pairs.

b) Print on the board:

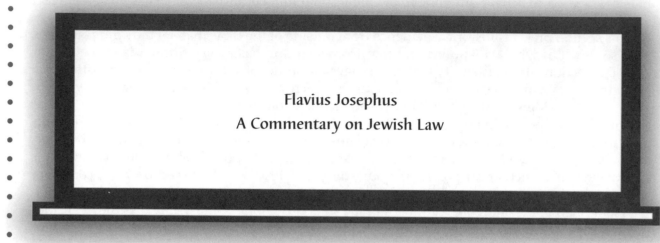

Flavius Josephus
A Commentary on Jewish Law

Inform your students that Josephus was a Jewish historian and that he essentially verifies that Jesus really lived in his collection of books the *Jewish Antiquities*. Point out that all of these references to Jesus from outside the Bible (new information for many students; see Warm Up "A") serve to make Christians confident that Jesus really entered history as a person; this makes Christianity more than just a philosophy or set of teachings. Christian faith is based on a real person who lived, died, and rose again to give us all eternal happiness.

c) Brainstorm with the students some of the reasons why it is important for Christians that non-Christian sources validate that Jesus really existed (see page 34).

Extending the Section

Encourage students to look up Thomas Aquinas' five ways of proving God's existence (see http://www.aquinasonline.com/Topics/5ways.html) and briefly delineate them for the class—particularly God as the "first mover" and "first cause." See what discussion ensues. Point out that we don't have to feel timid about believing in God. On the contrary, although we may empathize with people who doubt God's existence because of suffering or evil, in the end it's not believing in God that doesn't make sense. This course will help us grow in relationship with him and his Son, the Lord Jesus Christ.

Creative Learning

a) Invite students to compose a brief essay responding to the question "Did Jesus really live?"

b) Encourage students so inclined to compose an updated version of "One Solitary Life" (page 29).

SECTION 2: The Scriptures and Jesus and The Formation of the Gospels (pages 34-44)

Objectives

The goals of this section are to enable the students to:

➥ know how Jesus himself is the "new" testament;

➥ explain what is meant by the "canon of the Bible" and delineate the three criteria used by the early church before including a particular book in the New Testament canon;

➥ outline the three stages in the formation of the gospels.

Summary and Background Information

Although we do have information about Jesus that comes to us from outside of scripture, as addressed in the previous section, the vast majority of what we know about Christ we learn from the pages of the New Testament. This section answers some very basic questions about the New Testament and sets the stage for significant further study.

The concept of inspiration is addressed—what it means to say that the Bible is inspired by God. An overview of the New Testament's various books and dates is provided, and then a process or timeline for how the Gospels came to be is laid out. The process walks through three stages: that of the historical Jesus (6 B.C.–A.D. 30), the oral tradition (A.D. 30–50) and finally the actual writing of the Gospels and other New Testament works (A.D. 50–c.120).

It is worth pointing out that the Church was "up and running" for several decades before any of the New Testament was written. This runs counter to the notion that one could find something in the Bible that goes against any basic doctrinal or moral teaching of the Church. Studying scripture with the proper mindset not only enhances our relationship with God but also deepens our love for the Church.

Warm Up

a) Most of us enjoy cultural events and experiences of various sorts, even if it's just listening to music, watching a movie, or maybe even going to a play. Ask your students to reflect about the role that memory plays in singing song lyrics and in having a speaking part in a play. Conduct a brief discussion—encouraging them to acknowledge the tremendous human capacity for memorization.

b) Assign the exercise "Key Old Testament Readings" (page 37) with this variation: distribute the categories evenly among your students. When each student has read and summarized one selection in her or his journal, place the students in groups of six (one of each category per group) and ask them to report to the other members of their group about what they have read.

Using the Section

a) Ask for examples of how the word *covenant* came up during the "Key Old Testament Readings" exercise. Based on these examples, arrive at an agreed-upon definition of the word covenant. Assign the text under the heading "The Scriptures and Jesus" (pages 34-35). Ask students to write in their journals how Jesus himself is the "new" testament.

b) Review the history of the covenant theme in Scripture. Assign "Tracing God's Covenant" (pages 35-37).

c) Pause for a brief class discussion, "Why are there *four* written versions of the one gospel, the good news of Jesus?" Affirm all plausible answers. Review the material in the text section "The Scriptures as Inspired Writings" (pages 37-38).

d) Assign the text section under "Canon of the New Testament" (pages 38-39). In small groups, ask your students to discuss why the following would not have been included by the early church in the New Testament canon. Ask the students to name which of the three criteria applies to each:

A letter to "those who meet at Martha's house" is distributed within a five-mile area.

A "gospel of James" appears suddenly around the year 175.

A "second letter to the Hebrews" claims that Jesus ordered his followers to beat anyone who would not proclaim him to be God the Father disguised as a human.

Share the responses as a class and write on the board:

> ✓ Apostolic Origin ("gospel of James")
> ✓ Widespread Acceptance ("letter to those who meet at Martha's house")
> ✓ Conformity to the Rule of Faith ("2 Hebrews")

e) Assign the feature "The Gospel of Thomas" (page 39) and have the students note the reasons this gospel is not viewed by the Church as authentic.

f) Outline the stages involved in gospel formation covered on pages 41-44. List the following reasons the gospels were eventually written by the early Church:

> ✓ End of the world didn't come as soon as was first thought.
> ✓ Distortions were setting in.
> ✓ More instruction was needed.

Explain to them that these were the main reasons for the period of oral tradition following Jesus' public life transitioning to a time when the Gospels and other works were recorded in writing. (If you did Warm Up "A" you might remind them of the tremendous human capacity for memorization.) It is good to note that the Church existed for several decades—worshiping, teaching, and preaching—before the New Testament was written down.

g) Assign the entire text section under "The Formation of the Gospels" (pages 41-44) as a review.

Extending the Section

a) Ask the students to write a short journal entry explaining how Jesus is the "Word of God."

b) Point out that oral tradition is one thing, while plagiarism is another. Extend the section to the seventh commandment, "You shall not steal," pointing out that this applies to intellectual property, "bootlegging" or dubbing tapes for distribution, etc.

c) Assign "New Testament Books and Quick Facts" (page 41) and the accompanying journal assignment for homework.

Creative Learning

a) Ask your students to imagine the selections from "Key Old Testament Readings" (page 37) are being made into movies. What will their titles be? Who will star in them? Where and when might they be set?

b) Have the students devise mnemonic devices to remember the New Testament books. For example, "My Mom Loves Jelly" corresponds to the four gospels. See if the students can devise a longer mnemonic phrase that covers all twenty-seven books of the New Testament.

Section 3: How the Church Interprets the New Testament (pages 44-54)

Objectives

The goals of this section are to enable the students to:

➡ distinguish between the literal and spiritual senses of scripture;

➡ recognize five methods of studying the gospels;

➡ define the phrase *synoptic gospels* and outline an acceptable approach to the so-called synoptic problem.

Summary and Background Information

Catholics definitely have a unique way of interpreting our Bible; it is important to establish this up front and to give some sense of the different "lenses" through which the Church believes scripture can be studied profitably. The section seeks to accomplish these two tasks.

First, the Catholic tendency not to take all of the scripture literally is made clear. Parts of scripture, though, must be historically accurate (e.g., the Resurrection), so the pitfalls of an entirely subjective or relativistic approach to the Bible are also addressed. The Vatican II document *Dei Verbum* is mentioned and would be good background for students to reference as well.

The concept of biblical criticism is introduced and its main varieties—source criticism, historical criticism, form criticism, redaction criticism, and textual criticism—are explained briefly. While dwelling on these forms of criticism won't be particularly important, an acquaintance with them will serve your students well throughout the remaining chapters.

Finally, different translations of our Bible are discussed. *The New American Bible* is appropriately highlighted and its availability on-line is pointed out.

Warm Up

• • • • • • •

a) Ask the question "Why is it good to have more than one friend?" Conduct a brief discussion, trying to help your students see that in addition to giving us more ways and chances to show friendship and love, having a few good friends helps us know ourselves better. Each friend relates to us from a different perspective, shedding light on different aspects of ourselves.

b) Read or summarize the first two paragraphs of the section "How the Church Interprets the New Testament" (page 44). Call on students to briefly respond to the two questions presented in the text. Offer a short summary to the discussion based on the material in the next two text paragraphs. Print a short summary on the board as follows:

> ✓ Fundamentalists understand that everything written in the Bible is absolutely, literally, and historically true.
>
> ✓ Catholics understand that the Bible should be read prayerfully and critically.

Using the Section

• • • • • • • • • • • •

a) Expand on the term "fundamentalist" and the differences between a fundamentalist, Catholic, and secular understanding of the Bible. As a supplement you may wish to share the following comparisons:

Fundamentalist	Catholic	Secular
•• Bible is word of God	•• Bible is word of God in human words	•• Bible is a human creation only
•• Text is infallible	•• Text is incarnational	•• Text is equivalent to any other text
•• Concentrate on text	•• Concentrate on context	•• Read text as literature
•• Read text prayerfully	•• Read text prayerfully	•• Emphasis is on reader's subjective experience
•• Emphasis is on literal truth	•• Emphasis is on religious truth	

b) Assign the concluding paragraphs of the section "How the Church Interprets the New Testament" (pages 44-46). Print the following terms on the board:

Source Criticism

Historical Criticism

Form Criticism

Redaction Criticism

Textual Criticism

Refer to these terms, offering definitions, as the students read the subsections on pages 46-54.

c) Summarize the ways Catholic scholars study scripture, based on the *Dogmatic Constitution on Divine Revelation* (pages 45-46). Offer a brief explanation of two senses of scripture defined on page 46—the scriptural sense and literal sense. Assign the margin exercise (page 46). The document can be accessed at:

http://www.vatican.va/archive/hist_councils/ii_vatican_council/documents/
vat-ii_const_19651118_dei-verbum_en.html.

d) Assign the subsection "Source Criticism" (pages 46-47). Make sure to note the introduction of the terms *synoptic gospels* and the *Q source*. Point out that much of Mark's gospel appears also in Matthew and Luke. Be sure the students are familiar with the most common explanation for this observation introduced in the text.

e) Note the feature "Sample Contents of Q, M, L" (page 48). Consider allowing the students to work in small groups to complete the Journal Writing assignment, page 48.

f) Move to an explanation of historical criticism. Point out that the historical critic asks: "What really took place behind the given biblical text?" and "What is the historical context?" Assign the subsection (pages 48-49) for individual reading. Then quiz the students on the content. Ask: "Which criteria of historical criticism is applied in each of the following examples?"

❧ Both Matthew and Luke report Jesus was born during reign of Herod the Great in Bethlehem. (convergence)

❧ Jesus was the first to address God as "Abba." (originality)

❧ Jesus spoke Aramaic, a language different than the rest of the written gospel. (linguistic analysis)

❧ Throughout his ministry, Jesus upset the religious leaders of his day. (consistency)

g) Define form criticism from the text section, pages 49-50. Show the class a daily newspaper. Ask the students to list all the literary forms present in it. Assign the exercise "Form Criticism" (page 51 and page 206 of this Manual). Answers follow:

1. Mk 8:1-9 (nature miracle)
2. Mt 17:19-20 (riddle)
3. Lk 1:46-55 (hymn/prayer)
4. Jn 6:51 (revelation discourse)
5. Mk 1:23-26 (exorcism)

6. Lk 12:49 (controversy)
7. Lk 10:29-37 (parable)
8. Mt 10:1-12 (riddle)
9. Mk 7:24-30 (healing)

h) Define redaction criticism as "the examination of the editor compiling and adapting sources into a single unified work." Assign the subsection, "Redaction Criticism" (pages 51-52). Point out that redaction criticism asks (write on the board):

✓ How and why were the sources arranged the way they are?

✓ How did the editor's theological slant influence his arrangement of the material?

i) Display some of the many Bible translations available today, including some of those mentioned in the text (pages 53-54). Call on three students to come to the front of the class. Have each person look up the same assigned passage and read it from their version of the Bible. Comment on the differences.

Extending the Section

a) Assign the margin exercise on page 49. You may wish to have the students incorporate all three assignments into one report on the historical analysis of Matthew 4:12-17.

b) Regarding redaction criticism (the editor's work in forming the gospels), ask the students to rank by percentage to a total of 100 percent, the weight each of the following resources should have in a total gospel portrait of Jesus: healings, nature miracles, passion narrative, resurrection and appearance accounts, infancy narratives, kingdom of God sayings, parables, Jesus' teaching sermons, baptism of Jesus, biography of Mary, Peter, and John the Baptist.

c) Assign the exercise under "Genealogy of Jesus" (page 52). Hint: Remind the students that Matthew wrote for a Jewish-Christian audience, Luke for a Gentile-Christian audience.

Creative Learning

a) Invite the students to write a brief allegorical tale, a story with a moral, or an anagogic interpretation of a current event or phenomenon.

b) Jesus at age twelve (Lk 2:41-52) evokes many reactions. Ask the students to choose a form of expression (art, writing, etc.) and share any thoughts or feelings they'd like after reading this account.

c) In small groups, have the students compose skits showing a person living out all of the Beatitudes (Mt 5:3-6, 11-12; Lk 6:20-23) within a very defined amount of time (e.g., one week). The class can guess what Beatitude is being demonstrated as each skit is performed.

d) Play the song "American Pie" (Don McLean). Have the students guess at the meaning of some of the 1960s reference in the lyrics. (For example, the "day the music died" is commonly believed to be the day '50s star Buddy Holly died in a plane crash). Encourage them to check on the Internet for other possible interpretations of the lyrics. Connect this assignment with linguistic analysis that is part of historical criticism.

Conclusion

a) Allow time for the students to study the Summary Points and Selected Vocabulary terms (pages 54-55 and 56-57). Then quiz them on these items in preparation for the Chapter Test.

b) Assign the Review Questions (pages 55-56). Grade them and review them as preparation for the Chapter 1 Test.

Answers to Review Questions

1. Identify Tacitus, Suetonius, and Pliny the Younger.

    Tacitus was the Roman historian who named Christ in a report about the fires started in Rome under the reign of Nero. Suetonius offers a report of Jews being expelled from Rome, mentioning Christians as instigators. Pliny the Younger, a Roman writer and biographer, mentioned Christianity several times in a letter to the Emperor Trajan.

2. Why is Josephus important for proving that Jesus actually existed?

    Josephus was an impartial Jewish historian who attests that Jesus and his followers were very much on the scene in the first century.

3. What is our primary source of knowledge about Jesus?

    Our primary source of knowledge about Jesus is the New Testament.

4. What is the meaning of the word *testament*? How is Jesus himself the "new" testament?

    Testament means "covenant." Jesus is the "new" testament because he is God's perfect representative. The New Testament shows how his words and actions reveal God's active presence in the world.

5. List three examples that show how God was faithful to the Chosen People during the Old Testament.

    For example, Yahweh rescued Jews from slavery in Egypt, renewed his covenant with Moses on Mount Sinai, gave them the Promised Land, anointed a king.

6. What is *biblical inspiration*?

    Inspiration refers to the Holy Spirit teaching truth through the Bible without destroying the free and personal activity of the human writer.

7. Define the term *evangelist*.

    Evangelist means "gospel writer."

8. Define *canon of the Bible*. What three criteria did the early Church use before including a particular book in the New Testament canon?

    The "canon of the Bible" refers to the official list of books the Church considers its inspired writings. The Church included in the canon those writings that met the following criteria: apostolic origin, widespread acceptance, and conformity to the rule of faith.

9. What are the different types of writings in the New Testament?

    The different types of writing in the New Testament are: gospels, Acts of the Apostles, Pauline letters, Hebrews, Catholic epistles, and Revelation of John.

10. What were the three stages in the formation of the gospels?

    The three stages of gospel formation were the public life and teaching of Jesus, the oral tradition, and the New Testament writings.

11. Identify the terms *kerygma* and *didache*.

    Kerygma refers to "preaching to unbelievers." Didache refers to "teachings" for those who accepted Jesus.

12. Why did the early Church finally decide to write their scriptures?

    The Church decided to write the scriptures because 1) the end of the world was not coming as quickly as the early Christians at first thought it would; 2) distortions to the gospel message in oral form were setting in; 3) a written record of the apostles' preaching was needed for Christian instruction.

13. What is the historical-literary approach to studying the Bible?

    The historical-literary method refers to examining the biblical texts carefully in their historical and literary context.

14. What three rules of interpretation should Catholic biblical scholars follow when doing their work?

    Three rules of interpretation for Catholic biblical scholarship are: 1) pay attention to the content and unity of the whole scripture; 2) look at scripture within the living Tradition of the Church; and 3) "be attentive to the analogy of faith."

15. Explain the difference between the literal and spiritual senses of scripture.

    The literal sense refers to what the words of scripture actually mean using sound rules for interpretation. The spiritual sense refers to how the texts, realities, and events in the Bible can be signs.

16. What does source criticism address?

    Source criticism tries to determine what source or sources the gospel and other New Testament writers used to compose their works.

17. What is the so-called synoptic problem? Outline an acceptable approach to it.

    The "synoptic problem" refers to how the gospels of Matthew, Mark, and Luke can be "seen together." Putting the three gospels together shows how they can be compared. (See example on page 46 of Student Text.)

18. Identify Q, L, and M.

    "Q" comes from the German "quelle," meaning "source." "L" stands for Luke and "M" stands for Matthew. Each refers to unique sources of gospel material.

19. What does historical criticism attempt to do?

    Historical criticism attempts to discover what evangelists really wanted to say when they wrote a particular text. Another goal is to determine whether what the gospels report about Jesus can be traced directly to him.

20. Explain two methods scholars use to verify the historical reliability of sayings or events in the gospels.

    Methods for verifying historical reliability of Jesus' sayings or events include linguistic analysis, originality, convergence, and consistency.

21. List, define, and give an example of three different forms of writing found in the New Testament.

    Answers will vary. Forms of writing include miracle stories, parables, riddles, pronouncement stories, hyperbole, controversy, hymn/prayer, and revelation discourse.

22. Define *redaction criticism*.

    Redaction criticism focuses on the evangelists as editors: how and why they arranged the sources the way they did.

23. Identify the major theological concern of each evangelist. Identify the audience for which each evangelist wrote.

    Matthew wrote for a Jewish-Christian audience and stressed Jesus' fulfillment of Old Testament prophecies. Mark wrote for a suffering Christian community and presented Jesus as the Suffering Servant. Luke wrote for a Gentile-Christian community and highlighted Jesus as the universal Messiah. John wrote for various churches around the Roman empire, presenting a theologically developed portrait of Jesus.

24. What is *textual criticism*?

    Textual criticism compares the minor changes and mistakes copyists made down through the centuries so that the translations we have today are as accurate as possible.

25. List two important Catholic translations of the Bible into English.

    Two English translations by Catholic scholars include: New American Bible *and* The New Jerusalem Bible.

Chapter 1 Test

Assign and grade the Chapter 1 Test (page 207 of this Manual). The answers follow below:

Chapter 1 Test   Name:_____

All questions worth 4 points each.

Part 1: Matching. Please match the person or type of biblical criticism in Column B with the descriptions in Column A.

Column A		Column B
B	1. wrote of a riot in Rome caused by "Chrestus"	A. Pliny the Younger
C	2. Jewish historian who referred to Jesus	B. Suetonius
A	3. masterful letter writer who wrote to Emperor Trajan about Christians	C. Josephus
		D. Tacitus
G	4. tries to discover what comes from Jesus in the gospel texts	E. Lucian of Samosota
		F. source criticism
H	5. studies literary differences in the biblical texts	G. historical criticism
I	6. analyzes how gospel writers edited their works for their particular audiences	H. form criticism
		I. redaction criticism

Part 2: True or False. Mark **+** if the statement is true and **0** if the statement is false.

0   7. There are a total of twenty-three books in the New Testament.

+   8. *Gospel* refers to Jesus himself, the preaching about him, and the four written accounts.

+   9. A New Testament book was not considered inspired unless it had roots in the apostolic witnesses.

0   10. The gospel of Thomas is an inspired biblical work.

+   11. Early apostolic preaching involved *catechesis*, that is, further instructions for new converts.

0   12. *Q* was a source for the gospels of Matthew and John.

+   13. *M* was a unique source for Matthew's gospel.

Part 3: Short Fill-ins.

the gospels   14. What is our primary source of knowledge about the historical Jesus?

covenant   15. A __?__ is a special kind of contract marked by *hesed* (loving-kindness).

inspiration   16. Biblical __?__ refers to the Holy Spirit teaching truth without destroying the free and personal activity of the human author.

evangelist	17. Term for a gospel writer: __?__.
canon	18. The official list of books considered inspired is known as the __?__ of the Bible.
oral preaching	19. The three stages in the formation of the gospels are the historical Jesus, the New Testament writings, and __?__.
Luke	20. Matthew, Mark, and __?__ are known as the synoptic gospels.
New American or *New Jerusalem Bible*	21. Name a good English translation of the Bible done by *Catholic* scholars.
A.D. 65-73 (Mark)	22. Give an acceptable date for when the first gospel was written.

Part 4: Short Answers

23. Why did it take so long before the gospels were written?
Early Christians thought Jesus would return in their lifetimes.

24.-25. Discuss two reasons why the gospels were eventually written:

For example, eyewitnesses were dying, distortions were setting in, needed an objective record, needed a source to use for catechetical purposes, etc.

Prayer Lesson

•◆ The text beginning "Dear Jesus" (page 57) is intended for personal reflection.

•◆ Ask the students to record five resolutions to the Prayer Lesson in their journals.

two
·····

The New Testament World of Jesus

Introducing the Chapter

A primary goal of this chapter is to remind the students that as a historical person, Jesus actually walked on the earth in a specific time and place in history. From history, we know several things about Jesus: that he came from Nazareth, that he was a devout Jew, that he could read, and that he knew more than one language.

The chapter looks at important parts of Jesus' world that help us to understand more about him.

Palestine, the Holy Land, is explored. Its four major terrains and major cities are named and described in the context of how the geography impacted Jesus' life and ministry.

Jesus spoke a special dialect of Aramaic, a common language of his day. Because he studied in the synagogue, it is likely that Jesus also know some Hebrew, the language of the Jewish scriptures.

The importance of the synagogue and Temple and religious rituals and practices associated with each in the life of Jesus are discussed.

The chapter then moves into an overview of the political climate in first century Palestine. The harsh situation for Jews living under Roman rule in the years surrounding Jesus' life impacted the Jewish desire and expectations for a Messiah. When Jesus came, he met the expectations for some, but failed to meet the militaristic and powerful expectations of many more.

To further explain the religious and cultural climate in which Jesus lived, more explanation is offered about the Jewish messianic expectations, the covenant and Torah, and beliefs about judgment, resurrection, and the spirit world.

As the students move to deeper study of the New Testament, several names of Jewish sects will arise including the Sadducees, Pharisees, Essenes, and Zealots. Explanations of the origins and special beliefs of each of these sects are offered. Finally, the chapter focuses on other people of significance in the New Testament: tax collectors, common people, Gentiles, and women.

This chapter offers a necessary prelude to the more detailed study of the New Testament. But it is merely a prelude. The students are very willing to absorb these details at the beginning of a course. But try not to let the details get in the way of the real purpose of the course: meeting the living Lord in the pages of the New Testament.

Bibliography

• • • • • • • • •

Brown, Raymond E., S.S., Joseph Fitzmyer, S.J., and Roland E. Murphy, O.Carm. *The New Jerome Biblical Commentary*. Englewood Cliffs, New Jersey: Prentice Hall, 1990.
    You simply must obtain a copy of this one-volume gold mine for your own use during the course. The background articles alone are worth the price of the book.

Charpentier, Etienne. *How to Read the New Testament*. New York: Crossroad, 1989.
    An excellent introduction. You can use some of the ideas in teaching any course on the New Testament.

Coleman, Lyman. *Serendipity Youth Ministry Encyclopedia*. Littleton, CO: Serendipity House, 1985.
    Many exercises can be used to apply the New Testament to the lives of your students. Permission to photocopy the exercises is granted.

Fitzmyer, Joseph A., S.J. *The Dead Sea Scrolls and Christian Origins*. Grand Rapids, MI: William B. Eerdmans Publishing Company, 2000.
    Magisterial in scope. A collection of essays by one of the leading experts on the scrolls. Impressive scholarship.

Freyne, Sean. *The World of the New Testament*, New Testament Message 2. Wilmington, DE: Michael Glazier, 1980.

Harpur, James and Marcus Braybrooke. *The Collegeville Atlas of the Bible: A Visual Guide to the Word in Biblical Times*. Collegeville, MN: Liturgical Press, 1999.

Jeremias, Joachim. *Jerusalem in the Time of Jesus*. Minneapolis: Fortress Press, 1975.

Malina, Bruce J. *Windows on the World of Jesus: Time Travel to Ancient Judea*. Louisville: Westminster/John Knox Press, 1993.
    Fascinating glimpses into the world of Jesus on topics like honor and shame; interpersonal behavior; in-group, out-group, and intra-family relationships; loving-kindness; common values; and concept of time. Highly recommended.

Millard, Alan. *Discoveries from the Time of Jesus*. Oxford, England: A Lion Book, 1990.
    This outstanding, popularly written book is lavishly illustrated. Makes the New Testament world come alive.

Murphy, F. J. *The Religious World of Jesus*. Nashville: Abington, 1991.

Osiek, Carolyn. *What Are They Saying about the Social Setting of the New Testament?* New York: Paulist Press, 1992.

Pilch, John J. *The Cultural Dictionary of the Bible*. Collegeville, MN: Liturgical Press, 1998.

Sawicki, Marianne. *Crossing Galilee: Architectures of Contact in the Occupied Land of Jesus*. Harrisburg, PA: Trinity Press International, 2000.
    Draws on archaeology and anthropology to fix Jesus in his Galilean cultural context.

Videos

· · · · ·

Dead Sea Scrolls

Includes early footage on the discovery of the scrolls plus interviews with four current scholars. Fascinating and accurate documentary (50 minutes, Ignatius Press).

The Holy Land

"A journey to nearly 40 major sites as they appear today . . . with a reminder of what happened there in Biblical history" (56 minutes, Reader's Digest).

Jesus and His Times

A three-part series produced by Reader's Digest. Very well-done and supportive of traditional teachings about Jesus. The segments are entitled "The Story Begins," "Among the People," and "The Final Days." Each segment is approximately an hour long (173 total minutes, Critics Choice).

Jesus: The New Way

An excellent series produced by Dr. Tom Wright, noted British Biblical scholar who accepts the basic gospel message about Jesus, unlike so many of those in the Jesus Seminar who have a particular ax to grind. Segments could be used successfully with students or purchase for teacher background (six 30 minute programs on two videotapes with script, teacher's guide, and student worksheets, Vision Video/Gateway Films).

Rome: Footsteps of Peter & Paul

The footsteps of these two early apostles are retraced to landmarks like the Coliseum, Mamertine Prison, and Vatican City (60 minute video, Ignatius Press).

Steps into the Holy Land

Visual tour of the Holy Land including Bethlehem, Calvary, Nazareth, and Jerusalem (60 minute video, Ignatius Press).

Where Jesus Walked

A docudrama that leads the viewer on a pilgrimage through the Holy Land from Christ's birth to his resurrection (90 minute video, Ignatius Press).

Yeshua: The Land, The Promise, The Messiah

Presented by Dr. Oswald Hoffmann, *Yeshua* reveals ancient customs and beliefs with exceptional clarity and detail. Starts with Abraham and moves through Old Testament history to the time of Jesus. Well done, and despite that it was produced in the mid 1980s, it is still useful (five programs, approximately 50 minutes each, Vision Video).

Resources

· · · · · · · ·

Bible History Online

Great links to wonderful graphics.
http://www.bible-history.com/bhodb/links.cfm?cat=2&sub=3

Charlesworth, J.H. *Jesus and Jehohanan: An Archeological Note on Crucifixion.*

Originally published in the *Expository Times*, 1973; republished on the Internet by PBS Frontline.

http://www.pbs.org/wgbh/pages/frontline/shows/religion/jesus/crucifixion.html

de Lacey, Douglas R. *Pharisees*.
http://www2.evansville.edu/ecoleweb/articles/pharisees.html

Edersheim, Alfred. "Sketches of Jewish Social Life."
http://www.ccel.org/e/edersheim/sketches/sketches.htm

Excavations at Sepphoris
Fascinating site on the archaeological work done by scholars at the University of South Florida, among others.
http://www.colby.edu/rel/archaeology/Israel.htm

Holy Net
Graphically rich review of Jesus' life through a tour of the sites connected to his life. Good site.
http://www.holynet.cc/

Into His Own: Perspectives on the World of Jesus
Good information on the political, social, intellectual, and cultural climate of Jesus' time.
http://religion.rutgers.edu/iho/index.html

Maps on the Historic Jesus
Some helpful maps provided.
http://www.historicjesus.com/maps/index.html

Meier, John P. "The Historical Jesus and the Historical Samaritans: What Can Be Said?" *Biblica* **81; 2000.**
http://www.bsw.org/project/biblica/bibl81/comm05.html

Palestine in the Time of Jesus: Social Structures and Social Conflicts
Images and information provided to supplement K.C. Hanson and Douglas E. Oakman's text of the same name (Minneapolis: Fortress Press, 1998).
http://www.kchanson.com/PTJ/ptj.html

Windows into the World of Jesus
http://www.columbusmennonite.org/Bible/default.htm

SECTION 1: Jesus of Nazareth, Palestine: The Holy Land, and Language and Dialect of Jesus' Time (pages 59-67)

Objectives
• • • • • • • •

The goals of this section are to enable the students to:

➼ uncover basic knowledge about Jesus from the scriptures;

➼ demonstrate a basic familiarity with Palestine including the significance of Capernaum and Jerusalem;

➼ describe Jerusalem of Jesus' day including its relation to Samaria;

➼ Identify Jesus' native tongue and other languages he may have spoken.

Summary and Background Information

Knowing about the world of Jesus helps us understand the Bible better and enables us to know the Lord at a deeper level. This section provides excellent background information on the land Jesus inhabited and the languages that he and his contemporaries spoke and understood.

The Holy Land at the time of Christ is described in its geography, major regions, and prominent cities. Outstanding, useful maps invite students to acquaint themselves more deeply with Jerusalem and surrounding locales; an activity encourages them to use both map and Bible.

The section's end provides details about Aramaic, the language of Jesus. Other languages pertinent for studying Scripture—namely Hebrew, Greek, and Latin—are commented upon in a way that when combined with a basic familiarity with Aramaic will allow your students to appreciate certain aspects of the New Testament in a richer context.

Chapter 2 in the Student Text opens by examining some facts about Jesus revealed in the gospels. A short narrative encourages the students to think about what it means to really *know* Jesus.

Warm Up

a) Ask the students to comment on the following: "What does it mean to know Christ?" Accept responses that are descriptive of faith, as well as those that show a knowledge of information *about* Jesus. Point out the differences of what it means to "know Jesus" based on the text section "Jesus of Nazareth" (pages 59-60).

b) All of us are affected by elected officials, and some of us may even become one. Ask: "Who are some of your elected officials?" "What good reasons might a person have for wanting to hold an office or for accepting a political appointment?" Begin to relate the discussion to first-century expectations of the Jews for a Messiah.

c) Assign the exercise "The World of Jesus" (pages 60-61). You may wish to check answers only after the students have completed the section. *Answers:* 1—a; 2—c; 3—b (Both Jews and Romans believed there were other miracle workers besides Jesus. Jesus was unique, however. He did not use magical formulas, refused payment for his deeds, and responded to the faith of those in need.); 4—a (The thirty-three-foot papyrus rolls usually determined the length of the manuscripts in the ancient world. Luke's gospel ran the maximum length. This is why he needed another roll to write the sequel, the Acts of the Apostles.); 5—b (The New Testament only records Jesus writing once—in John 8:6—with his finger in the sand.); 6—b (Matthew and Mark inform us that Jesus was emotionally moved by people in distress—for example, Matthew 9:36; Mark 8:2. Luke 7:13 reports how Jesus took great pity on a widow. John reports how Jesus wept on hearing of Lazarus' death.); 7—a (A mother-son bond has always been considered extremely close. Sons are a mother's best insurance in old age. Achievements of sons often reflect upon the good deeds of the mother).

Using the Text

a) Introduce the text section "Palestine: The Holy Land" (page 61). As part of the introduction, show a current and detailed map of Palestine. Refer to contemporary political situations that occur in the area. Also display, as possible, travel information related to the area.

b) Continue the introduction of Palestine. Divide the students into small groups to make poster-size maps of the Holy Land. Ask them to use atlas maps to locate and include the following on their group map:

Cities	Bodies of Water	Provinces
Bethany	Jordan River	Northern (location of Nazareth)
Bethlehem	Dead Sea	Middle
Bethsaida	Mediterranean Sea	Southern (location of Jerusalem)
Caesarea Philippi	Sea of Galilee	
Cana		
Capernaum		
Emmaus		
Jerusalem		
Nazareth		
Masada		
Tiberias		

c) Assign for reading the subsection "Geography" (pages 61-62) which describes four major terrains. Print them on the board:

Terrains of Palestine:

✓ coastal plain
✓ mountain range
✓ Rift Valley
✓ Transjordan

Call on students to point out these terrains on a class map and include them on the group map they have created.

d) Summarize the text in the subsection "Important Regions and Cities" (pages 62-64). Have the students note on their map the regions the cities they have listed fall under. You may also wish to have the students identify the location of Perea, Decapolis, Phonecia, and Idumea and locate and share some information on their relevance to the Jesus' story.

e) Assign the "Map of the Holy Land" exercise (page 64 and page 208 of this Manual). *Answers:* Lk 24:13 (14); Lk 10:30 (11); Mt 11:20-22 (1); Jn 1:44 (6); Jn 21 (5); Lk 18:35-43 and Lk 19:1-10 (11)

f) Cover the material from the section "Language and Dialect of Jesus' Time" (pages 65-67). Summarize the essence of the section, that Jesus spoke Aramaic but may have used Hebrew and Greek and have been exposed to Latin. Make sure the students understand how the use of parallel statements, comparisons, and exaggeration can be used to study and compare Jesus' speech.

g) Assign the questions related to Matthew 5:29 (see page 67). Point out that the exaggeration used here by Jesus was meant to convey that no sacrifice is too great to avoid the pains of Gehenna.

h) Point out the letters "INRI" on a class crucifix. Have the students read the separate feature on the subject (page 67).

Extending the Section

• • • • • • • • • • • • • • • • •

a) Have the students do a report on the economics, politics, culture, and religion of one of the regions of the Holy Land as it functions today.

b) Ask the students to create a timeline of the following events from 100 B.C. to A.D. 100 in chronological order. Assign bonus points for any other events the students can add to their time-line:

- ❧ The destruction of the Temple (7)
- ❧ The birth of Jesus (6-4 B.C.)
- ❧ The Romans occupy Palestine (100 B.C.)
- ❧ Paul begins to write letters (51)
- ❧ The death of King Herod (4 B.C.)
- ❧ Pilate becomes procurator of Jerusalem (26-36)
- ❧ The reign of Tiberius (14-37)

Creative Learning

• • • • • • • • • • • • •

a) Assign the students to work in small groups to create a media presentation (magazine photos, news articles) describing the geography of the four regions of the Holy Land.

b) Have the students write profiles of themselves using the following information. This activity will provide a prelude to the material in the next section. Ask: "How do the following affect your personal makeup?"

- ❧ politics in your time
- ❧ geographic/climatic factors where you live
- ❧ economic factors
- ❧ religious influences in your culture

- ❧ secular influences in your culture
- ❧ ethnic heritage

SECTION 2: Religious Feasts and Practices of Jesus' Time and The Political Climate in First Century Palestine (pages 67-73)

Objectives

• • • • • • • •

The goals of this section are to enable the students to:

- ❧ distinguish between synagogue and Temple, including the role each played in religious feasts and weekly activities;
- ❧ describe in some detail the political scene of Jesus' day;
- ❧ explain the existence of slavery in Jesus' time and how his teaching applies to slavery.

Summary and Background Information

Politics and religion were as influential, controversial, and interesting in Jesus' day as ours. Knowing about the political and religious atmosphere in which Jesus lived helps us appreciate him and extend our relationship with him beyond ourselves to a community of faith and a life of responsible citizenship.

The religious feasts, role of the Temple, and place of synagogues in Jesus' environment open this section. Students will learn about Passover and other celebrations that were a part of the Lord's life.

A fairly detailed account of the day's political situation occupies much of the section. Rulers like Herod, events like the Maccabean Revolt, and groups like the tax collectors are discussed and explained briefly.

The sensitive issue of slavery wraps up this section with a reading of St. Paul's letter to Philemon in its entirety. This reading is good preparation for the rest of this text as very much of the New Testament is read in the course, learning about it and its principal focus: Jesus.

Warm-Up

a) Ask the students to name their three favorite days of the year. As a follow-up, ask: "How has this list changed in the past five years?"

b) Ask the students to rank the three "greatest" Christian religious feasts and name what each celebrates. For the purposes of this discussion, it's okay to accept different responses, but generally the three greatest Christian feasts are Easter, Pentecost, and Christmas.

c) Play all or part of a video that depicts the religious atmosphere Jesus faced in his day. For example, *Yeshua: The Land, The Promise, The Messiah.*

Using the Section

a) Assign students in triads to read *one* of the following sections: "Synagogue" (pages 67-69), "Temple" (page 69), and "Jewish Feasts" (pages 69-70). Allow time for reading. Then ask each person to summarize his or her reading to the other two people in the group.

b) Assist the students in making connections between synagogue services and worship practices the Church uses today (see margin exercise, page 69).

c) Assign the other three margin exercises on page 69. (Jesus criticizes the scribes and Pharisees in Matthew 23:2, 6. In Luke 13:14, Jesus is criticized himself for performing cures on the Sabbath.)

d) Summarize the text under the heading "The Political Climate in First Century Palestine" (pages 70-72). Write the following names on the board. Have the students use the text and a Bible dictionary to record information about each person in their notebook.

> ✓ Caesar Augustus
> ✓ Caesar Tiberius
> ✓ Nero Claudius Caesar
> ✓ Herod the Great
> ✓ Archelaus
> ✓ Herod Antipas
> ✓ Philip
> ✓ Pontius Pilate
> ✓ Felix
> ✓ Festus

e) Combine a study of "The Practice of Slavery" (pages 72-73) with the reading/exercise, "The Letter to Philemon" (page 73).

Extending the Section

a) Based on the letter to Philemon, assign a short essay entitled "Equality Within the Christian Community."

b) Ask the students to research and report on the role religion played in the abolition movement in the nineteenth century.

c) Invite a rabbi to class as a guest speaker. Ask him to explain the Jewish beliefs covered in this section.

Creative Learning

a) Many song lyrics speak of the theme of "passing over" from something bad to something good. Ask the students to bring in recordings of such songs. Play excerpts. Then point out that the Paschal mystery is the Passover that affects everyone. Some more technically-oriented students may be able to produce mixes or medleys that make playing these songs easy and smooth.

b) Have the students write a letter to the editor of a "Roman" newspaper from the point of view of a Jewish person living in Palestine during Christ's life. They should mention specific Roman practices and beliefs that would be offensive to Jews.

SECTION 3: Jewish Beliefs and Practices, Religious Sects in Jesus' Time, and Other People in the New Testament (pages 74-80)

Objectives

The goals of this section are to enable the students to:

➡ explain briefly four important Jewish beliefs in Jesus' day;

➡ identify the four major sects within Judaism of New Testament times;

➡ comment briefly on the role that tax collectors, "common people," Gentiles, and women played in Jesus' society.

Summary and Background Information

This section provides background on some of the major religious groups of Jesus' day, as well as some other notable people mentioned in the New Testament.

Before describing these groups, though, some important Jewish beliefs are commented upon. The long-expected Messiah, for example, is described in ways that make it clear why many people of Jewish faith simply didn't believe that Jesus was he. Jewish teachings about law, resurrection (or lack thereof), and angels are also aptly depicted.

The "denominations" within Judaism in Jesus' time are reviewed next. This may be the first time many of your students have heard any details about these groups who they've heard mentioned so many times in Scripture; this section, then, can be very informative for them.

The section and chapter end by going over a few more important New Testament-era groups. The stage is now nicely set for your students to delve into the Gospels after one more chapter—a specifically Christological one.

Warm-Up

a) Conduct a brief discussion that helps the class arrive at some consensus about what they perceive to be the most important beliefs of Catholic faith. Help them to differentiate between theological belief (e.g., belief in the Trinity or the resurrection of Christ) with religious doctrine (e.g., Church laws).

b) Point out how the Pharisees of Jesus' day could be very legalistic. For example, share some examples of activities not permitted by Pharisees on the Sabbath: tying or untying a rope, putting out a lamp, starting a fire, sewing two stitches, using medicine, walking more than 3,000 feet, going out while wearing an artificial leg. Have the students discuss why they think Jesus would have been frustrated and tested by such legalistic people.

Using the Section

a) Assign the text under "Jewish Beliefs and Practices"and under the heading "The Messiah" (page 74).

b) Have the students complete the worksheet "Jesus the Messiah" (page 209 of this Manual), comparing the Old Testament expectations of a messiah with those presented in Mark's gospel.

c) Ask the students to 1) define the Torah; and 2) explain what role the Torah has in the Jewish faith. After a brief discussion, read or summarize the material from the text section "The Covenant and the Torah" (pages 74-75).

d) Read or summarize the brief text section "Judgment and Resurrection" (page 75). Connect this material with a more in-depth study of the Church's belief about the resurrection (see the *Catechism of the Catholic Church*, especially 988-1014).

e) Have the students complete the text section "Spirit World" (page 76) together with the exercise "Angels" (page 76). *Answers*: Gabriel (Lk 1:11-22); Michael (Dn 10:13,21); ministered to Jesus (Mt 4:11); strengthened Jesus in time of prayer (Lk 22:43); they tell Mary about the risen Jesus (Jn 20:11-40); angels will help to gather the elect (Mk 13:27).

f) Assign the sections under "Sadducees" (page 77), Pharisees (pages 77-78), Essenes (pages 79-80), and Zealots (page 80) for individual reading. Have the class help you with a summary, as follows:

Sadducees—priestly class of Jews who often compromised with Roman power; conservative in religion

Pharisees—Jews who were religiously liberal with a pious commitment to the law; would not compromise with Roman rulers, written about harshly in New Testament

Essenes—apocalyptic group; lived strict aesthetic life; producers of the Dead Sea Scrolls

Zealots—sought independence from Rome through military means

g) Further summarize Jesus' debates between the Pharisees and Sadducees by taking the students through the exercise on pages 78-79. Each student should have a Bible, read the passages, and recite the answers to each reference.

h) Assign the entire section, "Other People in the New Testament" (pages 80-82). From their study of all of the "characters" in the New Testament, quiz the students on all of the groups mentioned, asking them to write a one-sentence description of the groups as well as a brief statement as to the relationship the group had with Jesus.

Extending the Section

a) Related to a study of the Torah, this may be an excellent opportunity to review the Ten Commandments. Have the students copy of the Ten Commandments in their notebook or journal. Ask them to work in pairs to practice memorization of the commandments. Check their competency in a friendly game or quiz format.

b) As a research project, have the students examine one or more non-mainline Christian denominations (e.g., Seventh Day Adventist, Christian Science, Church of Jesus Christ of Latter Day Saints, etc.) and report on its origins, founder, beliefs, worship practice, and scriptures.

c) Assign the report on the Dead Sea Scrolls suggested in the margin feature on page 80.

Creative Learning

a) Note the Chi-Rho symbol (page 74). Ask the students to research and depict in art form other symbols for Christ.

b) Invite the students to prepare a presentation on how angels have been portrayed artistically through the years. This could involved technology (e.g., a PowerPoint presentation) and/or a piece of original artwork.

c) Encourage interested students to role play a discussion between the Sadducees, Pharisees, Essenes, and Zealots about how to recognize the Messiah. Another option is for the students to develop a role play among the tax collectors, common people, Gentiles, and women discussing their impressions of Jesus and his identity.

Conclusion

• • • • • • • •

Assign the Summary Points and Review Questions (pages 82-84). Grade them and review them as preparation for the Chapter Test.

Answers to Review Questions

1. Where did Palestine get its name?

    Palestine was named by the Greeks after the Philistines, the seafaring pirates who once lived in the northern coastal areas.

2. What are the four geographic areas of Palestine?

    The four geographic areas of Palestine are the coastal plain, mountain range, Rift Valley, and the Transjordan.

3. List two major cities that figure into Jesus' life that are located in Galilee and Judea.

    Jesus grew up in Nazareth of Galilee. Jesus was born in Bethlehem of Judea and worshipped and was tried in Jerusalem.

4. Who were the Samaritans? Discuss two of their beliefs.

    The Samaritans descended from foreigners who intermarried with the old Israelite tribes at the time of Assyria's conquest of the northern kingdom. They only accepted the first five books of the Bible as sacred. They rejected the Temple at Jerusalem, believing God chose Mount Gerizim as the proper place of worship.

5. Describe first-century Jerusalem.

    First-century Jerusalem featured many recently completed building projects. Jews living in Jerusalem worked at many different trades. As the Temple was in Jerusalem, it was the center of religious worship.

6. What was Jesus' native tongue? What other languages may have been spoken in first-century Palestine?

    Jesus' native tongue was Aramaic. Other languages of first-century Palestine included Hebrew, Greek, and Latin.

7. What took place in synagogues?

    The synagogue served three main purposes: it was a house of prayer, it was a place of discussion for legal settlements, and it was the local school.

8. Describe a typical Sabbath service in Jesus' day.

    It was a simple service. Ordinary townsfolk conducted the service. The congregation faced Jerusalem and recited various prayers, beginning with the confession known as the Shema. Other prayers were recited. The key part of the service was the reading of the Torah in Hebrew, followed by selected readings from the Prophets. The leader of the synagogue explained the readings in a homily.

9. List three facts about the Jerusalem Temple.

    For example, there was only one Temple. It was where Jews offered sacrifice to God. It was the place where Jews believed God dwelled in a special way. Only the priestly caste had a role in Temple worship. Only the high priest could enter the most sacred space in the Temple, once a year, on Yom Kippur.

10. Which were the three great Jewish religious feasts? What did each celebrate?

Passover celebrated the Chosen People's liberation from Israel. Pentecost was held fifty days after Easter and celebrated Yahweh's giving of the Law to Moses. Tabernacles was a fall harvest celebration.

11. What is meant by *Pax Romana*?

Peace of Rome, the state of peace and security offered in the Roman empire.

12. Identify: Antiochus IV, the Maccabean Revolt, the Hasmoneans, Pompey.

Antiochus IV was the Seleucid ruler who committed many atrocities against the Jews. The Maccabean Revolt was the Jewish effort to recapture the Temple. The Hasmoneans were rulers of a brief independent Jewish state that followed the Maccabean Revolt. Pompey was the Roman general who conquered Palestine for the Romans in 63 B.C.

13. Describe the moral character of Herod the Great. Who were his three sons and what territories did they rule?

Herod was called a "half Jew." He was actually despicable, and murdered several of his relatives. His son Philip controlled lands to the north and east of the Sea of Galilee. Herod Antipus ruled Perea and Galilee. Archelaus gained most of Samaria, Idumea, and Judea.

14. What functions did Roman prefects like Pontius Pilate have?

The prefects' main functions were tax collecting, approving or denying the death sentences imposed by the Jewish tribunal, keeping the peace, and reporting to Rome about the general state of affairs.

15. What was a debtor slave?

A debtor slave was a person who could work off a debt by working as a servant for wealthy people.

16. In the letter St. Paul sent to Philemon, what did Paul want Philemon to do?

Paul encourages Philemon not to punish his slave and also hints that he should free him.

17. What was the common first-century Jewish belief concerning the Messiah?

Most Jews believed Yahweh would send a Messiah very soon. They expected the coming of the Messiah to be accompanied by an apocalyptic event.

18. Identify the Torah and explain what role it played in the Jewish religion.

The first five books of the Bible comprise the Torah. It is the heart of Jewish life, the revelation of God and what he expects as a response to his covenant love.

19. What is the meaning of the word "angel"?

Angel means "messenger."

20. Identify these Jewish sects: Sadducees, Pharisees, Essenes, and Zealots. List several of the beliefs of each.

Answers will vary. For example, the Sadducees only accepted the Torah as inspired scripture. The Pharisees believed in strict observance of the Law and avoided Gentile influence. The Essenes were an apocalyptic group that believed God would usher in his kingdom through a dramatic event. The Zealots believed in violence to overthrow the Romans.

21. What was the Sanhedrin?

The Sanhedrin was the major law-making body and supreme court of Judaism.

22. Identify Jonathan ben Zakkai.

Jonathan ben Zakkai was the rabbi who, with some Pharisees, regrouped the Jewish faith at Jamnia (present-day Jabneh near Tel Aviv) after the destruction of the Temple in A.D. 70.

23. From the point of view of Pharisees, who were "the people of the land?"

    The Galileans were often called "the people of the land."

24. Who were Gentiles?

    Gentiles were the nations of people who were not circumcised, non-Jews.

25. Describe the situation of women in New Testament times and how Jesus revolutionized it.

    Women generally had a low position in New Testament times. Jesus elevated the position of women, treated them as equals, and instructed husbands to love and cherish their wives. Many women were Jesus' disciples.

Chapter 2 Test

● ● ● ● ● ● ● ● ●

Assign and grade the Chapter 2 Test (page 210 of this Manual). The answers follow below:

Chapter 2 Test   Name:_____

All questions worth 4 points each.

Part 1: Matching. Please match the group of Jesus' Jewish contemporaries with the descriptions given below.

Groups

A. Samaritans   B. Essenes   C. Pharisees   D. Zealots   E. Sadducees

Descriptions

___C___ 1. many were scribes who valued oral interpretation of the Law

___E___ 2. centered their power in Jerusalem and collaborated with the Romans

___B___ 3. founded by the Teacher of Righteousness

___A___ 4. descended from foreigners who intermarried with northern tribes of the Chosen People

___D___ 5. one of Jesus' disciples belonged to this group

___C___ 6. Jesus was closest to them in belief and spiritual practice

___D___ 7. despised Roman rule and worked to overthrow it

___A___ 8. believed Mount Gerazim was the God-chosen proper place for worship

___E___ 9. a priestly, conservative, aristocratic group

___B___ 10. associated with Qumran and the Dead Sea scrolls

Part 2: True or False. Mark + if the statement is true and 0 if the statement is false.

___0___ 11. Jesus chose Cana in Galilee to be his headquarters during his public ministry.

___+___ 12. In Jesus' day, the feast of Pentecost celebrated Yahweh's giving of the Law to Moses.

___+___ 13. The Roman general Pompey conquered Palestine in 63 B.C.

___0___ 14. Pious Jews were happy to cooperate with the adoption of Hellenism in Palestine.

___+___ 15. Jewish contemporaries of Jesus saw Messiahship in terms of political power.

__+___ 16. Common people in our Lord's day were surprisingly knowledgeable about the Law.

__0___ 17. Jesus and early Christians preached for the abolishment of the institution of slavery.

Part 3: Short Fill-ins.

messenger	18.	What is the meaning of the term *angel*?
Torah	19.	What is the term for the Jewish Law found in the first five books of the Bible (Pentateuch)?
Sanhedrin	20.	The 71-member supreme legislative and judicial body of the Jewish people was known as the __?__.
Judea	21.	The three major regions of the Holy Land in our Lord's day were Galilee, Samaria, and __?__.
Aramaic	22.	The language Jesus spoke on a daily basis was __?__.
Antipas	23.	This Herod was ruler in Galilee for most of Jesus' life: __?__.

Part 4: Short Answers:

24.-25. List and discuss two of the most interesting things you learned about Jesus from your study of Chapter 2.

Award two points for each fact they list and two points if their discussion is coherent and well-organized.

Prayer Lesson

➥ Assign readers to read separate sentences of the passage from Romans 8:31-39, alternating after each sentence.

➥ Allow time for silent reflection.

➥ Assign the reflection questions for journal writing.

three

The Essential Jesus

Introducing the Chapter

Prior to examining the four gospel portraits individually, this chapter provides a broader overview of all four gospels.

The chapter begins by reviewing the meaning of the term *mystery*, a reference to both God's infinite incomprehensibility and to God's saving plan in human history. To the latter, the chapter examines Jesus' infancy and hidden life in Nazareth, especially comparing and learning from the theological insights of Matthew's and Luke's infancy narratives.

Jesus' baptism by John is covered. John is the forerunner of Jesus, baptizing in water while Jesus will baptize in the Holy Spirit. Jesus' own baptism is a miraculous event that signifies God's presence with Jesus, the promised Messiah.

The temptations of Jesus are discussed. Jesus' retreat into the desert for forty days is compared to the experience of the Chosen People in the desert for forty years. Jesus' faithfulness is contrasted with the unfaithfulness of the Israelites.

The next major section of the chapter focuses on Jesus the Teacher, exploring characteristics of his method and style. The gospels record several of these teaching techniques, including Jesus' use of parables and proclamations about God's kingdom.

The chapter continues by examining the miracles of Jesus. Four types of miracles are discussed: physical healings, nature miracles, exorcisms, and raisings from the dead. The connection between miracles and faith is also explored. A list of the specific miracles of Jesus are also named.

A final section examines ways Jesus' demeanor and message were contrary to the expectations of the religious and civil leaders of the day. From his steadfast faith to his Father's will, we are led to a participation in the Paschal mystery which rescues us from sin and death and brings us new life.

Bibliography

Brown, Raymond E. *An Introduction to New Testament Christology*. New York: Paulist Press, 1994.
    An outstanding introduction to the development of Christian faith in Jesus.

Dunn, James D. G. *Evidence for Jesus*. Philadelphia: Westminister, 1985.
    A terrific book on the topic of the historical Jesus.

Duquesne, Jacques. *Jesus: An Unconventional Biography*. Translated by Catherine Spencer. Liguori, MO: Liguori/Triumph, 1997.
    Very readable, but a bit shaky on some doctrinal issues, for example, the virgin birth.

Fitzmyer, Joseph A., S.J. *A Christological Catechism: New Testament Answers*, rev. ed. New York: Paulist Press, 1993.
    Enjoyable reading from an outstanding scholar.

Harrington, Daniel J., S.J. *Who Is Jesus? Why Is He Important?: An Invitation to the New Testament*. Franklin, WI: Sheed & Ward, 1999.
    A popular overview of the New Testament by a respected scholar and a clear writer. Book-by-book analysis that highlights what each New Testament writer has to say about Jesus. Great reading for the teacher.

Jeremias, Joachim. *New Testament Theology I: The Proclamation of Jesus*. London: SCM Press, 1971.
    Outstanding on the teaching of Jesus based on a study of the Aramaic words of Jesus.

Johnson, Luke Timothy. *Living Jesus: Learning the Heart of the Gospel*. San Francisco: HarperSan Francisco, 1999.

Keegan, Terence J. *Interpreting the Bible: A Popular Introduction to Hermenuetics*. New York: Paulist Press, 1985.
    Includes a very readable introduction to the topic.

Nolan, Albert. *Jesus Before Christianity*, rev. ed. Maryknoll, NY: Orbis Books, 1992.
    A good portrait from a South African liberation theologian.

Powell, Mark Allan. *Jesus as a Figure in History: How Modern Historians View the Man from Galilee*. Louisville, KY: Westminster John Knox, 1998.

O'Grady, John F. *The Four Gospels and the Jesus Tradition*. New York: Paulist Press, 1989.
    A clearly written work on how the early traditions about Jesus developed into the four individual portraits of the canonical gospels. Good reading.

Sanders, E.P. *The Historical Figure of Jesus*. New York: Penguin Books, 1993.
    A balanced and fair treatment from a solid Protestant scholar.

Sloyan, Gerald. *Jesus in Focus: A Life in Its Setting*, rev. ed. Mystic, CN: Twenty-Third Publications, 1994.
    Insightful reading from a respected Catholic author.

Witherington III, Ben. *The Jesus Quest: The Third Search for the Jew of Nazareth*, 2nd ed. Downers Grove, IL: Intervarsity Press, 1997.
    A fair and balanced study.

Videos

· · · · ·

The Bridge

An allegory on God's love for us in Christ. A father must decide to save train passengers or his son who is running on the railway tracks. Powerful (11-minute video, Ignatius Press).

Jesus: The New Way

An excellent series produced by Dr. Tom Wright, noted British Biblical scholar who accepts the basic gospel message about Jesus, unlike so many of the others in the Jesus Seminar. Segments could be used successfully with students or purchase for teacher background (six half-hour programs on two videotapes with script, teacher's guide, and student worksheets, Vision Video/Gateway Films).

The Nativity

Produced by the American Bible Society, this ten-minute video provides a contemporary approach to Luke 2:1-21. A twenty-four-page discussion and activity guide is included (Harcourt Religion Publishers).

So, Who Is This Jesus?

Overview of Jesus' life showing the places he lived in and visited (48-minute video, Vision with Values).

Yeshua: The Land, The Promise, The Messiah

Presented by Dr. Oswald Hoffmann, *Yeshua* reveals ancient customs and beliefs with exceptional clarity and detail. Starts with Abraham and moves through Old Testament history to the time of Jesus. Though produced in the 1980s, it is still relevant and useful. (5 programs approximately 50 minutes each, Vision Video).

Resources

· · · · · · · ·

Bauckham, Richard J. "All in the Family: Identifying Jesus' Relatives."
An interesting article from the April 2000 issue of *Bible Review*.
http://www.bib-arch.org/bswb_BAR/bsba2806kprdg1.html

Christ's Birth in Art.
http://www.picturesofJesus.com/nativityof Jesus/htm

Comparison of the Septuagint and Hebrew Old Testament, based on New Testament quotations.
http://students.cua.edu/16kalvesmaki/lxx/

Mason, Steve and Jerome Murphy-O'Connor. "Where Was Jesus Born?" *Bible Review*, February 2000.
http://www.bib-arch.org/brf00/born.html

SECTION 1: The Light of the World and Mysteries of Christ's Life
(pages 87-99)

Objectives

The goals of this section are to enable the students to:

➡ determine the importance of some of Jesus' teachings for their lives;

➡ understand the religious meaning of the word *mystery*;

➡ compare and contrast the infancy narratives of Matthew and Luke;

➡ summarize the main details of and reasons for Jesus' baptism;

➡ identify three temptations faced by Jesus.

Summary and Background Information

Luke may have had access of some sort to Mary, the Mother of Jesus, which would explain the presence of various details in his infancy narrative. Like Mary who kept all these things in her heart, your students in this section are introduced to some of the mysteries of Jesus' life so they might ponder them, treasure them, and get to know our Lord even better.

After the introductory exercise "How Do You Respond?" the *Catechism of the Catholic Church* is referenced as the mysteries of Christ's life are explored. Next, Jesus' infancy and hidden life are examined. Students are invited to pause and read Matthew 1–2 and Luke 1–2. A comparison and contrast follows that allows the students to appreciate how each evangelist contributes to the rich portrait of Jesus that is ours through scripture. The students' treasury of experience with God's Word grows and they are now prepared to enter more deeply into further mysteries.

Next, the person of John the Baptist is introduced along with a study of the baptism of Christ.

Finally, the students are assigned an activity that helps them to understand the meaning and relevance of Jesus being tempted by Satan.

Warm Up

a) Assign the exercise "How Do You Respond?" (page 88). Call on students to share their responses to the teachings and the follow-up questions with a partner.

b) To follow up, ask the students to react in writing to this statement: "Jesus never forces his love on anyone." Allow time for the students to share their reactions with a partner. Also call on one or two students to share with the entire class.

Using the Section

a) Work from the opening of the text section, "Mysteries of Christ's Life" (page 89). Print the following definition on the board:

> Mystery (theological meaning) refers to:
>
> ✓ God's infinite incomprehensibility
>
> ✓ God's plan for our salvation, revealed most fully in Christ's life, passion, death, and resurrection

Point out that God's mystery is not meant to frustrate us. Rather, God always rises above our best expectations. This is the beauty of God: he chooses to communicate with us in various ways, but most especially through his Son Jesus and through the Church. Hence, to know God more fully is to know Jesus more fully as revealed through the life of the Church.

b) Assign the text under "Jesus' Infancy and Hidden Life" (pages 89-93) up to the point where the students are asked to read the infancy narratives from Matthew and Luke. Review the stages of gospel formation.

c) Group the students with a partner. Assign each person either the Matthew or Luke infancy narrative for reading. Then call on the partners to review the narratives using the chart on page 91.

d) Summarize the two infancy narratives using the material on pages 91-93. Make some or all of the following points (develop PowerPoint presentation or write on board):

> Matthew's genealogy of Christ is placed at the beginning of the gospel to show that participation in this "new way" was an extension of Judaism.
>
> Luke's focus is the inclusion of all people, Gentiles and Jews, in fellowship with Jesus.
>
> The flight to Egypt (Matthew) allows Jesus to relive the Exodus experience.
>
> The announcement to and visit by the shepherds is consistent with Luke's theme that the poor and lowly are singled out for God's blessings.
>
> The courage of the Jewish magi not returning to King Herod (Matthew) was similar to the courage many young Jewish Christians needed to face their families as they abandoned their religion and tradition to follow Jesus.
>
> The Simeon and Anna meeting signifies that Jesus will bring unity among Jewish Christians and Gentile Christians.

e) Read and summarize the text section "Jesus' Baptism" (pages 93-96). Call on the students to locate and individually read each gospel account of Jesus' baptism (see Comparing Gospel Accounts: The Baptism of Jesus, page 96). Point out the significance of the following similarities (write on the board):

Open Sky—God has come to his people in Jesus.

Dove Descends—Symbol that suggests we are at the dawn of a new era.

Voice of the Father—God the Father is pleased with Jesus, his Son.

Ask the students to list reasons why Jesus was baptized, for example: his obedience to God the Father, to preview the Paschal mystery, and an example for us to be baptized and to become the Father's adopted children.

f) Assign the text "The Temptations of Jesus" (pages 97-98) and "Scripture Reading: Jesus Is Tempted" (page 98). Ask questions related to the two readings, for example: 1) What were the three temptations of Jesus? 2) How did Jesus respond to each temptation?

Extending the Section

a) Related to the exercise "How Do You Respond?" (page 88), have the students copy the related gospel passages into their journals and write a paragraph that explains what it means to them (see page 88, bottom).

b) Present information on the origins of December 25 as the date the Church celebrates Christ's birth. The feast appeared on the Roman calender in A.D. 336 but was likely celebrated years before, perhaps as a response to the pagan solstice "holiday of the sun." Also, the date of Annunciation had already been established on March 25. Celebrating Christ's birth nine months later was a logical next step.

c) Assign the exercise that goes with "Scripture Reading: Jesus Is Tempted" (page 98).

d) Have the students print the three theological and four cardinal virtues in their journals and summarize how each is applicable to their lives.

Creative Learning

a) Either individually or in small groups, have the students develop a scriptural rosary for the joyful mysteries. This entails finding scripture verses that correspond with each bead related to 1) the Annunciation, 2) the Visitation, 3) the Nativity, 4) Presentation at the Temple, and 5) Finding Jesus in the Temple.

b) Invite students to depict Jesus' baptism visually (drawing, painting, etc.) in ways that include the main details of the event discussed in this section.

SECTION 2: Jesus the Teacher (pages 99-104)

Objectives

The goals of this section are to enable the students to:

➡ recognize the qualities of Jesus as a teacher;

➡ overview the parables of Jesus;

➡ examine the "kingdom of God" proclamations of Jesus.

Summary and Background Information

Jesus has several qualities of an excellent teacher. These are explored in this section, including his authenticity, his love of life, ability to relate with the common people, and his authoritative posture.

More specific techniques of Jesus' teaching are also addressed. The text presents a definition and overview of Jesus' use of parables. As Jesus used them, parables compare something very familiar (seeds, wheat, animals, etc.) to something unfamiliar about God's kingdom. A list of the principal parables in the synoptic gospels is provided.

The section lists important proclamations of Jesus about God's kingdom. It is explained that the term kingdom (or reign) refers to God's active participation in life, both in heaven and on earth.

Warm Up

a) Ask the students to list the qualities of a good teacher. Have them also describe their most memorable and/or creative lessons taught by a teacher.

b) Remind the students that they already know many teachings of Jesus. Individually or in small groups, ask the students to create a list of items that begin with "Jesus teaches that. . . ." You may wish to make it a contest to see which students or groups come up with the largest and most accurate lists of teachings about Jesus.

Using the Section

a) Related to the opening discussion, summarize the qualities of Jesus as a teacher (pages 99-100).

b) Define parables as (write on board) **"a vivid story drawn from ordinary life that conveys religious truth."**

c) Assign the text section "Jesus' Proclamations about God's Kingdom" (pages 102-104). Contrast the biblical idea of *kingdom* with the current understanding of democracy. For example, under some controversy, the Pledge of the Allegiance says that we are "one nation under God." Ask the students to name some ways the United States can be understood to be both "under God" and "separate from God."

Extending the Section

a) Have the students summarize the parable in Luke 18:9-14 and complete the questions that follow on page 104.

b) The kingdom, reign, or rule of God is mentioned throughout the Old Testament. Have the students complete the worksheet "Old Testament Search: The Kingdom of God" (page 211 of this Manual).

c) Ask the students to respond: "How does the Lord's Prayer contain a definition of God's kingdom? Why do you think Jesus needed to use metaphor to describe God's kingdom?"

d) As a journal assignment, have the students read and interpret three or four parables not discussed in this section.

Creative Learning

a) Have each student teach the class something—anything that can be taught in a two-minute period. Challenge their creativity. Possible topics for the students to consider include:

- how to score in wrestling
- how to shoot foul shots
- how to remember the notes in a treble clef
- how sound waves travel
- how to perform CPR
- how to juggle
- how to change guitar strings

Grade the students on their ability to teach the chosen lesson.

b) Have the students form groups and act out a parable of their choosing.

Jesus the Miracle Worker and Jesus' Obedience to His Father's Will (pages 104-110)

Objectives

The goals of this section are to enable the students to:

- discuss at least four points about what miracles reveal about Jesus;
- look at how Jesus fulfilled his Father's expectations for the Messiah, not necessarily those of religious and civil leaders;
- identify the Paschal mystery.

Summary and Background Information

The miracles of Jesus—a stumbling block for some modern minds—are examined in this section, as is the summation of Jesus' ministry in the Paschal mystery. You do a great service for your students by making this mystery more accessible, understandable, and applicable for them.

But first, miracles. A thorough analysis of Jesus' miracles kicks off this section. As usual students are encouraged strongly to read about many of these miracles first-hand in their Bible. Four categories of miracles are explored. The relationship between miracles and faith is also covered.

"Jesus' Obedience to His Father's Will" concludes the section and chapter. Jesus the miracle-worker allows himself to be seen as Transfigured—and then proceeds to Jerusalem, allowing himself to be murdered. In this section your students begin to see, with your help, that even God-made-man is not immune to suffering. The Paschal mystery, the summation of Jesus' life and mission and the road to our salvation, is defined in context.

Warm Up
• • • • • • •

a) Share an optical illusion or magic trick with the students. Or, secretly find out some information about a student that is not embarrassing. "Miraculously" share it with the class. Then open a discussion about miracles. Ask the students to define a miracle from their own experience.

b) Point out how science has a way of explaining many things that might once have been considered miraculous. For example:

•❖ once-deadly diseases like polio have been wiped out by inoculations;

•❖ damaged hearts are replaced with transplants;

•❖ eyes are repaired with laser surgery;

•❖ space probes uncover many mysteries of the universe.

c) Use the following questions as discussion starters or journal entries: 1) Do you think miracles happen today? 2) Have you ever had a miraculous experience? 3) What would you label a miraculous experience?

Using the Section
• • • • • • • • • • • • •

a) Begin by distinguishing between the biblical and scientific understanding of *miracle*:

biblical—an event that produces and/or signifies faith

scientific—a suspension of the laws of nature

b) Assign the text section "Jesus the Miracle-Worker" and sub-section, "Miracles and Faith" (pages 104-105). Summarize the types of miracles listed in the section:

TYPES OF MIRACLES

✓ healing

✓ natural

✓ exorcisms

✓ raisings from the dead

c) Read and summarize the text sub-section "The New Testament Concept of Miracle" (pages 105-107). Point out that miracles show God's power and serve as signs that God's kingdom is at hand. Ask the students to share with you some of the related teachings that come from these lessons.

d) Briefly define Paschal mystery. See the glossary of the *Catechism of the Catholic Church* and cited paragraphs.

e) Assign for reading the text section "Jesus' Obedience to His Father's Will" (pages 108-110). Point out the ways listed for how Jesus contradicted society's expectations for a Messiah. For example:

✓ Jesus fulfilled the Law, but emphasized the spirit of the Law.

✓ Jesus associated with outcasts.

✓ Jesus respected women.

✓ Jesus' words and teachings were one-of-a-kind.

✓ Jesus forgave sin.

Extending the Section

a) Assign the separate exercise, "The Miracles of Jesus" (pages 107-108). Have the students write their response in essay form, share with a partner, and then turn in for grading.

b) Ask the students to read some of the other miracle stories listed on pages 107-108 and name different reactions to Jesus. These include: astonishment, strong requests to leave, praise, reverence, hatred, and belief. Call on students to share what they believe their response would have been to Jesus' miracles.

c) Assign the students to write in their journals what they believe about Jesus. To probe further, ask: "What does discipleship mean to you? What do you expect of the Messiah? How faithful of a disciple are you?"

Creative Learning

a) Have the students locate and share news articles of something they believe has miraculous overtones. For example: a man diagnosed with dyslexia perseveres and graduates from college; a woman's life-threatening tumor suddenly cannot be found with an MRI, two siblings separated by adoption find each other late in life.

b) Ask the students to compose a brief prayer of adoration to Jesus.

c) Assign individuals or small groups to use a video camera and to record the responses of several people of all ages and genders to the questions: "What is a miracle?" or "Describe a miracle."

Conclusion

a) Allow time for the students to study the Selected Vocabulary definitions (page 113). Then quiz them orally or in writing on the definitions.

b) Assign the Summary Points and Review Questions (pages 111-113). Grade them and review them as preparation for the Chapter Test.

Answers to Review Questions

1. Discuss two religious meanings of the word *mystery*.

   Mystery refers to God's infinite incomprehensibility. Second, the New Testament uses the word "mystery" to refer to God's saving plan.

2. List five ways Matthew's and Luke's infancy narratives differ.

   Answers will vary. For example, Matthew traces Jesus' ancestry to Abraham, Luke to Adam. In Matthew, the angel's message is to Joseph. In Luke, the angel speaks to Mary. Luke includes Jesus' presentation in the Temple, Matthew does not. Matthew includes the Holy Family's pilgrimage to Egypt. Primarily, Matthew writes for Jewish Christians, Luke writes for Gentile Christians.

3. What major theological points were Matthew and Luke making in their infancy narratives?

   Matthew wanted to connect Jesus as the Messiah called forth in the Old Testament. Luke portrayed Jesus as the Messiah of all, including Gentiles.

4. Define *midrash*. Give an example of how Matthew used midrash in his infancy narrative.

   Midrash is a Jewish literary form that relates past scriptural events to help interpret the present event. For example, the Slaughter of Innocents by King Herod is not a documented historical event, but it reminds the reader of Moses' brush with death as an infant.

5. What is the meaning of the Epiphany?

   Epiphany refers to the time when Jesus is manifested as Messiah, Son of God, and Savior of the World.

6. In Luke's infancy narrative, what was the significance of Jesus' circumcision and his presentation in the Temple?

   Jesus' circumcision signifies his incorporation into the Jewish people. The presentation in the Temple reveals him to be the firstborn son who belongs to God.

7. In Luke's gospel, why does Jesus manifest himself first to the shepherds?

    Luke is communicating in a strong way Jesus' mission to the lowly.

8. What three significant events took place at Jesus' baptism?

    The opening of the sky represents that God has come to his people. The dove is a symbol of joy, inno-cence, freedom, power, and peace. It suggests the dawn of a new age. The voice of the Father showed that God was pleased with his son.

9. Why did Jesus, the sinless one, get baptized by John?

    The sinless Savior identified with all humans in their spiritual need.

10. Cite the evidence that makes it almost certain that Jesus was baptized.

    The criterion of embarrassment applies here. It would have been embarrassing to the early Church to have to teach that the sinless one was humbled in baptism unless it really happened.

11. Name the three temptations of Jesus. What did each mean?

    Satan tempted him to change stones to bread, take over rule of the Temple, and worship him. Jesus refused, showing his obedience to his Father.

12. Discuss at least two qualities that made Jesus an excellent teacher.

    For example, Jesus was authentic, he pursued people, he loved life and related to people at their level, he used colorful, down-to-earth language, and he spoke with authority.

13. Name and define the characteristics of parables. Why did Jesus teach in parables?

    Parables compare something very familiar to an unfamiliar idea about God's kingdom. Jesus used parables because such stories were able to convey truth in a more interesting, memorable way than simply teaching cold facts.

14. List five key parables of Jesus.

    Answers will vary. See pages 101-102 of the Student Text.

15. What is the meaning of the term *kingdom* (or *reign*) of God?

    The term kingdom (or reign) of God refers to God's active participation in life, both in heaven and on earth.

16. List and discuss three important themes in the teaching of Jesus.

    The central theme of Jesus' preaching was the coming of God's kingdom. The kingdom of God has several features, including: the kingdom is here now, the kingdom is of a loving God the Father, the kingdom is for everyone, the kingdom is a free gift from God, the Church is the beginning of God's kingdom, the kingdom is united in the Holy Spirit, and the kingdom involves a life of service.

17. What are the four categories of miracles performed by Jesus? Give an example of each.

    The four categories of Jesus' miracles are physical healings, nature miracles, exorcisms, and raising from the dead. Examples will vary.

18. How did the New Testament understand the concept of miracle?

    The New Testament concept of miracle assumes that God continues to work in human history.

19. What did the miracles reveal about Jesus?

    Jesus' miracles reveal God's power. They are signs of the coming of God's kingdom.

20. Name one way that Jesus was a sign of contradiction to his contemporaries.

    For example, Jesus emphasized the spirit of the Law in addition to fulfilling the Law, Jesus freely asso-ciated with outcasts, and Jesus treated women with respect.

21. What is the meaning of the Transfiguration?

The Transfiguration was the event where Jesus showed forth his divine glory.

22. Why did Jesus go to Jerusalem toward the end of his ministry? What did it reveal about him?

Jesus traveled to the place that was a place of death for several prophets. His actions there revealed that his life would climax in his death and resurrection.

Chapter 3 Test

• • • • • • • • •

Assign and grade the Chapter 3 Test (page 212 of this Manual). The answers follow below:

Chapter 3 Test   Name:_____

• •

All questions worth 4 points each.

Part 1: Matching. Please match the mystery from Jesus' life in Column B with its description in Column A.

Column A

			Column B
C	1.	Simeon and Anna recognize the Messiah	A. Transfiguration
E	2.	serves as a model for our baptism	B. circumcision of Jesus
A	3.	Jesus' full glory is manifested during his earthly ministry	C. presentation in the Temple
B	4.	signified Jesus' incorporation into Abraham's descendents	D. hidden life of Jesus
			E. baptism of Jesus
D	5.	Jesus learns obedience from his parents	F. temptations of Jesus

Part 2: True or False. Mark + if the statement is true and 0 if the statement is false.

+ 6. A key purpose of Matthew's infancy narrative is to show how Jesus fulfilled Old Testament prophecies about the Messiah.

0 7. Luke traces Jesus' genealogy to Adam to show how Jesus is the father of all Jews.

+ 8. Luke's infancy narrative stresses the relationship between John the Baptist and Jesus.

+ 9. The Lucan infancy narrative highlights Jesus' coming for the downtrodden.

0 10. According to the strictest methods of historical scholarship, scholars conclude that Jesus' baptism was a story made up to inspire early Christians to get baptized.

0 11. The temptations of Jesus in the desert show how Jesus, like all humans, was a sinner.

0 12. When he taught, Jesus often quoted famous Jewish teachers of his day.

+ 13. Jesus revealed himself to be an outstanding debater in his attempts to win over his opponents.

+ 14. Jesus worked miracles primarily to force people to believe in him.

+ 15. Jesus' miracles prove his mastery over Satan and the forces of darkness.

Part 3: Short Fill-ins.

midrash	16. What is the term for a literary form that relates past scriptural events to help explain and interpret present events?
parables	17. ___?___ are vivid picture stories told by Jesus to convey religious truth.
mystery	18. The term ___?___ refers to God's infinite incomprehensibility and his plan for salvation and redemption in Christ Jesus.
kingdom of God	19. The term ___?___ describes God's process of reconciling and renewing all things through his Son. It was proclaimed by Jesus and begun by his life, death, and resurrection.
Amen	20. The Hebrew word that means "certainly."

Part 4: Short Answers with Discussion.

21-25. List and briefly discuss five major points in the teaching of Jesus.

For example, the reign of God is here; God is a loving merciful Father; God loves everyone; repent; believe in the good news; imitate Jesus' life of service; the Lord is present in the Church; The Lord is present in the Holy Spirit; accepting Jesus requires accepting the cross. You may wish to accept any specific teaching of Jesus too, for example, the Golden Rule. Assign two points for each summary point given and two for each cogent explanation of the teachings listed.

Prayer Lesson

➨ Ask the students to investigate the Lord's Prayer. Have them answer in writing the question presented in the text: "How might Matthew and Luke have adapted Jesus' instruction on prayer to their own audiences?"

➨ For the reflection assignment, ask the students to write an explanation for each rating in their journals.

➨ The resolution questions (page 115) can also be used for journal writing.

➨ Pray the Lord's Prayer together to conclude a class session.

four

The Gospel of Mark: Jesus the Suffering Servant

Introducing the Chapter

The major focus of this text is the study of the four gospels. These are the books which allow us the most detailed glimpse into the life of Jesus Christ and the good news he preached.

Each of the next four chapters have some common elements: background on the author, the focused Christology, the date of its writing, the intended audience, and a simplified outline of the gospel. There are several break points in the chapter where the students should be assigned to read directly from the gospel. Because Mark is the short-est of the gospels, it is recommended that all the students be assigned to read the gospel in its entirety.

A major theme of Mark's gospel is defining Jesus as the Suffering Messiah. Christ gradually reveals himself to his disciples amidst their mis-understanding of his identity and mission. The gospel presents the question "What does it mean to be a disciple of Jesus Christ?" This is a crucial question for the students to ponder as well.

Bibliography

Achtemeier, Paul J. *Mark*. 2nd rev. ed. Proclamation Commentary. Philadelphia: Fortress Press, 1986.
   An excellent series of commentaries.

Barta, Karen A. *The Gospel of Mark*. Wilmington, DE: Michael Glazier, Inc., 1988.
   Volume 9 in the "Message of Biblical Spirituality" series, this book focuses on the dramatic story of Jesus in Mark's gospel.

Benson, Dennis. *Creative Bible Studies*. Loveland, CO: Group Books, 1985.
   Over 400 group activities covering all the gospels and Acts. Good source for some creative teaching ideas for the course.

Brown, Raymond E. *The Death of the Messiah: From Gethsemane to the Grave*, two volumes in the Anchor Bible Reference Library. New York: Doubleday, 1994.
   Outstanding work. This work is referenced often in the Student Text.

Flanagan, Patrick J. *The Gospel of Mark Made Easy*. New York/Mahwah, NJ: Paulist Press, 1997.

Gundry, R.H. *Mark*. Grand Rapids, MI: Eerdmans, 1993.
   An essential commentary recommended by Fr. Ray Brown in his *An Introduction to the New Testament*.

Harrington, Wilfrid. *Mark*. Wilmington, DE: Michael Glazier, 1979.
   A clear and scholarly text on Mark's gospel.

Kilgallen, John J. *A Brief Commentary on the Gospel of Mark*. New York/Mahwah, NJ: Paulist Press, 1989.

Kingsbury, Jack Dean. *The Christology of Mark's Gospel*. Philadelphia: Fortress Press, 1989.

LaVerdiere, Eugene. *The Beginning of the Gospel: Introducing the Gospel According to Mark*, two volumes. Collegeville, MN: Liturgical Press, 1999.
   Written by well-renowned scripture scholar.

Montague, George T., S.M. *Mark: Good News for Hard Times*. Ann Arbor, MI: Servant Books, 1981.
   Engaging commentary.

Keegan, Terence J. *A Commentary on the Gospel of Mark*. New York: Paulist Press, 1981.

The NIV Serendipity Bible for Study Groups. Second edition. Zondervan Bible Publishers, 1989.
   The work contains hundreds of questions that will help students discuss biblical passages in small groups. There is an opening exercise or questions, a "dig" section for analyzing the text, and a "reflection" segment for application of the text to one's life. More extended exercises are provided for each of the gospels.

Senior, Donald, C.P. *Understanding the Gospel Healing Stories*. Cincinnati, OH: St. Anthony Messenger Press, 2001.
   Analyzes the miracle stories as stories of liberation and inclusion.

Sweetland, Dennis. *Mark: From Death to Life*. New York: New City Press, 2000.
   A most readable and insightful commentary.

Van Linden, Philip, C.M. *The Gospel According to Mark*. Collegeville Bible Commentary. Collegeville, MN: The Liturgical Press, 1983.

Videos

· · · · ·

Dateline Jerusalem

"Special news report" takes viewers to Jerusalem during Holy Week as it reports on Jesus' arrest, trial, crucifixion, and resurrection. The politics and intrigue of first-century Palestine provide the background (two 60-minute tapes, Ignatius Press).

Evangelists Speak for Themselves

Fr. William Burke portrays the gospel witness before a contemporary audience (Luke—45 minutes; John—58 minutes; Mark and Matthew—75 minutes in two separate segments; Pflaum).

How Jesus Died: The Last 18 Hours

A stunning medical account of Jesus' sufferings at Calvary (35-minute video, Videos with Values).

Jesus

Stars Jeremy Sisto who presents an appealing view of the human Jesus. However, the production allows incorrectly that Jesus' mother knows more about his identity than he does. Further, the Jesus portrayed shows way too much reluctance about embracing his ministry. However, today's youth find this portrayal interesting, believable, and easy to discuss in light of the gospels (2000; 173-minute CBS made-for-TV movie, Amazon.com).

Jesus and the Shroud of Turin

Tries to debunk skeptical scholars in making the case of the Shroud being an authentic relic that dates from the time of Jesus (52-minute video, Ignatius Press).

The Last Supper

The Last Supper is dramatized at authentic locations in the Holy Land. Emphasizes both Christian tradition and Jewish roots (60-minute video, Ignatius Press).

Meditation on the Passion of Jesus

One-man performance by the youth outreach group RADIX. From the biblical to the modern-day Christ, it shows the suffering that comes from abortion, contraception, and pornography. Invites viewers to meet Christ in the Eucharist (60-minute video, Ignatius Press).

The Silent Witness

Documentary reporting the scientific investigations on the Shroud of Turin. An award-winning film (55-minute video, Ignatius Press).

The Stations of the Cross

Combines the spoken word, music, and beautiful visual images to walk us through the stations. Meditations provided by Bishop Donald Wuerl (58-minute video, Ignatius Press).

Resources

· · · · · · · ·

Michael Spencer's "Gospel of Mark" Homepage

http://www.geocities.com/Athens/Forum/2736/

The Miracles of Jesus

Explained by a believer, Hampton Keathley IV, Th.M., a 1995 graduate of Dallas Theological Seminary.

http://www.bible.org/docs/nt/topics/miracles/toc.htm

Shroud of Turin

Interesting website by one (Daniel R. Porter) who accepts the Shroud of Turin as a true relic.

http://shroudstory.com/

Section 1: Faith Perspective and Background on Mark's Gospel (pages 117-120)

Objectives

The goals of this section are to enable the students to:

➥ consider how the perspective of faith helps us to know Jesus in a new way;

➥ recognize several key details of Mark's gospel, including date and purpose;

➥ examine an outline of Mark's gospel and read its contents.

Summary and Background Information

The Jesus portrayed by Mark's gospel is the Suffering Servant. As it was during Jesus' time on earth, this is a stumbling block of faith for some, the key to salvation for others.

This section introduces the gospel by exploring several sayings of Jesus, asking the students to compare how popular culture today would respond to his message.

Next, a brief background on the gospel is provided. An outline introduces the students to all the major sections. An assignment encourages the students to read the gospel in its entirety.

Warm Up

a) Assign for reading the text under the heading "Faith Perspective" (pages 117-118). Ask the students to tell or write about how a new perception of a person changed how they felt about that person.

b) Ask the students to consider how they have been prodded to follow the example of others, in both good and bad situations. For example, ask:

➥ Have you ever teased somebody because "everybody else" was doing it?

➥ How you ever told one friend a lie so you could do something with another friend?

➥ Have you ever helped a classmate with schoolwork because you've observed someone you respect doing the same?

➥ Have you ever refused alcohol at a party because others were doing the same?

Call on students to name examples of negative and positive leadership among teenagers.

Using the Section

a) Assign the exercise "Life-Changing Sayings" (pages 118-119). Allow time for students to discuss their responses with a partner. Call on one student to be "on the spot" and to answer the two follow up questions on page 119 in front of the class. Choose other students to be on the spot as time allows.

b) Use the margin exercise (page 119) as an introduction to the identity of Mark. You may wish to choose seven different students to read the seven passages. Then proceed by reading or summarizing the first two paragraphs under "Background on Mark's Gospel" (page 119).

c) Use the introductory notes for Mark's gospel in the *New American Bible* to help supplement the discussion on when the gospel was written. Summarize with information like the following:

THE GOSPEL OF MARK

Author: uncertain, but most likely a person of Jewish background

Date: approximately A.D. 65-70

Place: Rome or Syria

Purpose: to bolster the faith of Christians who are being persecuted

c) The central question "Who is Jesus?" introduced in the text section "Gospel Focus" (page 120) is at the heart of Mark's gospel. As a short discussion activity, ask the students to list adjectives that they believe describe Jesus. Write their suggestions on the board. At the end of the discussion, note which adjectives do and do not fit the authentic profile of Jesus as Suffering Messiah.

d) As a way to wrap up the section, ask the following questions: "Who was Mark? What do we know of him? Why does Mark's gospel have no infancy narrative? Why does Jesus tell his disciples to keep his messiahship a secret?"

Extending the Section

a) Assign the gospel of Mark for reading. This is best done as a home assignment. See suggestions on page 120. Allow opportunity in a future class session for the students to share the verses that are both meaningful and confusing for them.

b) Related to the reading assignment above, divide the class into six groups. Ask them to prepare a report on Mark's gospel based on one of the following themes:

Discipleship
Suffering
Miracles
Jesus and the Authorities
Titles for Jesus
Reactions to Jesus

Creative Learning

a) Have the students use various art media (painting, pencil sketches, sculpture) to create their impressions of the winged lion often used as a symbol for St. Mark.

b) Have the students locate articles featuring famous contemporary people who publicly witness their Catholic faith. Have them share these articles with one another.

c) Encourage the students to interview a person engaged in Christian ministry and report on how the person perceives their ministry being connected with Christian discipleship.

SECTION 2: Mark's Gospel Reveals Jesus, Jesus the Healer and Miracle Worker (pages 121-125)

Objectives

The goals of this section are to enable the students to:
- explore what the prologue of Mark's gospel reveals about Jesus;
- understand the meaning of *authority* related to Jesus' teaching;
- examine the pattern of Jesus' miracle stories in Mark's gospel;
- understand the nuances of the Messianic secret;
- look at Part 2 of the gospel as it focuses on the way of discipleship.

Summary and Background Information

This section begins with a portrayal of Jesus. Several elements of Christology are explored. Mark's gospel presents Jesus as an authoritative teacher whose message centers on the kingdom of God. The section begins with a closer look at the prologue of the gospel and what it reveals about Jesus.

Mark's gospel also records a distinct pattern of miracle story. An examination of his pattern is offered: introduction, display of faith, Jesus' response, result of the miracle, and reaction to the miracle.

A running part of the narrative of Mark's gospel is the Messianic secret, that is, Jesus' disciples' lack of understanding of the true meaning of Jesus as the Suffering Servant and of the meaning of discipleship. The "way of discipleship" is covered in depth on pages 128-130.

Also, a separate feature examines the meaning of the most frequently used title in the gospel for Jesus: Son of Man.

Warm Up

a) Assign the worksheet "Scripture Search" (page 213 of this Manual) at the beginning of a session. Allow the students to work individually or in small groups. *Answers:* 1. Jesus and his disciples arrive somewhere; 2. Jesus predicts his death; 3. The disciples misunderstand; 4. Jesus explains; 5. Jesus tells the people involved not to tell anyone what has happened; 6. sower and seed, seed at harvest, mustard seed; 7. "This is the time of fulfillment. The kingdom of God is at hand. Repent and believe in the gospel"; 8. Abba.

b) Discuss with the students the challenges and difficulties of keeping a secret. Ask them to describe a contemporary person who may keep his or her identity secret in order to perform a good deed.

Using the Section

a) Read or summarize the opening text under "The Jesus of Mark's Gospel" and the subsection "What the Prologue Reveals About Jesus" (pages 121-122). Make sure the students understand how Mark's readership has been informed of the central message of the good news: that Jesus is the Son of God.

b) Write the definition of authority on the board (see page 122):

Authority means:

✓ the right to command;

✓ someone with official power;

✓ the source of reliable information;

✓ the ability to gain the respect of others and influence what they do;

✓ and knowledge, skill, or experience worthy of respect.

Assign the text section, "Jesus the Authoritative Teacher" (page 122-124). Call on student volunteers to share how Jesus meets these various definitions of authority.

c) For each of the conflicts Jesus experienced in Mark 2:1–3:6 ask the students to research and name the Old Testament laws that Jesus was apparently in violation of.

d) Note how the parable of the sower (Mk 4:1-20) and the mustard seed (4:30-32) would have been a source of encouragement to early Christians who were suffering for the faith. Assign a short journal entry asking the students to tell how these parables offer them encouragement.

e) Assign the text section "Jesus the Healer and Miracle Worker." Write the pattern of miracle stories on the board. Have the students examine the pattern using Mark 2:1-12.

PATTERN OF JESUS' MIRACLES
Introduction
Display of Faith
Jesus' Response
Result
Reaction to the Miracle

f) Follow up with the exercise on the miracle of the calming of the storm from Mark 4:35-41. Check the students' understanding of the five points: 1. violent storm at sea (introduction); 2. disciples wake Jesus (display of faith); 3. Jesus demands the sea be still (response); 4. Sea is still (result); 5. Jesus questions the disciples faith; disciples wonder about Jesus' identity (reaction).

g) Assign the text section "The Messianic Secret" along with accompanying feature "Son of Man" (pages 127-128). To accompany the reading, focus on the passage from Mark 10:45, explaining that this passage completely reveals the mission of Christ. Ask the students to look up the passage and tell you Christ's mission: The mission of the Son of Man is not to be served but to serve and to give his life as a ransom for many.

h) Read or summarize the text section, "The Way of Discipleship" (pages 128-130) that focuses on the second part of Mark's gospel, the road leading to Jerusalem and Jesus' trial, death, and subsequent resurrection.

i) Assign the subsection, "Arrival in Jerusalem" (page 132). Encourage the students to re-read Mark 11:1–13:37.

Extending the Section

a) Mark uses a literary device called "framing." A more significant story is placed in the middle of another story. Ask the students to read Mark 5:21-43 and compare the two parts of the stories. Note the woman's great faith compared with the lack of faith of those surrounding the sick child.

b) Assign the margin exercise, the "Suffering Servant" (page 128). In addition to having the students read Isaiah 52:13–53:12 assign Mark 8:27-35. Ask the students to answer these questions: "How are the two prophecies of Isaiah interpreted by Jesus? How did Jesus redefine kingship to include service?"

c) Call on the students to reflect further on the parable of the sower (Mk 4:1-20). Ask: Name the persons who have planted the Word of God in your life. Who are the "birds" who have snatched the seed of God away from you? What might cause a person of faith to begin to practice the faith but then give up? Who are "thorns" to your faith life? What do you hope to accomplish as "good soil?"

d) Assign the exercise on the parable of the Tenants (pages 124-125). *Answers:* God the Father, Jesus, Jewish authorities, Gentiles.

e) Play the conclusion of the video *Oh God!* (with George Burns) beginning with the trial scene (approximately 15 minutes). The conclusion of the movie shows some of the ways people react when confronted by miracles. Have the students comment on their reactions.

Creative Learning

a) Encourage small groups of students to develop short skits depicting the narrative in Mark 2:1–3:6. Allow the students to perform the skits, noting differences in the interpretation.

b) Point out examples of how faith can help a person accomplish great things. For example, a basketball coach has faith that a player will make a free throw, a child has faith a father will make it home in a snowstorm. Have the students suggest other examples of the power of faith.

c) Have the students write a short essay offering their opinion on the following statements of Jesus as a model for living: "Whoever wishes to save his life will lose it, but whoever loses his life for my sake and that of the gospel will save it" and "Whoever does not accept the kingdom of God like a child will not enter it."

d) Related to the story of the rich man (Mk 10:17-31), ask the students to form small groups and develop skits that depict what happened next to the rich, young man (see page 131). Assign the other parts of the exercise for individual work.

SECTION 3: The Paschal Mystery in Mark's Gospel (pages 132-141)

Objectives

The goals of this section are to enable the students to:

- define the term Paschal mystery;
- put the Paschal mystery in the context of what happened to the historical Jesus;
- understand the theological importance of the Paschal mystery.

Summary and Background Information

While the crucial importance of the Paschal mystery has already been introduced, this section explores this central teaching of faith in greater detail.

Mark's passion narrative has been called the heart of the gospel; the other thirteen chapters have often been thought of as an apt introduction to the passion narrative.

Prior to covering the individual events of the passion story, the text looks at actions and teachings of Jesus that led some of Jesus' enemies to see him as a threat. In short, the religious authorities thought of Jesus as a false prophet who claimed to be God.

Jesus' decision to be crucified was the means of our salvation. It proved beyond a doubt his immense love for us. A separate feature provides the students an opportunity for imaginative prayer, to pray with the events of the passion narrative from Mark 14:1–15:47.

Warm Up

a) Give each student five index cards and have them print the following on each card: card 1—one positive personality trait they possess; card 2—one positive academic, intellectual, or creative skill they possess; card 3—one positive physical skill they possess; card 4—their most prized possession; card 5—the names of four people who are very important to them. When completed, have them sit facing a partner. Each person should fan out the cards so that the blank side faces their partner. Direct each person to pick one card from each other's hand. Then allow time for discussion: "How would losing this affect your life? How could something positive come from this loss?" Connect this activity to Jesus' giving up his will to follow his Father's will and ultimately giving up his life for our salvation.

b) As journal entries, assign the students to write on at least one of the following:

- How would you respond if you found out you only had one week to live?
- How would you feel if someone close to you betrayed you?
- Describe one hardship in your life that you offered up to God.
- Under what circumstances would you be willing to die for your faith?

Using the Section

• • • • • • • • • • • •

a) Assign chapters 22–24 of Luke's gospel. Have the students list five differences between Luke's version of Jesus' passion and Mark's version (see page 141).

b) Read paragraph 571 from the *Catechism of the Catholic Church* aloud to the students. Print part of the statement on the board:

> "The Paschal mystery of Christ's cross and Resurrection stands at the center of the Good News. . . . "

Ask the students to discuss ways they can share this central message with others through their words and actions.

c) Read or summarize the text section "The Paschal Mystery in Mark's Gospel" on pages 132-133. Ask the students to look up and read Psalm 22 and identify three specific passages that coincide with Jesus' passion and death.

d) Regarding the text section "Historical Background" (page 133), call on the students to provide a coherent response to the question of why Jesus was put to death.

e) The section "Theological Background" (page 134) has to do with who is responsible for putting Jesus to death. It is important for the students to understand that all of us—as sinners—bear a responsibility for Christ's death.

f) Assign the margin exercises on page 140 as journal writing. Call on volunteers to share their "obituary" for Jesus.

Extending the Section

• • • • • • • • • • • • • •

a) Ask the students to investigate recent developments in Catholic-Jewish relations. Searching within the Vatican website (http://www.vatican.va/) reveals many recent documents on the issue.

b) Assign the students to read more background information on the reasons for the various endings of Mark's gospel and to write their own opinion on why the original ended as abruptly as it did.

Creative Learning

• • • • • • • • • • • •

a) Read the introduction to "Meditating on the Passion Narrative" (pages 135-140). If possible, provide a new setting for the students to undertake this imaginative form of prayer. Make sure each student has his or her own copy of the Bible.

b) Arrange for the students to photograph samples of particular stations of the cross from many different local churches. Have them display the photos so that they can be available to all for viewing.

Conclusion

a) Call on several student volunteers to share with the class a summary of the main theological purpose of Mark's gospel.

b) Allow time for the students to study the Selected Vocabulary definition (page 143). Then quiz them orally or in writing on the definitions. Include on the quiz other terms the students have recorded definitions for during the course of study for this chapter.

c) Assign the Summary Points and Review Questions (pages 141-143). Grade them and allow the students to review them in preparation for the Chapter Test.

Answers to Review Questions

1. Identify the author of the Gospel of Mark.

   With most certainty, we can say that Mark is a Christian who came out of a Jewish background.

2. Where, when, and why was the Gospel of Mark written?

   The gospel was written in Rome or Syria, likely between A.D.64-70. The gospel was written to encourage Jesus' disciples to follow in the Lord's path of suffering for the sake of the kingdom.

3. What is the basic narrative framework of Mark's Gospel?

   Mark gives a geographical framework for presenting the gospel that includes Jesus' baptism, his preaching and performing miracles in Galilee, his journey to Jerusalem, and his preaching, rejection, and crucifixion there.

4. What is the symbol for the Gospel of Mark?

   The winged lion is the symbol of St. Mark the Evangelist.

5. What is Jesus' basic message about the kingdom of God? What is his relationship to this message?

   Jesus announces that the kingdom is at hand, that people should repent, and that he is God's agent in establishing the kingdom.

6. What does it mean to be a person who speaks with authority? Discuss several ways Jesus was an authoritative teacher.

   A person with authority speaks with the right to command, has official power, is the source of reliable information, has the ability to gain respect of others and influence them, and has knowledge, skill, or experience worthy of respect. Examples will vary.

7. How did Jesus differ from other teachers in relationship to his students?
   Jesus gathered his own disciples. Other teachers were sought out by disciples.

8. Interpret the meaning of one of the parables in Mark 4.

   Answers will vary.

9. Name and explain the basic elements of the typical miracle story in Mark's Gospel.

   An introduction presents the setting and situation. Jesus is witness to a display of faith. Next, Jesus responds to the problem. The result of the miracle follows. Most miracles conclude with a reaction to the miracle.

10. What do Jesus' miracles reveal about his identity?

Jesus' miracles reveal his identity as God's Son.

11. What is the messianic secret?

The so-called messianic secret is Mark's description of Jesus asking even his own disciples to keep quiet about his true identity.

12. Why does Jesus call Peter "Satan" in Mark 8:31-33?

When Jesus calls Peter "Satan" he makes it very clear that even his closest disciples are tempting him to walk the wrong path.

13. What was Jesus' favorite title for himself? What does it mean?

Jesus may have preferred "Son of Man" over other titles because he could shape its own meaning. He may well have used "Son of Man" to emphasize his claim to be human like us, but also his supernatural identity as one sent by God.

14. What is the meaning of the term *Paschal mystery*?

The Paschal mystery refers to Jesus' passion, death, and resurrection.

15. List and discuss some things Jesus did and taught that angered the religious leaders of his day.

Jesus performed exorcisms, he forgave sin, healed on the Sabbath, claimed to teach with authority, disregarded cleanliness and dietary laws, associated with sinners and tax collectors, taught that God is merciful of sinners, cleansed the Temple, and predicted it would be destroyed.

16. Who is responsible for Jesus' death?

The real culprits for Jesus' death are all of us—sinners.

17. Why did Jesus die?

Jesus died to prove his immense love for us. His death was the perfect sacrifice for our salvation.

18. What does Jesus do at the Last Supper?

Jesus celebrated a Passover meal with his apostles and instituted the Eucharist.

19. Interpret the meaning of the naked young man who ran away in the Garden of Gethsemane.

Answers will vary. For example, some scholars interpret the identity of the man to be Mark himself.

20. Why did some Jewish religious leaders want Jesus crucified? Why could they not inflict capital punishment themselves?

Jesus was accused of blasphemy by the religious leaders. Under Roman rule, the laws in Judea allowed only the Roman prefect to inflict the death penalty for crimes of a non-religious nature.

21. Did Pilate find Jesus guilty? Why did he order execution? Identify Barabbas.

Though Pilate knows that Jesus is innocent, he hands him over for crucifixion. He did so after caving into pressure from the crowds. Barrabas was a killer convicted in a civil disturbance who was released by Pilate.

22. What is significant about the centurion's proclamation at the moment of Jesus' death?

The expression is ironic because it is a lone Gentile who interprets Jesus correctly and recognizes his true identity.

23. Why is it important that Jesus *really* died?

Jesus died to fulfill his Father's will and his prediction that the Messiah would be handed over, suffer, and die before being raised from the dead.

24. Suggest a reason Mark ends his gospel the way he does.

Answers may vary. One theory is that Mark is trying to draw his audience into the narrative. Another is that Mark is trying to invite the readers to substitute themselves for the women at the empty tomb.

Chapter 4 Test

• • • • • • • • •

Assign and grade the Test on Chapter 4 (pages 214-215 of this Manual). The answers follow below:

Chapter 4 Test   Name:_____

All questions worth 4 points each.

Part 1: Multiple Choice. Write the letter of the best choice in the space provided.

___A___   1. Mark's Gospel was probably written around:
      A. A.D. 70
      B. A.D. 76
      C. A.D. 80
      D. A.D. 85

___C___   2. The symbol for the evangelist Mark is:
      A. an eagle
      B. a man
      C. a lion
      D. a bull

___A___   3. Mark compares John the Baptist to which prophet?
      A. Elijah
      B. Jeremiah
      C. Ezekiel
      D. Amos

___D___   4. Jesus' miracles included all of these *except:*
      A. exorcisms
      B. healings
      C. raisings from the dead
      D. legerdemain

___E___   5. Jesus was seen as a threat by the authorities because of his:
      A. forgiveness of sin
      B. disregard of cleanliness laws
      C. association with sinners
      D. his cleansing of the Temple
      E. all of these

___B___   6. The high priest at the time of Jesus' crucifixion was:
      A. Joseph of Arimathea
      B. Joseph Caiaphas
      C. Nicodemus
      D. Annas

Part 2: True or False: Mark **+** if the item is true and **0** if the item is false.

__+__   7. Jesus was a teacher of authority in the sense that he had original teachings.

__0__   8. Because he respected the Torah, Jesus forbade healing on the Sabbath.

__+__   9. Mark emphasizes Jesus' miracles as demonstrations of God's power (*dynamis*) breaking into human history.

__+__   10. For Jesus, repentance and faith are intimately linked.

__0__   11. By cursing a fig tree, Jesus symbolically reprimanded *Gentiles* for their lack of faith.

__+__   12. The title *Son of Man* emphasizes both Jesus' human and supernatural natures.

__0__   13. Jesus requires his followers to give up their wealth to follow him.

Part 3: Short Fill-ins:

____learner____   14. The term *disciple* means ___?___ .

___blasphemy___ 15. By claiming to forgive sin, Jesus' opponents accused him of ___?___ [name of sin].

____sinners____ 16. Complete this quote: "Those who are well do not need a physician, but the sick do. I did not come to call the righteous but ___?___ ."

____allegory____ 17. What literary term fits this definition: "A story in which people, things, and events have symbolic meanings that represent something else."

Suffering Servant 18. For Jesus, the Messiah is a ___?___ ___?___ .

_____cross_____ 19. Complete this quote: "Whoever wishes to come after me must deny himself, take up a ___?___ , and follow me."

_____child_____ 20. Complete this quote: "Amen, I say to you, whoever does not accept the kingdom of God like a ___?___ will not enter it."

Part 4: Short Answers: (4 points each)
Give one reason why Jesus instructed people not to reveal his identity.

Because most people misunderstood the nature of Messiahship. He wanted people to approach him in true faith.

Analysis: "It is like a mustard seed that, when it is sown in the ground, is the smallest of all the seeds on the earth. But once it is sown, it springs up and becomes the largest of plants and puts forth large branches, so that the birds of the sky can dwell in its shade" (Mk 4:31-32).

_____Jesus_____   22. Who is the speaker?

_____parable_____   23. What literary form is this an example of?

___kingdom of God___ 24. To what is the mustard seed compared?

25. What is the meaning of this story?

Though God's kingdom starts small, it will grow large and embrace all people.

Prayer Lesson

➥   Have the students share their responses with a partner.

five

The Gospel of Matthew: Jesus the Teacher

Introducing the Chapter

Chapter 5 highlights the gospel of Matthew's teaching on the Christian life. Matthew presents the teachings of Jesus, especially in the noted passages from the Sermon on the Mount, the kingdom of God parables, and the commissioning of the disciples.

As with the other chapters on the individual gospels, Chapter 5 begins with background information on the author, location, and date of the writing. A basic outline of the gospel is offered on pages 151-152.

A good portion of Mark's gospel is quoted in Matthew. The chapter compares the two gospels as well as pointing out material that is unique to the gospel of Matthew.

The next portion of the chapter addresses Jesus' discourses recorded in the gospel. The topics of the discourses include love and forgiveness, standing up to ridicule, pursuing God's kingdom, trusting God, and sharing with the needy.

Parables about the kingdom are also looked at in more detail, especially the parable of the sower. The gospel also looks at the founding of the Church.

Finally, Matthew continually references the Old Testament. Jesus is seen as the new Moses who presents a new law of love. The gospel repeatedly refers to Jesus' prophetic fulfillment. All of this makes sense when we consider Matthew's attempt to proclaim the good news of Jesus to a *Jewish*-Christian audience.

Bibliography

Allison, Dale C. *The New Moses: A Matthean Typology*. Minneapolis: Fortress Press, 1993.

_____. *The Sermon on the Mount: Inspiring the Moral Imagination*. Companions to the New Testament. New York: Crossroad, 1999.

Betz, Hans Dieter. *The Sermon on the Mount: A Commentary*. Hermeneia Series. Minneapolis: Fortress Press, 1995.

Brown, Raymond E., S.S. *The Birth of the Messiah*, rev. ed. New York: Doubleday, 1993. Outstanding commentary on the infancy narratives of Luke and Matthew.

Carter, Warren. *What Are They Saying About Matthew's Sermon on the Mount?* New York: Paulist Press, 1994.

Dodd, C. H. *The Parables of the Kingdom*, rev. ed. New York: Scribners, 1965. Remains a highly regarded work on the parables.

Garland, David E. *Reading Matthew: A Literary and Theological Commentary on the First Gospel*. Reading the New Testament Series. New York: Crossroad, 1999.

Hughes John Jay. *Stories Jesus Told: Modern Meditations on the Parables*. Liguori, MO: Liguori, 1999. Excellent commentary on some of the key parables.

Harrington, Daniel, S.J.. *The Gospel of Matthew*. Sacra Pagina, 1. Collegeville, MN: The Liturgical Press, 1991.

Jeremias, Joachim. *The Parables of Jesus*. New York: Scribners, 1963. A seminal work.

Lambrecht, J. *The Sermon on the Mount*. Wilmington, DE: Michael Glazier, 1985. A scholarly work on the topic.

Perkins, Pheme. *Hearing the Parables of Jesus*. New York: Paulist Press, 1981. An excellent introduction to the parables.

Powell, Mark Allen. *God with Us: A Pastoral Theology of Matthew's Gospel*. Minneapolis: Fortress Press, 1995.

Schnackenburg, Rudolf. *The Moral Teaching of the New Testament*. New York: Seabury, 1979.

Senior, Donald. *Matthew*. Abington New Testament Commentary. Nashville: Abington, 1998. The best of Catholic scholarship.

_____. *What Are They Saying about Matthew?*, rev. ed. New York: Paulist Press, 1996.

Stock, Augustine. *The Method and Message of Matthew*. A Michael Glazier Book. Collegeville, MN: Liturgical Press, 1995.

Witherup, Ronald D. *Matthew: God with Us*. New York: New City Press, 2000. A spiritual commentary based on the best of New Testament scholarship. Very readable.

Videos

· · · · ·

Evangelists Speak for Themselves

Fr. William Burke portrays the gospel witness before a contemporary audience (Luke—45 minutes; John—58 minutes; Mark and Matthew—75 minutes in two separate segments; Pflaum).

The Fourth Wiseman

Artaban (Martin Sheen) pursues the Messiah for thirty-three years, missing him at every turn. Along the way, our hero uses his gifts to help those in dire need. He finally meets Jesus on Easter Sunday. Heart-warming story (72-minute video, Ignatius Press).

Godspell

Dated, but still useful for some of the depictions of the parables. Presents Jesus as a counter-cultural clown. The bouncy disciples following Jesus around New York City is a bit much to take after the terrorist attacks of 9/11/01 (1973; 102-minute feature film, Amazon.com).

The Gospel According to St. Matthew

A low-budget, dubbed-into-English, black-and-white production dedicated to Pope John XXIIII by its director—the Italian, Marxist-atheist Pier Pasolini. The camera-work has a "you-are-there" documentary style to it as it captures the poor villages of rural southern Italy and the cast of extras, all of whom were non-actors. The Jesus of this film is portrayed by a Spanish student, Enrique Irazoqui, with a narrow face, high forehead, stubbly beard, sad expression, and piercing black eyes. Limited to depicting only Matthew's gospel, the film presents an angry Christ of the people who tries to whip up the populace into some kind of revolutionary frenzy. This Jesus has emotion, but he definitely reflects the politics of the director (1964; 136-minute feature film, Amazon.com).

Jesus of Nazareth

The acclaimed Zeffirelli film with an all-star cast. Robert Powell portrays Jesus. Many hold this to be the best of all Jesus films. Jesus is dignified, idealistic, in control, polished, and visionary. The film does a good job showing Jesus as one divine person with two natures. It neither overemphasizes his divine nature nor his human nature, as films have a tendency to do. The miracles are handled tastefully, showing how the Father worked through his Son (371-minute feature film on VHS or DVD format, widely available, for example, Ignatius).

Joseph

Explores St. Joseph via art and interviews with Catholic authors, priests, and teachers (60-minute video, Ignatius).

King of Kings

The famous Jeffrey Hunter version that highlights a blue-eyed, blond Jesus who is, at times, moody and confused and, at other times, compassionate and self-possessed. The story highlights Judas and Barabbas as political revolutionaries with Jesus presented as a pawn in their game. The Jesus in this film is strong, self-controlled, yet at times gentle (1961; 171-minute video, Amazon.com, Critics Choice).

Resources

How to Interpret Parables
http://www.discipleship.net/parables.htm

Matthew: Introduction, Argument, and Outline
http://www.bible.org/docs/soapbox/matotl.htm

Jeremias, Joachim. *The Lord's Prayer.*
English translation of the classic work on the Our Father originally published by Fortress Press in 1964; republished on the Internet by Religion Online.
http://www.religion-online.org/cgi-bin/relsearchd.dll/showbook?item_id=1118

Jeremias, Joachim. *The Sermon on the Mount.*
English translation originally published by the Athlone Press in 1961; republished on the Internet by Religion Online.
http://www.religion-online.org/cgi-bin/relsearchd.dll/showbook?item_id=1117

Section 1: Attitudes of Being and Background on Matthew's Gospel (pages 145-154)

Objectives

The goals of this section are to enable the students to:

➥ realize that happiness is an "attitude of being";

➥ identify various details related to Matthew's gospel including its authorship, audience, date, purpose, and themes;

➥ look at several themes in Matthew's gospel, including teachings on judgment, messiahship, discipleship, Church, and morality;

➥ examine differences between Matthew's gospel and Mark's gospel.

Summary and Background Information

"Jesus: the Teacher" is the focus of the chapter. Jesus' most famous and important teachings were addressed in the Sermon on the Mount, including the Beatitudes. This chapter introduces the Beatitudes as an "attitude of being" and reminds the students that God only wills for our happiness and perfection.

The section opens with a story and an exercise, "Living the Beatitudes," that asks the students to rate their progress in living the Beatitudes through this time in their lives.

Relevant background information on the gospel of Matthew is offered. An outline of the gospel is included on pages 151-152. Finally, as much of the information from Matthew's gospel is also in the gospel of Mark, a comparison between the two gospels helps us to understand that Matthew was a Jewish-Christian who was writing for a predominantly Jewish-Christian audience.

Warm Up

a) Write statements like these on the board:

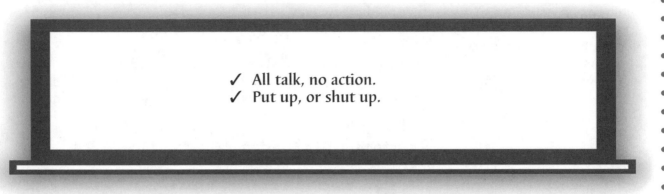

> ✓ All talk, no action.
> ✓ Put up, or shut up.

Ask the students to tell what meanings they associated with these statements. Then have them read the opening scripture quote (page 144) and relate the statements to its meaning. Point out that Jesus teaches us that we are to use our deeds to influence the world for good.

b) Select nine students and have them each read one Beatitude (Matthew 5:1-11) as an opening prayer.

Using the Section

a) Read and discuss the opening story under "Attitudes of Being" (page 145). Call on volunteers to react to the truth in Frankl's statement. "I choose how I will react to what happens to me."

b) Assign the reading "Living the Beatitudes" with the accompanying exercise "The Beatitudes in My Life" (pages 146-147). Allow the opportunity for the students to share their responses with a partner. Have them complete the assignment on suffering for their Christian convictions (page 147) as journal writing.

c) Print a summary of Matthew's gospel on the board or use as a PowerPoint presentation. For example:

Gospel of Matthew

Authorship: a Jewish-Christian, perhaps a former scribe

Audience: Greek-speaking Jewish-Christian community in Syrian Antioch

Date: c. A.D. 85

Purpose: to show that Christians may claim Yahweh's promises to the Chosen People and that Gentiles are also welcome

Summarize the material by having the students read the material under "Background on Matthew's Gospel" (pages 148-151).

d) Compare Mark 14:43 and Matthew 26:47 (see page 149). Ask the students to note that Matthew does not include the scribes as those who came to arrest Jesus and to understand a possible reason for doing so: the author of Matthew may have been a scribe.

e) Note the reasons for the conclusion that Matthew's gospel was originally intended for a Jewish-Christian audience.

f) Assign the text section "The Outline of Matthew's Gospel" (page 151-152).

g) Read or summarize the subsection "Comparing the Gospels of Matthew and Mark" (pages 152-154). Conclude by asking the students to answer in writing: "Why was it necessary for Matthew to write another gospel?"

Extending the Section

a) Assign the exercise on page 151. The students should write how Jesus fulfills the prophecy, not simply recant the passage. For example, Matthew 1:22-23 is fulfilled when Joseph and Mary do indeed name their son Jesus.

b) For the oral report suggested as part of "The Outline of Matthew's Gospel" (pages 151-152), instruct the students to summarize the reports by completing the worksheet "Characters and Events of Matthew" (page 216 of this Manual) as they listen to the reports of their classmates.

c) Have the students research the answers to the following questions:

> ✓ Why is Matthew's gospel listed first in the New Testament?
>
> ✓ Why would Matthew emphasize *prophetic fulfillment* throughout his gospel?
>
> ✓ Why would the author of Matthew, writing to a Jewish-Christian audience, divide the teaching of Jesus into five sections?

d) Assign the margin exercise on page 154. *Answers:* Micah 5:2 is quoted in Matthew 2:6. Jesus' mercy and compassion is being appealed to Mt 9:27, 15:22, and 20:30.

Creative Learning

a) Have the students do a report on modern-day Nazareth, Jesus' hometown.

b) Using their choice of art medium, have the students create a depiction of the Annunciation to Joseph, the nativity, the flight to Egypt, or the massacre of infants from the first two chapters of Matthew.

c) Assign a book report on *Man's Search for Meaning* by Viktor Frankl.

SECTION 2: Jesus: The Teacher (pages 154-155)

Objectives

The goals of this section are to enable the students to:

➡ view Jesus as a sole teacher worthy of our obedience;

➡ understand Jesus as a new Moses who brings a new law to God's people;

➡ note Matthew's arrangement of five main teachings or discourses by Jesus and their content.

Summary and Background Information

As introduced in Chapter 4, Jesus is a teacher *par excellence*. The gospel of Matthew highlights Jesus' role as teacher.

Matthew's gospel is an appropriate one to focus on Jesus as teacher as Matthew significantly added to Mark's gospel by including many of Jesus' specific teachings collected from the Q source as well as from Matthew's own unique traditions, called "M."

Matthew arranges Jesus' teachings into five discourses, following the pattern of the Jewish Torah.

Jesus' famous Sermon on the Mount is examined first. Ample opportunity to apply the content of Jesus' teaching to everyday, contemporary life is provided through a series of exercises and activities. Jesus' instructions on the nature of mission may seem less directly applicable. It will be important that you help your students see that his words are addressed not only to the Apostles and early Church, but also to each of us today.

The other subsections discuss requirements of discipleship, the kingdom of God parables (including a detailed look at the Parable of the Sower), Jesus' founding of the Church, and his eschatological discourse having to do with the final judgment.

Warm Up

a) Put an agree-disagree "continuum" on poster paper on the floor or taped to a wall. The continuum should include the following phrases: strongly agree, agree, somewhat agree, disagree, and strongly disagree. Ask the students to stand. Read the following statements one at a time. Pause after each statement and allow the students to stand near the phrase that best describes how they feel about that statement. Call on students expressing a variety of feelings to explain their position before moving on to the next question.

Statements

➡ Good can come from suffering.

➡ Everyone is out for themselves.

➡ Most poor people could help themselves if they really wanted to.

➡ I could forgive someone who murdered one of my family members.

➡ I would stick up for an unpopular classmate who was being treated unjustly.

➡ I would die for my Christian beliefs.

Make a connection between this discussion and the main themes of the Beatitudes.

b) Ask the students to write one three-sentence paragraph that sums up their philosophy of life. Allow a chance for everyone to share this paragraph with the class, either orally or displayed in some way in the classroom.

Using the Section

a) Introduce the section "Jesus the Teacher" by reminding them of some of the qualities of excellent teachers previously discussed on page 87 of this Manual.

b) Assign the text section "Discourse One: The Sermon on the Mount" (pages 155-158) and Matthew 5–7. Divide the class into three groups, with one group taking responsibility for Matthew 5:13-48, another for Matthew 6:1-34, and a third for Matthew 7:1-29. When the reading is completed, form teaching triads where each person summarizes his or her section for the other two.

c) Call on a student to be "on the spot" and come before the class. Ask the person one or more of the questions on page 158. Then call on more people, as time permits, to be on the spot.

d) Read or summarize the subsection "Discourse Two: Sharing the Faith with Others" (pages 158-160). Also ask the students to read Matthew 10.

e) Review with the students the meaning of *parables*. Say something like "A parable is a story where familiar things are used to describe something unfamiliar." In addition, Jesus told parables that always had a surprising twist or finish to them. Read or summarize the first three paragraphs of "Discourse Three: Parables about the Kingdom" (pages 160-162). Assign the students to work in small groups or with a partner to read and discuss the four parables cited on page 161. For a point of discussion, ask them to share what each parable tells about the kingdom of God.

f) Assign the text section "Discourse Four: Jesus Founds and Instructs the Church (Mt 18)" (pages 162-165). In addition, have the students read Matthew 16. Ask them to explain Peter's importance in the Church.

g) Summarize the fifth discourse from "Discourse Five: The Final Judgment (Mt 25)" (pages 164-165). Also have the students read Matthew 25:31-46 and note the corporal works of mercy cited in the passage. Generate a discussion using the following questions:

Do you believe in a hell?

Do you believe God judges us? What part do we play in determining our eternal destiny?

What would the world be like if you had never been born? better? worse?

Extending the Section

a) Have each student select one of these four topics for doing a short report: 1) Sermon on the Mount; 2) kingdom of God parables; 3) the Church in Matthew's gospel: 4) divine judgment. The reports should include the following:

- An explanation of Matthew's treatment of the them (resource—biblical text)

- Critical information on the passages in Matthew (resource—biblical commentary)

- Personal reflections on the theme

b) Ask the students to memorize the Beatitudes and recite them from memory.

c) Assign the worksheet "Jesus' Teachings" (page 157 and page 217 of this Manual). Then ask the students to write a brief explanation of their highest and lowest marks.

d) As the Parable of the Sower has previously been analyzed in part of a class discussion, assign the separate feature (pages 161-162) and accompanying assignment for homework. Allow time in a future class for the students to share their analysis of the parable.

e) Regarding Matthew's emphasis on Church, ask: "Why do you think the gospel of Matthew was chosen to be the first book of the New Testament? If Mark was written earlier, why wasn't it placed first?" Help the students to understand that because of Matthew's emphasis on the Church, the Catholic Church placed the gospel of Matthew first when arranging the canon.

Creative Learning

a) Assign students to create a video, slide show, photo album, or musical arrangement that illustrates a contemporary interpretation of the Beatitudes or Sermon on the Mount. Allow time for the students to share their projects with the class. The students can work individually or in a small group.

b) Related to Jesus' call to discipleship have the students work together on a service project. For example: sponsor a car wash to raise money for a homeless center, sponsor a "hunger day" at school when students give up lunch to donate money to the poor, agree to sponsor a meal at a homeless shelter, catechize younger children in a parish school or religious education program. See also page 165.

c) Assign "The Church" exercise (page 164 and page 218 of this Manual). To follow up on the assignment, ask the students to interview a parish leader (e.g., pastor, pastoral associate, parish council representative) or school leader (e.g., principal, teacher) on his or her standards for Church membership. At a future class session, compile one list of all the suggestions that were gathered.

Section 3: Jesus Challenges Judaism (pages 166-167)

Objectives

The goals of this section are to enable the students to:
- put into context the criticism leveled at Judaism in the gospel of Matthew;
- define anti-Semitism as a form of prejudice;
- learn the seven "woes" exclaimed by Jesus against the scribes and Pharisees.

Summary and Background Information

This short section references the apparent criticisms leveled against Judaism by the author of Matthew. The gospel records several incidents, for example, when Jesus denounces the scribes and Pharisees. In the condemnation of Jesus, Matthew seems to attribute the guilt to the entire Jewish people.

Judaism of the first century was a complex web of many religious "cousins" (including Jewish Christians) who were trying to win people to their view of faith. As a follower of Jesus and a Jew, Matthew was likewise trying to win people over to his point of view. In doing so, he used the strongest language possible.

The section offers a counterpoint to the prejudice of anti-Semitism and echoes Pope John Paul II's words that to be anti-Semitic is to be anti-Christian in behavior.

Warm Up

• • • • • • •

a) Assign the margin exercise on page 167 that asks the students to read Matthew 23 and list two warnings. Allow time for discussion.

b) Call on students to share their understanding of Judaism, including experiences knowing Jewish friends and their knowledge of Jewish holidays and customs.

Using the Section

• • • • • • • • • • • • •

a) Related to the students' reading of Matthew 23, summarize the message in the first two paragraphs under "Jesus Challenges Judaism" (page 166). Note the following key points from Matthew 23:1-12:

> Jesus shows respect for the authority of the Jewish leaders and the Law.
>
> Jesus warns leaders who tried to impress others through superficial external titles rather than trying to be humble.

b) Assign the text section "The Seven Woes" (pages 166-167) as well as Matthew 23:13-36 from the Bible. Define "woe" as a word that expresses the horror of sin and punishment for those who commit it.

Extending the Section

• • • • • • • • • • • • • • • •

a) Invite a group of Jewish teenagers to class to share some of their core beliefs and practices with the students.

b) Have the students write a practical pledge for how they will live Christianity today.

Creative Learning

• • • • • • • • • • • •

a) Assign the students to write seven woes that express horror and condemnation of sins (not sinners) that take place in their world today.

b) Ask the students to write a poem or song lyrics that express the stern warning of the seven woes.

Conclusion

a) Allow time for the students to study the Selected Vocabulary definitions (page 170). Then quiz them orally or in writing on the definitions. Include on the quiz other terms the students have recorded definitions for in their notebooks or journals.

b) Assign the Summary Points and Review Questions (pages 167-169). Grade them and review them as preparation for Chapter 5 Test.

Answers to Review Questions

1. Why is the Gospel of Matthew often called the "First Gospel?"

    Church traditions involving the composition of Matthew as well as the gospel of Matthew being listed first in the New Testament canon contribute to it being known as the "first gospel." It was most likely known as the first gospel because it contains detailed teachings, especially in the area of Christian ethics.

2. Identify the probable author of the Gospel of Matthew.

    The author of the gospel is anonymous. He was most likely a Jewish-Christian who probably knew Hebrew and perhaps a little Aramaic.

3. Offer evidence that Matthew wrote *after* Mark.

    The gospel of Matthew contains about 80 percent of Mark's gospel. Traditions that cited Matthew as the first gospel may have been referring to one of Matthew's sources, not the gospel itself.

4. Give a probable date for the composition of Matthew's Gospel.

    Scholars believe Matthew was written in Greek for a predominantly Greek-speaking Jewish-Christian community probably in Antioch in Syria, sometime in the 80s, perhaps A.D. 85.

5. List two reasons why Matthew wrote his gospel.

    Matthew wanted to show 1) how the Church could legitimately lay claim to Yahweh's promises to Israel and 2) how the Church should include Gentiles in the community.

6. Discuss several examples of how Matthew's Gospel is the most "Jewish" of the four gospels.

    Matthew cites several Old Testament prophecies and other passages. Jesus is compared to Moses. The number of discourses (five) parallels the books in the Torah.

7. List at least three key themes treated in Matthew's Gospel.

    Besides portraying Jesus as the Messiah called forth from the Old Testament, Matthew also reminds his readers that Gentiles are welcome in God's kingdom. Other themes include judgment, Jesus as Emmanuel, discipleship, Church, and right instruction.

8. Why may the author of Matthew have divided his gospel into five major sections?

    The division reminds us of the first five books of the Old Testament (Pentateuch) and a comparison between Moses and Jesus.

9. Discuss the meaning and significance of these two titles of Jesus, both found in Matthew's infancy narrative: Son of David, Emmanuel.

    Son of David is a title that connects Jesus with his Jewish roots. The title Emmanuel refers to Jesus as the promised one who fulfills the promises made to Israel.

10. What might Matthew have had in mind by including women in his genealogy of Jesus?

The inclusion of women—all either foreigners, or Gentiles—shows the gospel will eventually be preached to all people.

11. Contrast the ending of Mark's Gospel with that of Matthew.

While Mark criticizes the apostles for their "hardened hearts," Matthew presents a more flattering picture of the apostles after the resurrection. Matthew also includes two resurrection appearances and the story about the empty tomb.

12. Discuss two specific teachings from the Sermon on the Mount.

Answers will vary. For example, Christians are salt of the earth and light of the world, Christians observe a new standard of law, Christians have a right attitude, Christians do not judge others and they pray in trust.

13. Write the Golden Rule. Give two examples of how you can practice it in your own life.

The Golden Rule is: "Do to others whatever you would have them do to you." Examples will vary.

14. What is a parable? What is an allegory? Why did Jesus teach in parables?

A parable is "a short story drawn from ordinary life that makes a comparison with a religious message." An allegory is a sustained comparison where many story elements correspond to some reality outside the story. Jesus taught in parables to confound outsiders and to present truths about the kingdom to the disciples in ways that show how God works.

15. What advice does Jesus give Church leaders in Matthew 18?

Leaders must not be obsessed with power and authority. They must be humble, never lead others to sin, pursue the sinner, put no limits on forgiveness, imitate God the Father who forgives, confront troublemakers privately first, pray together as a community for the Church's needs.

16. How does Matthew's Gospel support the establishment of the pope as the Christ-appointed leader of the Church?

Jesus is very clear in Matthew 16:18-19 that the Church be based on Peter, the rock.

17. What is the *eschaton*? What are some qualities of "apocalyptic" writing?

Eschaton means "end time." Apocalyptic writing includes strong beliefs like: God is ultimately in charge during times of trial, there is an ongoing war between forces of good and evil, God will bring judgment on the righteous and punish the wicked, disciples should remain faithful, and disciples should be prepared for God's return.

18. Interpret the parable of the talents (Mt 25:14-30).

The parable of the talents teaches that we should make good use of the time the Lord has given us.

19. According to Matthew 25, on what will we all be judged?

Jesus' criterion is this: "Whatever you did for one of these least brothers of mine, you did for me" (25:40).

20. Why is it not correct to say Matthew 23 is anti-Semitic?

Matthew 23 is not an attack from outside Judaism. It is more a bickering of Jewish insiders who were trying to win over their fractured religious body to the world-changing view that Jesus is the Christ, the Son of God.

Chapter 5 Test

• • • • • • • • •

Assign and grade the Chapter 5 Test (pages 219-220 of this Manual). The answers follow below:

Chapter 5 Test   Name:_____

• •

All questions worth 4 points each.

Part 1: Matching. Please match the theme of the parable in Column A with the parable listed in Column B.

	Column A	Column B: Parable
__F__	1. Always be ready for Christ's return.	A. Yeast
__D__	2. Despite being opposed, God's kingdom will grow immensely.	B. Pearl of great price
		C. Weeds among the wheat
__A__	3. God's kingdom grows mysteriously.	D. Sower
__B__	4. Sacrifice all for God's kingdom.	E. Judgment at end of time
		F. Wise virgins

Part 2: True or False. Mark **+** if the statement is true and **0** if the statement is false.

__+__ 5. Matthew's Gospel is listed first in the New Testament because it links well the Old Testament to the New Testament.

__+__ 6. Matthew includes a number of women in his genealogy of Jesus to show that the gospel will be preached to all people.

__0__ 7. Matthew tends to paint a *harsher* view of the apostles than does Mark.

__0__ 8. Jesus endorses a concept of *lex talionis*, that is, reasonable retalitation.

__0__ 9. The Sermon on the Mount permits divorce in the case of physical abuse.

__+__ 10. Matthew's Gospel stresses how Jesus fulfills Old Testament prophecies about the Messiah.

__+__ 11. Apocalypse means "revelation."

__+__ 12. "Eschatological" has to do with death and the end of the world.

__+__ 13. To be anti-Semitic is to be anti-Christian.

Part 3: Multiple Choice. Write the letter of the best choice in the space provided.

__B__ 14. Which is the Hebrew word for "hell"?
  A. Talitha koum
  B. Gehenna
  C. Golgotha
  D. Beelzebul

__A__ 15. Matthew has as one of its sources all of the following *except*:
  A. Luke
  B. *Q*
  C. *M*
  D. Mark

   __A__ 16. This title means "God is with us":
          A. Emmanuel
          B. Son of Man
          C. Son of David
          D. Yahweh

   __C__ 17. The title "Son of David" in Matthew especially emphasizes that Jesus is:
          A. God's Son
          B. the Lord
          C. the Messiah
          D. the Son of Man

   __D__ 18. The quote, "You are Peter, and upon this rock I will build my church . . . . I will give you keys to the kingdom of heaven . . ."
          A. establishes Peter as the earthly leader of Christ's church.
          B. shows Christ's intent to found a hierarchial church.
          C. gives Peter and his successors the power to forgive sin and teach authoritatively.
          D. all of these
          E. none of these

Part 4: Short Fill-ins

    __Jesus__   19. Who is the founder of the Christian church?

    __scandal__   20. Bad example that leads others to sin is   __?__ .

21. "Blessed are the poor in spirit, for theirs __is the kingdom of heaven__."

22. "Blessed are the merciful, for __they will be shown mercy__."

23. Write out the Golden Rule: __"Do to others whatever you would have them do to you."__

Part 5: Short Reflection.

"You are the salt of the earth. You are the light of the world."

What do these words of Jesus mean? __Christ calls on his disciples to live their lives such as to__ __make a difference in the world and attract others to the kingdom.__

Give four examples of how you can be salt and light in your world: (Award one point for each answer given.) *Answers will vary.*

Prayer Lesson

- Assign the Prayer Lesson as individual, silent prayer.
- Encourage the students to write answers to each question in their journals.
- Also, ask the students to write the plan to improve their response to God suggested in the Resolution (page 171).

six

The Gospel of Luke and Acts of the Apostles: Jesus the Savior

Introducing the Chapter

While Luke's gospel tells the story of Jesus, the Acts of the Apostles (by the same author) tells the story of the early Church. This chapter shows how the gospel of Luke and Acts of the Apostles fit together. The style, language, and organization of the two books are similar. Both were addressed to Theophilus, and both highlight the journey to Jerusalem. The chapter also takes up the issues of authorship, audience, and date of the writing. The outline of Luke is simple and focuses on Jerusalem.

The chapter also examines several common themes in Luke and Acts. Among these are Jesus as prophet, the Church's role in continuing Jesus' prophetic ministry, the role of the Holy Spirit in salvation history, prayer, joy, and peace, and the special role of Mary and women.

In the final sections, the chapter explores Luke's picture of Jesus as the compassionate Messiah who identifies with the poor and lowly, and as the universal Savior who reaches out to all people, Gentile or Jew, man or woman.

A more detailed synopsis and outline of Acts of the Apostles is offered in conclusion.

Bibliography

• • • • • • • • •

Luke

Byrne, Brendan, S.J. *The Hospitality of God: A Reading of Luke's Gospel.* Collegeville, MN: The Liturgical Press, 2000.
A fascinating commentary that stresses the theme of God's bounteous love.

Conzelman, Hans. *The Theology of St. Luke.* New York: Harper, 1960.
The classic work on Luke's gospel.

Fitzmyer, Joseph A., S.J. *The Gospel According to Luke.* Anchor Bible, 28. Garden City, NY: Doubleday, 1981, 1985.
Among the most scholarly and best available.

Ford, Richard Q. *The Parables of Jesus.* Minneapolis: Fortress Press, 1997.

Grassi, Joseph A. *The Hidden Heroes of the Gospels: Female Counterparts of Jesus.* Collegeville, MN: Liturgical Press, 1989.
Reviews the theological themes of each gospel and illustrates how women exemplify those themes. Excellent resource on showing how women are ideal disciples.

Johnson, Luke Timothy. *The Gospel of Luke.* Sacra Pagina 3. Collegeville, MN: Liturgical Press, 1991.

Karris, Robert J., O.F.M. "The Gospel According to Luke," in *The New Jerome Biblical Commentary.* Englewood Cliffs, NJ: Prentice-Hall, 1990.
A helpful commentary with a detailed bibliography.

_____. *What Are They Saying about Luke and Acts?* New York: Paulist Press, 1979.
A good introduction to the unity of these two works.

_____. *An Invitation to Luke.* Garden City, NY: Doubleday, 1977.
A very readable edition.

Kilgallen, John J. *A Brief Commentary on the Gospel of Luke.* New York: Paulist, 1988.

Knight, Jonathan. *Luke's Gospel.* New York: Routledge, 1998.

Kodell, Jerome, O.S.B. *The Gospel According to Luke.* Collegeville Bible Commentary. Collegeville, MN: The Liturgical Press, 1982.
A short and still-useful commentary.

McBride, Dennis. *The Parables of Jesus.* Liguori, MO: Liguori/Triumph, 1999.
Insightful overview of parables and excellent discussion of some leading stories told by Jesus.

Powell, Mark Allan. *What Are They Saying about Luke?* New York: Paulist Press, 1989.
Excellent overview of current Lucan research.

Scott, Bernard Brandon. *Hear Then the Parable: A Commentary on the Parables of Jesus.* Minneapolis: Fortress Press, 1991.

Tannehill, R.C. *The Narrative Unity of Luke-Acts: A Literary Interpretation.* Philadelphia: Fortress, 1986.

Acts

Brown, Raymond. *The Churches the Apostles Left Behind*. New York: Paulist, 1984.

Bruce, F.F. *The Book of Acts*. Grand Rapids, MI: Eerdmans, 1981.

Dillon, Richard J. "Acts of the Apostles," in *The New Jerome Biblical Commentary*. Englewood Cliffs, NJ: Prentice-Hall, 1990.
Excellent commentary.

Fitzmyer, Joseph A. *The Acts of the Apostles*, Anchor Bible 31. New York: Doubleday, 1998.

Johnson, Luke Timothy. *The Acts of the Apostles*. Collegeville, MN: Liturgical Press, 1992.

Karris, Robert J. *Invitation to Acts*. Garden City, NY: Doubleday, 1978.

Kilgallen, John J. *A Brief Commentary on the Acts of the Apostles*. New York: Paulist Press, 1988.
Pastoral orientation.

Powell, Mark Allan. *What Are They Saying about Acts?* New York: Paulist Press, 1992.

Tannehill, Robert C. *The Narrative Unity of Luke-Acts: A Literary Interpretation*. 2 volumes. Philadelphia: Fortress Press, 1991-1994.

Van Linden, Philip, C.M. *Gospel of Luke & Acts: The Spiritual Vision of Luke-Acts*. Wilmington, DE: Michael Glazier, 1986.

Videos

A.D.

Recreates the turbulent years following the death of Christ. Acclaimed made-for-TV mini-series depicts the years A.D. 30-69. Comes with a 52-page study guide for a twelve-week course (3 tapes, 360 minutes, Ignatius Press).

Evangelists Speak for Themselves

Fr. William Burke portrays the gospel witness before a contemporary audience (Luke—45 minutes; John—58 minutes; Mark and Matthew—75 minutes in two separate segments; Pflaum).

A Father and Two Sons

A ten-minute modern rendering of the age-old tale of the Loving Father. Produced by the American Bible Society (Harcourt Religion Publishers).

Greatest Story Ever Told

Filmed against the stunning background of the red-cliff mesas of Utah, this film stars the distinguished Swedish actor, Max von Sydow. Light imagery is used to great effect. The portrayal of Lazarus' raising from the dead, against the background music of Handel's *Messiah*, is stunning. Distracting, though, are the cameo appearances of Hollywood stars who appear frequently as bit players. Von Sydow's impeccable appearance, mesmerizing Swedish accent, and piercing blue eyes present an unearthly, controlled, mystical Christ who is easy to admire but hard to warm up to. Jesus' divinity is clearly stressed (1965; 199-minute feature film, Amazon.com).

Jesus

A widely distributed film on the life of Jesus that is very faithful to the gospel of Luke. Used with success with students for years. Brian Deacon stars as Jesus. Based on the gospel of Luke, and promoted by evangelical Christians, this film does a fine job presenting the gospel and a human Jesus who laughs, dances at wedding parties, and enjoys being with his disciples. The film shows a human Jesus, yet one who is still divine and sure of his mission. The most marketed of any film made about Jesus, it has been used for mission outreach throughout the world and dubbed in over six hundred languages! It has its own website where students can watch the movie on-line: http://www.jesusfilm.org/ (1979; 120-minute feature film, Ignatius Press).

Mary of Nazareth

From acclaimed French film director Jean Delannoy. A perspective on the life of Jesus from the eyes of the Blessed Mother (115-minute video, Ignatius Press).

The Neighbor: The Parable of the Good Samaritan

A twelve-minute video rendering of Lk 10:25-37. Produced by the American Bible Society (Harcourt Religion Publishers).

The Visual Bible: Acts

Filmed on location in the Middle East and Africa. Exact quotes from the biblical text. Includes portrayals by notable actors such as Richard Kiley (Matthew), Dean Jones (Luke), James Brolin (Peter), and Jennifer O'Neill (Lydia) (four 50-minute videos, Ignatius Press).

Resources

Acts-L WWW Homepage
http://www.baylor.edu/ACTSL/

The Good Samaritan
Have your students check out this outstanding website from the New Media Bible people.
http://www.newmediabible.org/1goodsam/

Gospel of Luke
A website with many links related to Luke's gospel.
http://www.geocities.com/gospelofluke/

Gospel of Luke
http://www.abu.nb.ca/courses/NTIntro/Luke.htm

Luke: Introduction, Outline, Argument.
An introduction by Daniel Wallace, Ph.D.
http://www.bible.org/docs/soapbox/lukeotl.htm

SECTION 1: Lost and Found and Background on Luke's Gospel and the Acts of the Apostles (pages 173-180)

Objectives

The goals of this section are to enable the students to:

➼ understand the portrayal of Jesus in the gospel of Luke as one who intimately knows the loving heart of his Father;

➼ recognize details related to Luke-Acts, including author, audience, date, and purpose;

➼ be familiar with the outline of the gospel and Acts and how each focuses on Jerusalem.

Summary and Background Information

This section opens with an introduction of the Luke/Acts connection. It also focuses on some of the prominent parables of Jesus included in Luke's gospel. The students are asked to read, summarize, and note the themes from some of the Lucan parables.

The remainder of the text section focuses on key elements of the background of the gospel. Several deductions are made. For example, it is deduced that the author of Luke did not know the historical Jesus in person. Also, the author did write for Gentile churches, most likely those founded by St. Paul. The main sources of the gospel and Acts are also discussed.

Finally, information about why Luke wrote the gospel is discussed in relation to clues mentioned in the prologue.

Warm Up

a) Print a portion the following gospel quotations from Luke on the board and see how many the students can finish:

"Behold I am the handmaid of the Lord. May it be done according to your word" (Lk 1:38).

"Stop judging and you will not be judged" (Lk 6:37).

"Why do you notice the splinter in your brother's eye, but do not perceive the wooden beam in your own" (Lk 6:41).

But he said to the woman, "Your faith has saved you; go in peace" (Lk 8:8).

"Ask and you will receive; seek and you will find; knock and the door will be opened to you" (Lk 10:9).

Then the veil of the temple was torn down the middle. Jesus cried out in a loud voice, "Father, into your hands I commend my spirit" (Lk 23:46).

Then the two recounted what had taken place on the way and how he was made known to them in the breaking of the bread (Lk 24:35).

b) Play a short Bible quiz game. Make sure each student has his or her own Bible. Ask questions with answers that can be found in Luke or Acts. Divide the group into two teams. Award points to the team that can cite the chapter and verse where the answer can be found.

Using the Section

a) Assign a complete reading of the gospel of Luke (to be completed by the end of the study of Chapter 6). Have the students take notes on their reading, perhaps dividing the gospel by theme or by noting specific times how Jesus deals with 1) the poor, 2) Gentiles, 3) women, 4) Samaritans, and 5) sinners and outcasts. Another method is to assign students specific sections of Luke and Acts (see page 176) and have them report to others after reading.

b) Read the opening text under "Lost and Found" and the chapter objectives. Discuss with the students any experience they had like the one described: being literally found after being lost or finding someone in their care who had been lost.

c) Assign the text activities involving Lucan parables (pages 174-175 and pages 221-222 of this Manual). Allow the opportunity for the students to discuss their feelings on Parable Themes and Reflections with a partner.

d) Ask a series of short questions based on the material in the section "Background on Luke's Gospel and the Acts of the Apostles" (pages 175-178). For example:

True or false: Tradition identifies Luke as a Jewish-Christian (false).

True or false: The author of Luke and the Acts of the Apostles are the same. (true)

True or false: Luke may have accompanied St. Paul on some of his missionary journeys. (true)

What year is the most probable date of the composition of Luke-Acts? (85)

What does the name Theophilus mean literally? ("lover of God")

What other gospel did Luke use as a source? (Mark)

True or false: The Good Samaritan and Prodigal Son parables appear only in Luke. (true)

True or false. Luke is unconcerned with historical details. (false)

What city is most prominent in Luke and Acts? (Jerusalem)

e) Note Luke's master plan in delineating three periods of salvation history (see page 178). Write on board:

> **Luke's Three Stages of History**
>
> Stage 1: Age of Promise (ends when Jesus is born)
>
> Stage 2: Time of Jesus (focal point of history)
>
> Stage 3: Age of the Church (starts at Pentecost)

f) Assign the separate feature, "The Outline of Luke's Gospel" (pages 178-179).

g) Have the students complete the summary of the gospel passages on page 175 in their journals.

Extending the Section

a) Assign reading of the *Catechism of the Catholic Church* on the Holy Spirit, a key element in both Luke and Acts. Have the students focus in particular on *CCC* 683-741 and write summary reports on what they have read.

b) Included in the "L" source are five miracle stories unique to Luke. Have the students read and summarize those stories: Luke 5:1-11; 7:11-17; 13:10-17; 14:1-6; 17:11-19.

Creative Learning

a) Have the students go through the entire gospel and create a map that chronicles Jesus' journey to Jerusalem.

b) The author of Luke set out to write a masterpiece, the premier work that told the story of Jesus and the good news. Have the students answer orally or in writing the following questions related to Luke's gospel:

➥ What do you hope will be your life's masterpiece?

➥ Who are people you feel are excluded from being a part of the Church?

➥ If you could know one thing about Jesus' hidden years (ages 13 to 30), what would it be?

SECTION 2: Common Themes in Luke and Acts (pages 180-189)

Objectives

The goals of this section are to enable the students to:

➥ recognize Jesus' role as prophet and how the Church continues that role;

➥ examine the themes of the Holy Spirit, prayer, joy, peace, and the special role of Mary and women in Luke and Acts;

➥ identify the Marian doctrines of the Immaculate Conception, Perpetual Virginity, and Mother of Christ and Church.

Summary and Background Information

Several common themes in Luke and Acts are explored in this section. The first theme examined is Jesus as prophet with the Church continuing his prophetic ministry throughout history. Luke is sometimes called "the gospel of the Holy Spirit" because of the many mentions of the Spirit leading Jesus in his ministry in the gospel. The section continues to remind the students of the Spirit's role in this gospel as well in their own lives.

In addition, the themes of peace, joy, and prayer are closely explored.

Next, the role of women in the gospel (in particular the role of Mary, the Blessed Mother) are elucidated. The role of Mary also leads the students to a theme to be covered in the next section: God's preferential love for the poor.

Warm Up

a) Read Luke 4:1-44 for an opening prayer. Explain that this passage underscores the themes of the Holy Spirit and prayer, and shows Jesus' ministry is for the oppressed.

b) Introduce the themes to be covered in this section. Divide the class into four groups, assign one theme, and have each group read and report on how Luke treats the theme.

Holy Spirit: 1:35; 2:27; 3:22; 4:1; 23:46

Joy and Peace: 1:14; 2:10; 10:17; 15:7; 24:52

Prayer: 3:21; 5:16; 9:18; 21:36; 24:34

Women: 8:21; 10:38-42; 24:9-12; 18:1-8; 2:52

Using the Section

a) Introduce the themes to be covered in this section by reading the opening text under "Common Themes in Luke and Acts" (page 180).

b) Continue by reading or summarizing the text subsection "Jesus the Prophet (Lk 4:14-44)" (pages 180-181). Note the threefold importance of these passages:

✓ First, they reveal what Jesus thought of himself and how he conceived his mission.

✓ Second, the scene at Nazareth foreshadows Jesus' public life.

✓ Third, the synagogue scene also foreshadows the role of the Holy Spirit and the importance of prayer.

c) The text section "The Church Continues Jesus' Prophetic Mission (Acts 1–2) (pages 181-183)" focuses on lessons from the Acts of the Apostles. Identify characteristics of an ideal Christian community as defined in Acts: Christian fellowship, prayer, breaking bread, and the teaching of the apostles. Ask the students to share how each of these characteristics remains present in today's Church.

d) Assign the margin exercise (page 182) as a short in-class assignment. *Acts 1:15-26 Answers:* Joseph (Barsabbas) and Matthias; prayer; drawing lots. *Acts 2:1-12 Answers:* wind, tongues as of fire, speaking in tongues; the gift of tongues enabled the Apostles to be understood no matter the language of the listener.

e) Use "The Role of the Holy Spirit in Salvation History" (page 183-184) to trace how the gospel of Luke and Acts stress the vital role of the Spirit. Assign the margin questions on page 184. *Answers:* Spirit allows us to prophesy. The Spirit is given through the laying on of hands. The Spirit fills us with joy.

f) Read or summarize the text section, "Prayer," (pages 184-185). Then ask the students to complete the assignment on page 186. Next, call on three or four students to sit on a panel to share their responses to the questions. As time allows, call on other students to take a place on the panel.

g) Cover the section "Joy and Peace" (pages 185-186). Witness to the sense of joy that is contained in the gospel. Speak to some of these ideas:

●◆ God's reign will triumph and evil will lose.

●◆ God loves us unconditionally—no matter what we do or say.

●◆ God can forgive our sins.

●◆ Christ has died for us, to show us the way to heaven.

●◆ Christ has risen; he has conquered death—and we can share in this.

●◆ Heaven awaits the followers of Jesus, but the peace and joy of heaven can begin on earth.

h) Summarize the material in "The Special Role of Mary and Women" and the feature "What the Church Believes About Mary" (pages 186-189). Assign the students to read Mary's Magnificat (Lk 1:46-55). Ask them to explain why they believe Luke found this ancient hymn appropriate to include in the gospel.

Extending the Section

● ● ● ● ● ● ● ● ● ● ● ● ● ● ● ●

a) Ask the students to do at least *one* of the assignments offered on page 181. Allow opportunity for the finished work to be checked in class.

b) Have the students design a chart in their notebooks of the movement of the Holy Spirit. For example:

Luke 1:35 Spirit's power conceives Jesus in Mary

Luke 2:27 Spirit enables Simeon to recognize Jesus

Luke 3:22 Spirit descends on Jesus (baptism)

Luke 4:1 Spirit leads Jesus to the desert

Luke 23:46 Jesus gives up his spirit at death

Acts 2:3-4 Spirit descends on the Apostles

c) Assign the students to research and print in their notebooks or journals the text of at least one of the following prayers:

●◆ Prayer of St. Patrick

●◆ Generosity Prayer of St. Ignatius

●◆ Peace Prayer of St. Francis

●◆ Serenity Prayer

d) Quiz the students on the following information related to Mary:

Name the countries of the following Marian apparitions: Guadalupe (Mexico), Fatima (Portugal), Lourdes (France).

Name the dates of these Marian feasts: Solemnity of Mary, Mother of God (January 1), Immaculate Conception (December 8), Annunciation (March 25), Assumption (August 15).

Name Mary's mother and father. (St. Anne and St. Joachim.)

Mary is the patron saint of the United States under what title? (Immaculate Conception.)

Creative Learning

a) Assign a short essay titled "Joy." Ask the students to use examples from personal experience to describe what joy means to them. (See also page 189.)

b) Ask the students to imagine that they have been assigned to write a definitive account of Jesus' life. Tell them to each write down the ten most important events from Jesus' life (miracles, teachings, parables, etc.) that would have to go in the story, ranking them in importance from 1 to 10. When they have finished, collect, read, and compare several of the lists.

SECTION 3: Jesus: A Compassionate Messiah and Universal Savior and Overview of the Acts of the Apostles (pages 189-199)

Objectives

The goals of this section are to enable the students to:
- relate to Jesus as a compassionate Messiah and universal Savior;
- interpret parables like Lazarus and the Rich Man, the Good Samaritan, and the Prodigal Son;
- give several examples of how Jesus is the faithful martyr;
- identify the five main sections of Acts of the Apostles and recall several pivotal events in Acts.

Summary and Background Information

Luke's gospel emphasizes the compassionate Messiah who cares especially for the poor and disadvantaged (described as the *anawim*). Jesus teaches that love for the poor, represented by concrete deeds, is a requirement of discipleship. This section highlights Jesus' teaching in this regard, focusing also on his teaching to "love your enemies" and to be "friends of sinners."

The section also addresses Jesus' role as Universal Savior, the one who brings about our salvation.

Finally, the section offers a brief overview of the entire Acts of the Apostles. Included is a description of how the Church handled the debate over allowing Gentiles to join the community. Paul, the Apostle to the Gentiles, is introduced. He will figure more prominently when his epistles are studied later in the course.

Warm Up

a) To review the prevalence of the Spirit in Luke and Acts, print the following scrambled words having to do with the Holy Spirit on the board. Ask the students to unscramble them.

ROPO (poor)

MIODWS (wisdom)

DNIW (wind)

DLLFIE (filled)

NKOESP (spoken)

NTDINOAE (anointed)

b) Continuing to make the connection between Luke and Acts, have the students read both Luke 24:13-35 and Acts 8:26-40 and note the similarities between both incidents.

Using the Text

• • • • • • • • • •

a) Emphasize the portrait of Jesus as the compassionate Messiah. Read the story of Lazarus and the rich man (Lk 16:19-31) to help make this point. Continue the exposition by covering the opening text under "Jesus: A Compassionate Messiah and Universal Savior" and the subsection "Compassionate to the Poor" (pages 189-190).

b) Continue in the same fashion with a portrait of Jesus as "Friend of Outcasts" (page 191) by re-telling the story of Zacchaeus (Lk 19:1-10).

c) Begin a discussion on perceived enemies of the students and the difficulty they might find in loving these people.

d) Encourage the students to re-read Luke 15. Point out that it is often known as the "heart" of Luke's gospel because of its emphasis on parables that deal with God's great compassion and joy over repentant sinners. Summarize the teachings in the parables discussed (lost sheep, lost coin, lost or prodigal son):

God's love is relentless in pursuit of one who has lost his or her way.

God's love exceeds anything we can imagine.

God is merciful to everyone, and in a special way to the lost, lowly, outcast, and sinner.

e) Assign the exercise "Jesus and Money" (page 194) for in class work. Call on students to share their applications of each statement.

f) Luke's gospel concludes with emphasis on Jesus as a martyr. Read or summarize the text section "The Martyred Lord" and Luke 23–24. For the Emmaus story (Lk 24:13-35) consider choosing a student to serve as narrator to read the passage while three other students mime the parts of Jesus and the two disciples.

g) Introduce the "Overview of the Acts of the Apostles" by reading the opening paragraph on page 196. To cover the material, divide the class into four groups with each group responsible for reading the text and cited scripture for "Mission in Jerusalem," "Missions to Judea and Samaria," "Mission to the Gentiles," and "The Missions of Paul to Rome" (pages 196-199). When completed, arrange for one student from each group to form new "teaching groups" and to report on their material to the others.

h) Note the similarities between Paul and Jesus (see page 199). Assign the margin exercise on page 199.

Extending the Section

a) Review the interpretation of the Good Samaritan parable as an allegory (page 192). Assign the students to write their own version of the parable, including modern elements and an allegorical interpretation.

b) Assign the margin exercise "Stephen—First Martyr" (page 196). There are many similarities between Jesus' death and Stephen's death, including Stephen's uttering of the same last words of Christ, "Lord [Jesus], receive my spirit" (Acts 7:59).

c) Have the students give a detailed report on how the gospels of Mark, Matthew, and Luke are truly synoptic ("seen together") citing research gleaned from biblical commentaries.

d) Assign the margin exercises on page 197 and page 198 as individual work. *Answers to page 197 exercise:* Cornelius was a Roman centurion. Peter had a vision of him being commanded to eat unclean animals. The message was that Gentiles were to be considered clean and accepted members of the Church. *Answers to page 198 exercise:* The council responded to the opinion of the apostles and presbyters. Peter and James spoke at the council. The decision was to allow Gentile members and not trouble them with keeping all of the Jewish law. Rather, they had to avoid pollution from idols, unlawful marriage, the meat of strangled animals, and blood. The decision opened the way for universal membership in the Church.

e) Review the path of Paul's three journeys using a PowerPoint presentation or overhead map featuring the entire Roman empire.

Creative Learning

a) Invite a member of the Missionaries of Charity to speak to the class on their ministry of service and compassion to the poor.

b) Call on groups of students to develop a role play for one of the stories or parables from Luke (e.g., rich man and Lazarus, Zacchaeus, parable of the Prodigal Son).

Conclusion

a) Call on students to share their summaries of Acts 22 (see page 199).

b) Allow time for the students to study the Selected Vocabulary definitions (page 202). Then quiz them orally or in writing on the definitions. Include on the quiz other terms the students have recorded for their notebooks or journals.

c) Assign the Summary Points and Review Questions (pages 199-202). Grade them and review them in preparation for the Chapter 6 Test.

Answers to Review Questions

1. List at least three themes taught by the parables of Jesus. Name a parable that illustrates each theme.

    Answers will vary. See pages 174-175 of the Student Text.

2. Identify the author of Luke's Gospel. Offer evidence that he also wrote the Acts of the Apostles.

    The author of Luke's gospel was a Gentile-Christian who might have been attracted to Judaism. The style, language, and organization of the gospel and Acts are very similar. Both works are addressed to the same person, Theophilus.

3. When was Luke-Acts probably written?

    The year 85 is often listed as the probable date of composition.

4. What were the sources for Luke's Gospel?

    The author used three main sources: Mark's gospel, Q, and L (sources unique to Luke).

5. Identify *Theophilus*.

    Theophilus was the subject of the dedication of Luke and Acts. Theophilus may have been a definite person or a symbol for all Christians.

6. Why did Luke write his Gospel?

    Luke wants to show all Christian readers that their instruction in the Christian faith was sound. He wanted to strengthen their faith.

7. How is Jerusalem a symbol in Luke's Gospel?

    Jerusalem is the start of the Christian journey and the place from which the Christian message must be taken out.

8. Explain the significance of Jesus' teaching in the synagogue at Nazareth.

    The teaching revealed what Jesus thought of himself and how he conceived his mission. It foreshadowed Jesus' public life. It underscores the role of the Holy Spirit and the importance of prayer.

9. How did the early Church continue Jesus' prophetic ministry?

    The Church continued Jesus' prophetic ministry through fellowship, praying for each other, celebrating the Eucharist, and apostolic witness or succession.

10. What is Luke's understanding of salvation history?

    Luke stresses the vital role of the Holy Spirit in salvation history. He views salvation history in three stages: Stage 1—Age of Promise; Stage 2—The Time of Jesus; and Stage 3—The Age of the Church.

11. Give several examples of how the Holy Spirit plays a role in both the Gospel of Luke and Acts.

    Answers will vary. For example, Mary becomes Mother of God through power of Holy Spirit, the Spirit descends on Jesus in form of dove; Jesus prays full power of Spirit and teaches us how to pray in the Spirit.

12. What role did prayer play in Jesus' life? in the life of the early church?

    Jesus prayed on several important occasions. For example, at his baptism, before he chose his apostles, and while hanging on the cross. The Church continues this constant prayer. For example, they prayed in the Upper Room while awaiting the Holy Spirit, while performing miracles in Jesus' name, and while praying for new Church leaders.

13. Give some examples of the part women played in Luke-Acts. What does their inclusion say about Jesus and his teaching?

    Jesus' attitude toward women was positive and revolutionary. He healed women, had women disciples, and made women central characters in his parables. Jesus' treatment of women echoes the respect and love he has for all people, especially the most vulnerable.

14. List three ways Mary has a special role in the writings of Luke.

    Mary is the model of Christian faith. Her response of "yes" to God enables Jesus to come to humanity. She prayerfully meditates on the meaning of her son and is faithful to him to the end.

15. Identify these Marian doctrines: *Immaculate Conception, Assumption,* and *Mary Ever Virgin.*

    Immaculate Conception—Mary was without sin from the first moment of her existence. Assumption—At the time of her death, Mary was assumed body and soul into heaven. Mary Ever-Virgin—Mary was always a virgin, "before, in, and after" the birth of the Lord.

16. Interpret the meaning of these three parables: Lazarus and the Rich Man, the Good Samaritan, and the Prodigal Son.

    Lazarus—Those who have plenty in this life must share with those who have less. Good Samaritan—We must love everyone, even our "enemies." Prodigal Son—The return of sinners brings great joy in heaven. God loves sinners.

17. What were some gifts given to the disciples on Pentecost Sunday?

    On Pentecost Sunday the disciples were given the gift of the Holy Spirit which immediately manifested itself in the gift of tongues and the increase in Church membership.

18. Who was the successor to Judas Iscariot? How was he chosen?

    Matthias was Judas' successor. He was chosen by lots.

19. Identify Stephen.

    Stephen was the first Christian martyr.

20. What important decision was made at the Jerusalem Council in A.D. 49? What did it mean for the future of Christianity?

    The difficulties of following all of Jewish law were removed from Gentiles entering the Church. The decision paved the way for Christianity to spread to the ends of the earth and to all people.

21. Who was Barnabas?

    Barnabas was a traveling companion of Paul who was sent to minister to the Church in Antioch.

22. Where were Christians first called by that name?

    Antioch.

23. List at least two ways in the Acts that Jesus' life was a model for Paul.

    For example, each began ministry in a synagogue. Both ministered and were arrested in Jerusalem. Both predicted their sufferings. Both were innocent of charges but sentenced by weak leaders.

24. What is the meaning of Acts of the Apostles ending in Rome?

    The ending in Rome hints at a third work, perhaps the "Acts of Christians."

Chapter 6 Test

• • • • • • • • •

Assign and grade the Chapter 6 Test (pages 223-224 of this Manual). The answers follow below:

Chapter 6 Test   **Name:**_____

All questions are worth 4 points each.

Part 1: Matching. Please match the mystery from Jesus' life in Column B with its description in Column A.

Column A

Column B

<u>L</u> 1. tax collector who converted to Christ; short in stature

<u>H</u> 2. "brother of the Lord," leader of Jewish-Christians in Jerusalem

<u>F</u> 3. companion of Paul on missionary journeys

     4. greatest Christian saint; prayed the Magnificat

<u>I</u> 5. first Christian martyr

<u>G</u> 6. Gospel of Luke and Acts are dedicated to him

     7. Apostle to the Gentiles

<u>B</u> 8. replaced Judas as an Apostle

A. Stephen
B. Matthias
C. Cornelius
D. Good Samaritan
E. Prodigal Son
F. Barnabas
G. Paul
H. James
I. Mary
J. Theophilus
K. Demetrius
L. Zaccheus

Part 2: Multiple Choice. Write the letter of the best choice in the space provided.

<u>A</u> 9. Jesus was like Old Testament prophets. He did all of the following *except*:
   A. He spoke in tongues.
   B. He used attention-getting actions.
   C. He warned of God's judgment on evil-doers.
   D. He performed miracles.

<u>D</u> 10. Jesus' parables are important because:
   A. they contain the heart of his message.
   B. they show him to be a remarkable teacher.
   C. they reveal how he dealt with his opponents.
   D. All of the above.
   E. None of the above.

<u>C</u> 11. The gospel of Luke highlights this city as a central symbol of God's salvific activity:
   A. Rome   B. Antioch   C. Jerusalem   D. Capernaum

<u>B</u> 12. According to Acts, the ideal Christian community included all of these *except*:
   A. *koinonia*
   B. excommunication of known sinners
   C. celebrating the Eucharist
   D. studying the teaching of the apostles

___A___   13. The theme of this parable is to share your gifts with poor people:
- A. Lazarus and the rich man
- B. The Lost Coin
- C. The Prodigal Son
- D. The Unjust Judge

___C___   14. The theme of this parable is God's incredible love for sinners:
- A. Lazarus and the rich man
- B. The Good Samaritan
- C. The Prodigal Son
- D. The Friend at Midnight

Part 3: True or False. Mark **+** if the statement is true and **0** if the statement is false.

___+___   15. Luke wrote primarily for a Gentile-Christian audience.

___0___   16. The author of Luke's gospel knew the historical Jesus.

___+___   17. Acts of the Apostles is properly known as the "Gospel of the Holy Spirit."

___0___   18. Unlike the gospel of Matthew, the gospel of Luke downplays the role of women in Jesus' ministry.

___+___   19. The doctrines of the Ascension and the Assumption both refer to Jesus' going to heaven.

Part 4: Short Fill-ins.

___witness___   20. The term *martyr* means ___?___ .

___age of the Church___   21. For Luke, the three periods of salvation history included: the age of promise; the time of Jesus; and the ___?___ .

___Pentecost___   22. The Jewish feast of ___?___ is considered the "birthday of the church."

___Immaculate Conception___   23. This doctrine of the ___?___ of Mary holds that from the first moment of her existence, Mary was free from any alienation caused by original sin.

Part 5: Short Responses

24. What is the lesson of the parable of the Good Samaritan?
    Everyone is our neighbor, even our enemy. We must love everyone.

25. If Jesus were retelling the parable of the Good Samaritan today, who might he choose to be the hero of his story? Why?
    Accept as correct anyone who is an "outsider," an "enemy," or "outcast" in our society. Why? Because a Samaritan was despised by Jesus' contemporaries.

Prayer Lesson

➠ As noted, review with the students the steps for imaginative prayer on page 135.

➠ Quiet the room. Allow time for silent reflection based on Luke 7:36–50. Choose a good reader to read the passage as the students sit quietly. Also engage the narrator to read the questions on page 202.

➠ Allow time for the students to complete the Reflection and determine how they will live out the Resolution to the Prayer Lesson (page 203).

seven

The Gospel of John: Jesus the Word of God

Introducing the Chapter

The gospel of John presents a special challenge to high school teachers and students. It can be the most difficult gospel to study. Theologically, the gospel of John is the most highly developed of the gospels. Because of this, a key in understanding the gospel is to look at themes with universal appeal that arise from both the Book of Signs (miracles) and Book of Glory (Jesus' farewell discourses and death and resurrection).

The chapter opens by examining the background of the gospel authorship, date, audience, and outline—and the major themes that are introduced in the prologue of the gospel, in John 1. A fuller understanding of *Christology* is also developed, with a comparison of "ascending Christology" of the synoptics with the "descending Christology"—that is, "Christology from above"—that is more the focus of John's gospel. The opening section of this chapter also introduces several titles for Jesus.

Following, the chapter is organized around the Book of Signs and the Book of Glory. The miracles of Jesus have a different perspective in John than in the synoptics. They reveal Jesus' identity, the purpose of his Incarnation, his heavenly glory, and his relation to God the Father. Each of the seven signs is explored. The Book of Glory shows how Jesus' passion, death, and resurrection reveal God's love for us. In the Last Supper discourses, Jesus prepares his apostles for these events.

In conclusion, the chapter compares the resurrection appearances in John's gospel with those of the synoptics.

Bibliography

• • • • • • • • •

Brodie, Thomas L. *The Gospel According to John: A Literary and Theological Commentary*. New York: Oxford University Press, 1997.

Brown, Raymond E. *The Gospel According to John*. Anchor Bible 29. Garden City: Doubleday, 1966, 1970.
   Part of the Anchor Bible series. A classic commentary which tends to stress the historical value of John and points out its similarities to the synoptic gospels.

_____. *The Community of the Beloved Disciple*. New York: Paulist Press, 1979.

_____. "The Resurrection of Jesus," in "Aspects of New Testament Thought," pp. 1373-1377, in *The New Jerome Biblical Commentary*. Englewood Cliffs, NJ: Prentice-Hall, 1990.
   A readable presentation with a fine bibliography.

Culpepper, P. Alan. *The Gospels and Letters of John*. Nashville: Abington, 1998.

Davis, Stephen and Gerald O'Collins, eds. *The Resurrection: An Interdisciplinary Symposium*. New York: Oxford University Press, 1997.

Flanagan, Neal M., O.S.M. *The Gospel According to John and the Johannine Epistles*. Collegeville, MN: The Liturgical Press, 1983.
   Another fine, short commentary in the Collegeville series.

Marrow, Stanley B. *The Gospel of John: A Reading*. New York: Paulist Press, 1995.

Moloney, Francis. J. The Gospel of John. Sacra Pagina, Volume 4. Collegeville, MN: Liturgical Press, 1998.

Osborne, Kenan B. *The Resurrection of Jesus: New Considerations for Its Theological Interpretation*. New York/Mahwah, NJ: Paulist Press, 1997.
   A helpful study which analyzes each of the texts in turn. Relates Jesus' resurrection to contemporary Christological concerns and themes.

O'Collins, Gerard. *Interpreting the Resurrection*. Mahwah, NJ: Paulist Press, 1988.
   Excellent defense of the traditional teaching on the resurrection.

The Navarre Bible: St. John. Second Edition. Dublin: Four Courts Press, 1992.
   Provides both the RSV and the New Vulgate texts. Traditional commentary with good spiritual insights from Blessed Josemaria Escriva de Balaguer.

Perkins, Pheme. "The Gospel According to John," in *The New Jerome Biblical Commentary*. Englewood Cliffs, NJ: Prentice-Hall, 1990.
   Perkins is a clear and informed commentator.

_____. *Resurrection: New Testament Witness and Contemporary Reflection*. Garden City, NY: Doubleday, 1984.

Schnackenburg, Rudolf. *The Gospel According to St. John*, three volumes. New York: Herder & Herder/Crossroad, 1968, 1980, 1982.
   Ranks with Brown as one of the great commentaries on John's gospel.

Senior, Donald, C.P. "The Miracles of Jesus," in "Aspects of New Testament Thought," pp. 1369-1373 in The *New Jerome Biblical Commentary*. Englewood Cliffs, NJ: Prentice-Hall, 1990.
Includes an excellent bibliography.

Weber, Gerard P. and Robert Miller. *Breaking Open the Gospel of John*. Cincinnati, OH: St. Anthony Messenger Press, 1995.
A straightforward introduction to the gospel.

Witherington III, Ben. *John's Wisdom: A Commentary on the Fourth Gospel*. Louisville, KY: Westminster John Knox, 1995.

Videos

• • • • •

Evangelists Speak for Themselves

Fr. William Burke portrays the gospel witness before a contemporary audience (Luke—45 minutes; John—58 minutes; Mark and Matthew—75 minutes in two separate segments; Pflaum).

Jesus Christ Superstar

Based on Webber and Rice's rock opera, the film version stars Ted Neeley as an energetic Jesus who cries, craves companionship, and is typically harsh and angry. The rock lyrics of the early 1970s are anguished and fit the blaring musical score well. Many critics found the film anti-Semitic in its harsh portrayal of the Jewish leaders and were turned off by a flower-child portrayal of Jesus who, with wispy beard and flowing white gown, sings in a falsetto voice. A glaring omission in the film is the lack of a clear reference to Jesus' resurrection. All believers know there is no Jesus story without the resurrection. Though popular with teens in the '70s, today's students often find this film dated and silly (1973; 107-minute feature film, Amazon.com).

Jesus Christ Superstar

This updated version stars Glenn Carter as Christ. Sean Axmaker in a review for Amazon.com states: "[The film] takes the show out of ancient Jerusalem to an indeterminate mix of modern New York (complete with graffiti-scrawled walls and T-shirt garbed disciples) and timeless Rome. The grandly abstract sets, rainbow lighting, and striking costumes are more theater than cinema . . . . The setting folds fascism, intolerance, and revolution into a portrait out of time, robbing the play of its powerful historical grounding but injecting it with energy and insight. . . . "

It's an entertaining, thoughtful, and well-sung production. Edwards avoids the tepidity of Norman Jewison's solemn 1973 film, driving forward with energetic editing and swooping cameras, and guided at all times by the dramatic, exhilarating score (2001; 107-minute feature film, Amazon.com).

The Resurrected Life

Gives insight on how the resurrection can change individual lives. A four-part program that covers these topics: crucifixion, resurrection, transformation, and reconciliation (60-minute video, Ignatius Press).

Resurrection

Based on a story by the popular author, Max Lucado, this "what-if" story highlights Claudius, a Roman soldier at Christ's death who refuses to participate in a cover-up of the resurrection (50-minute video, Vision with Values).

Resurrection

A ten-minute video produced by the American Bible Society providing a new translation of John 20:1-31. A 32-page discussion/study guide is provided (Harcourt Religion Publishers).

Resources

McDowell, Josh. "Evidence for the Resurrection."
This is a paper that is published on the Telling the Truth website.
http://www.leaderu.com/everystudent/easter/articles/josh2.html

Johannine Literature Web
A site worth exploring. Highly recommended.
http://bellarmine.lmu.edu/~fjust/John.htm

SECTION 1:
No Greater Love, Background on the Gospel of John, and The Word of God (Jn 1) (pages 205-215)

Objectives

The goals of this section are to enable the students to:
- ➥ uncover several basic details about the gospel of John, including authorship, date of origin, and three major themes;
- ➥ understand the meaning of "descending Christology" or "Christology from above";
- ➥ learn several titles for Jesus contained in John's gospel.

Summary and Background Information

"For God so loved the world that he gave his only Son, so that everyone who believes in him might not perish but might have eternal life." These rich words from the prologue of John's gospel (3:16) were once termed by Martin Luther the "heart of the Bible, the gospel in miniature."

God's great love for us, his willingness to see out our friendship are beautiful themes of the fourth gospel. As John's gospel was written near the turn of the second century, the theology of the Christian faith had grown richer in understanding. In the same way, John's Christology is "from above," a descending Christology that stresses very strongly Jesus' heavenly origins, his fundamental identity as Son of God, and his preexistence as the Word of God.

Warm Up

• • • • • • •

a) Have the students read John 3:16. Tell them that at one time fans at Super Bowls and other sporting events would hold up a sign with this verse printed on it. Ask: "Why do some think this verse sums up the entire gospel?"

b) As John's gospel was written thirty to forty years after the death and resurrection of Christ, ask the students for their perspective of a famous historical event that took place thirty or forty years ago. Ask how the perspective they have described may differ from one that was shared immediately after the event took place.

Using the Section

• • • • • • • • • • • • •

a) Assign the opening text under "No Greater Love" (pages 205-206). Have the students read the entire text of Jesus' speech to Nicodemus (Jn 3:1-21) in the context of what is meant by "new birth from above."

b) Begin a general discussion on friendship. Ask the students to list positive aspects of friendships. Write on the board, for example: **sharing common interests, trust, fun, companionship**. Related the discussion to friendship with Jesus and how these aspects related to their relationship with him. Assign the exercise "Friendship with Jesus" (pages 206-207 and page 225 of this Manual). Allow the opportunity for the students to discuss their marks and their overall relationship with Jesus with a partner.

c) Briefly introduce the language and structure of John's gospel, comparing them to the synoptics. For example, contrast images in the language such as light and dark, life and death. As to structure, have the students page through the gospel and note the structure of event—dialogue—monologue followed by long theological discourses.

d) Assign the text section "Background on the Gospel of John" (pages 207-209). Summarize as follows:

Authorship: attributed to John because of the "beloved disciple" reference; probably written by several authors over a period of time

Audience: Jewish-Christians who were expelled from synagogues after the Roman revolt

Date: A.D. 90-100

Length: Twenty-one chapters (two additional endings were likely added to original)

Characteristics: long theological discourses

Themes: divinity of Jesus; belief in Jesus leads to eternal life; division of gospel into Book of Signs and Book of Glory

e) Ask the students to examine the "Outline of the Gospel of John" (page 210) and "Themes in John" (page 211). Assign students various parts of the gospel to read, asking them to point out places where the themes can be found.

f) Cover the entire text section "The Word of God (John 1)" (pages 212-215) as one unit. Compare John 1:14 (Word-made-flesh) with Genesis 1 (Word fashions the world—creation). Point out how the gospel of John portrays the incarnation as a new beginning of creation itself.

g) Along with the subsection "Theme 3: Who Is Jesus" note the "Other Titles for Jesus in John's Gospel," (pages 214-215), with the students writing the references in their journals. To follow up, ask the students to name their favorite title for Jesus and why.

Extending the Section

• • • • • • • • • • • • • • • • •

a) Have the students research the life of St. Maximillian Kolbe, reporting how he gave up his life for another man. Compare this story to the one told in the introduction, and to the life of Christ.

b) Assign one or more of the exercises on friendship suggested on page 207.

c) Assign the margin exercise on page 209 on the Beloved Disciple. *Answers include:* What are some signs that Jesus favored this disciple? (John on many occasions is termed the "beloved" disciple.)

Describe the Beloved Disciple in relationship to Peter. What might his stepping aside to allow Peter to enter the tomb first signify? (This text reinforces Peter's primacy in the Church.)

d) Have the students research some features of the feasts described in the Book of Signs (see page 212).

e) Point out other titles of Jesus from the synoptics, such as: Divine Physician (Mt 9:12-13); Holy One (Mk 1:24); Daybreak (Lk 1:78); and Ruler (Mt 2:6).

Creative Learning

• • • • • • • • • • • • •

a) Ask each student to make an effort to join a new group as part of a class experiment on friendship and making friends. For example, they may sit with a different group of people at lunch, attend a youth group meeting for the first time, or hang out with a completely new set of people on one weekend night. Have them report on the situation based on the following questions:

➡ How did you introduce yourself?

➡ How did someone make you feel welcome?

➡ How did you let the group know something about yourself?

➡ How can what you know about making friends help you in a new situation?

b) Have the students create their own personal title for Jesus and design it using the medium of their choice.

c) Encourage the students to create a crossword puzzle using the titles of Jesus with accompanying scripture references. Duplicate and share the finished projects with the class.

SECTION 2: The Book of Signs (Jn 1:19–12:50) (pages 215-221)

Objectives

The goals of this section are to enable the students to:
- understand the unique definition and use of miracles in the gospel of John;
- name and explain the meaning of the seven signs;
- explore the connection between faith and an understanding of the signs in John's gospel.

Summary and Background Information

This section focuses on the Book of Signs from John 1:19–12:50. The gospel focuses on the significance of these events and offers interpretation of them through the use of reflections, narratives, and discourses.

A common theme in the seven signs is the power of Jesus' life-giving words and actions. The accounts of the seven signs serve as an apt lead-in to the Book of Glory, which will reveal the greatest of all signs—the Paschal mystery of Christ that results in our salvation.

Also in this section, a separate feature examines the account of the woman caught in adultery (8:1-11). The story was a later addition to John's gospel.

Warm Up

a) Discuss both the external and internal changes that take place in Jesus' miracles. For example, external changes (those others can see) would include the calming of a storm, making a blind person see, healing the wounds of a leper. Internal changes in the same events might include the calming of fears, making a person see the "truth," and healing a person of his or her sin. Discuss the miraculous and powerful nature of both types of changes associated with miracles.

b) Introduce the Book of Signs (Jn 1:19–12:50). Point out that the Book of Signs is organized around seven wondrous deeds of Jesus that are representative of his life and ministry. Ask the students to write a journal entry about one positive sign from their own life (e.g., a good deed) that is representative of who they are.

Using the Section

a) Read or summarize the introduction to the section "The Book of Signs (John 1:19–12:50)" (pages 215-216). John's gospel structures the Book of Signs into seven sections. After explaining the event, John provides a discourse that helps the reader comprehend the significance of Jesus. Divide the class into six groups (signs four and five are treated together) and have each group (1) read the biblical text; (2) read the accompanying commentary in the Student Text (pages 216-220); and (3) choose a representative from the group to give a brief report to the class that includes answers to these questions:
- What is the context for the miracle?
- What is being signified?

• Does Jesus explain what he does? If so, how does he interpret it?

b) Read the final two paragraphs of the section on page 220. Explain how John 12 functions as a conclusion to the Book of Signs.

c) Assign the separate feature "Woman Caught in Adultery (John 7:53–8:11)" (page 221). Consider calling one student to the front of the class to be "on the spot." Address one of the questions to the student for response. As time allows, call others students to be on the spot with the same and other questions.

Extending the Section

• • • • • • • • • • • • • •

a) Read the margin feature on page 217. Ask the students what fact Jesus' celebration of three Passovers in Jerusalem reveals about his ministry (its duration was three years). Ask them to complete the questions that follow their reading of Jesus meeting with the Samaritan woman (Jn 4:1-26).

b) Have the students choose one or two verses from the Book of Signs that are especially meaningful to them. Then call on students randomly to share their passage and explain why it is so meaningful.

Creative Learning

• • • • • • • • • • • •

a) Related to the seven signs, have the students write their thoughts in their journals on the following entries:

• Reflect on Mary's trust and confidence in Jesus in the wedding at Cana.
• Reflect on our need to see in order to believe in the cure of the official's son.
• Reflect on how healing is often painful related to the cure of the paralytic.
• Reflect on our society's wastefulness and extravagance related to the feeding of the five thousand.
• Reflect on our fears related to Jesus walking on water.
• Reflect on the power of evil at work in the world related to the healing of the blind man.
• Reflect on our ability to show emotion related to Jesus' crying prior to the raising of Lazarus.

b) Have the students work on a mnemonic device, poem, song, rap, or other visual or audio exercise that names and briefly covers the details of all seven signs covered in the Book of Signs.

SECTION 2: The Book of Glory (John 13:1–20:3) (pages 222-228)

Objectives

• • • • • • • •

The goals of this section are to enable the students to:

• read and understand major teachings in the gospel of John's Book of Glory;
• note the symbolism of Jesus' celebrating the Last Supper on the day Jews killed lambs for the Passover meal;
• compare the resurrection narratives and consider it as a major revelation of God the Father.

Summary and Background Information

After a recounting of the seven signs, John's gospel moves its setting to the Upper Room where Jesus' Last Supper discourses help to interpret the meaning of the passion, death, and resurrection narratives that follow. This section is the opening of the Book of Glory; the other section covers the events surrounding Jesus' death and resurrection. An epilogue in Chapter 2 covers Jesus' resurrection appearances.

This section begins by covering the Last Supper discourses. These address several themes including unity, love, and service. An activity on Christian Leadership offers the start of an excellent way to put these qualities into practice.

The resurrection appearances in the gospel are also covered and a comparison is made between these narratives and those found in the synoptics. A point-by-point summary of the meaning of the resurrection serves as a lead-in to a personal faith exercise, "Do You Believe?" (page 228).

Warm Up

a) The section covers several truths including the following:
- Jesus calls us to serve, not to be served.
- Jesus calls us friends.
- Jesus calls us to unity.

Offer personal testimony on how these truths resonate in your own life. Then call on student volunteers to share similarly.

b) One of the most perplexing questions of our faith is "Why did Jesus die?" Present the question to the students. Then have them look up and read three answers to the question from John's gospel:

> John 8:21-30 (Jesus does what is pleasing to the Father.)
>
> John 12:23-24 (Jesus is like the grain of wheat that must die in order to bring new life.)
>
> John 16:28 (Jesus desires to return to the Father.)

Summarize the discussion by writing the following on the board: **Jesus' motivation for accepting death was to do God's will.** Read Luke 22:41-42 to support this conclusion.

Using the Section

• • • • • • • • • • • • •

a) Assign the opening paragraph of "The Book of Glory (John 13:1–20:31)" and the subsection "The Last Supper Discourses (Jn 13–17)" (pages 222-224). Ask the following questions to gauge the students' understanding of the section:

What is the symbolic meaning of the Last Supper occurring on the day the Jews killed the lambs for Passover? (Jesus is the Lamb of God whose sacrifice on the cross freed all people from sin.)

What was the act of humility in which Jesus began the meal? (He washed the feet of his disciples.)

What was the new commandment Jesus offered? (To love one another.)

Why does Jesus want us to stay close to him? (Because he is the "way and the truth and the life.")

Who is the Paraclete? (The Paraclete is the Holy Spirit, who Jesus promised to send to his disciples.)

What does Jesus ask for in his Last Supper prayer? (Jesus asks that through his death and resurrection, we may all be brought into the glory of eternal life.)

b) Assign the students to work in pairs to do the exercise "Jesus' Use of Allegory" (page 224 and page 226 of this Manual). Check the following answers:

Who is the vine? (Jesus)

Who is the vinegrower? (God the Father)

What does the pruning process represent? (removing sinners from among God's people)

Who are the branches? (the faithful)

What happens if the branches remain attached to the vine? (We will have life in Christ.)

What does the fruit represent? (our full potential as God's creation)

c) Assign the text subsections "The Resurrection of Jesus (Jn 20–21) (CCC, 639-658)" (pages 225-226) and "The Resurrection Narratives Compared" (pages 226-227). Write the following on the board:

> ### The Resurrection Narratives Agree on the Essentials:
> ✓ an empty tomb
> ✓ women witnesses
> ✓ takes place on Sunday
> ✓ heavenly messengers present
> ✓ disbelief removed by Jesus' appearances
> ✓ Jesus' preparation for his ascension and the coming of the Holy Spirit

Cover each point, allowing the students to locate examples of each from the gospel text.

d) Assign the exercise "The Synoptic Gospels on the Resurrection of Jesus" (page 226). Check answers below:

Answers

Who actually witnessed the resurrection itself? (no one)

When does it take place? (Sunday)

What was the reaction of the women in all cases? (amazement, surprise)

Where in Galilee did Jesus appear? (mountain)

Where in Jerusalem did Jesus appear? (Upper Room)

e) Summarize the text section "The Meaning of the Resurrection" (page 228) by making the following points. Write on the board:

The resurrection:

✓ proves Jesus' claim to be God's Son;

✓ accomplished our salvation;

✓ gives us new life,

✓ promises us eternal life with God.

Extending the Section

a) The Last Supper discourses (Jn 13–17) speak of service, love, and unity. Have the students review these chapters and cite quotations they think are most important, symbolic, or poetic.

b) Have the students compare Christian belief in the afterlife to the beliefs of Native American religions, Hinduism, Buddhism, Judaism, Islam, and Greek and Roman mythology.

c) Assign the Christian Leadership activity (page 224 and page 227 of this Manual). Ask the students to work in small groups to discuss both the qualities of leadership present in Jesus and those they believe they possess. Ask each student to explain his strongest leadership characteristic and the one that he or she thinks needs the most improvement.

d) Assign 1 Corinthians 15:3-7, which is the earliest written testimony of the resurrection. Note for the students its liturgical formula.

e) Read or summarize the separate feature "The Ascension of Jesus (CCC, 659-67)" (page 227). Ask: "What does it mean for Christ to be seated at the right hand of the Father?" Refer them to CCC 663 for the answer.

Creative Learning

a) Form a panel with three to five students. Conduct a discussion based on their beliefs in Jesus and the resurrection using the "Do You Believe?" statements on page 228.

b) Have the students keep a scrapbook with news stories that describe people who have experienced a "little resurrection," for example: a conversion, a new start at life, recovery from an illness, etc.

Conclusion

a) Allow time for the students to study the Selected Vocabulary definitions (pages 230-231). Then quiz them orally or in writing on the definitions. Include on the quiz other terms the students have recorded definitions for in their notebooks or journals.

b) Assign the Summary Points and Review Questions (pages 229-230). Grade them and review them as preparation for the Chapter 7 Test.

Answers to Review Questions

1. Who wrote the gospel of John? Identify the Beloved Disciple.

   John's gospel was likely written in several stages and edited by different people. The Beloved Disciple is traditionally identified as John, one of the apostles.

2. When and where was it probably composed? What was the evangelist's reason for composing it?

   The gospel was likely composed between 90-100. The gospel may have been written in Antioch or Alexandria. The gospel was written to combat false ideas about Jesus' full humanity and his divinity and to oppose followers of John the Baptist who claimed he was the messiah.

3. List three ways John's Gospel differs from the synoptic gospels.

   For example, there are new characters (e.g., Nicodemus, Lazarus, man born blind, and a Samaritan woman). Jesus attends three Passovers. Jesus' teaching takes place in the form of long discourses.

4. Discuss three major themes in John's Gospel.

   Key themes include: Jesus Christ, Word of God, Son of God; Faith; Love; Holy Spirit; and Resurrection.

5. What does it mean to say John's Gospel has a "Christology from above?"

   John emphasizes Jesus' heavenly origins, his fundamental identity as the Son of God, and his preexistence as the Word of God.

6. How is Jesus the Word of God?

   Word of God, a concept understood by Jews and Gentiles, connects with Jesus as God's word who has existed forever. At the time of the incarnation, the Word became flesh.

7. How does the author of John's Gospel understand the term *miracle*?

   John's gospel understands miracle to be "signs" of God that reveal Jesus' identity, the purpose of the Incarnation, his heavenly glory, and his relation to his heavenly Father.

8. What is the symbolic meaning of Jesus' first miracle at Cana? What role did Mary play in this sign? How can we learn from her?

   Jesus' attendance at the wedding was a sign of his blessing on marriage as a sacrament of divine love. Mary interceded for the wedding hosts to Jesus. We can learn that she will intercede for us on our behalf. We can also learn from her modeling of faith.

9. What do we learn about Jesus from his discourse with the Samaritan woman?

   Jesus reveals that he is the Messiah, the source of eternal life.

10. Why did so many of Jesus' followers abandon him after the sign of the bread?

    They had trouble understanding and believing how Jesus could be the Bread of Life.

11. Discuss a possible meaning of Jesus' walking on water.

   For example, that Jesus is indeed God's Holy One and that despite the storms that come our way in life, the disciples of Jesus need never fear.

12. Discuss the meaning of Jesus' raising Lazarus from the dead.

   This sign prefigures Jesus' own death and resurrection and teaches that Jesus is the way to life, the resurrection, God, and that faith is essential for our gaining eternal life with him.

13. What is the symbolic meaning of Jesus' celebration of the Last Supper one day before the Passover feast?

   As this was also the day lambs were slaughtered for Passover, Jesus reveals that he is the Lamb of God who takes away the sin of the world.

14. In what way did Jesus fulfill a priestly role in our salvation?

   In his prayer at the Last Supper, Jesus assumes a priestly role by interceding for us by praying to his Father on our behalf.

15. Describe the meaning of the resurrection appearances of Jesus in John's gospel.

   The resurrection is a major revelation of God the Father. John's gospel emphasizes Jesus' commissioning of the leaders to continue his work of resurrection and love.

16. Why do the four gospels have different resurrection stories?

   There are differences among the resurrection stories because eyewitnesses often give dissimilar accounts of what they have seen. Though the evangelists chose different stories in some cases, they agree on the essential points surrounding the resurrection.

17. On what essential points about the resurrection do all the gospels agree?

   The gospels agree on these essential points about the resurrection: it took place early on Sunday morning, women were present at the tomb, the stone had been rolled away and the tomb was empty, a messenger or messengers were at the tomb, Jesus appears to his disciples, and Jesus prepares his disciples for his ascension and the descent of the Spirit.

18. Discuss three important implications of the resurrection of Jesus.

   The resurrection proves Jesus' claims to be God's Son. The resurrection accomplishes our salvation. The resurrection gives us new life, justifies us in God's grace, and adopts us into God's family. Jesus' resurrection is the promise of our eternal life with God.

19. What is meant by the Ascension of Jesus?

   The ascension of Jesus refers to the time when Jesus stopped appearing to the disciples in visible form and his glorified body took its rightful place in heaven as equal to the Father.

Chapter 7 Test

Assign and grade the Chapter 7 Test (pages 228-229 of this Manual). The answers follow below:

Chapter 7 Test   Name:_____

All questions are worth 4 points each.

Part 1: Matching. Please match the title of Jesus from John's gospel in Column B with its description in Column A.

Column A		Column B
__D__	1. Jesus is willing to die for his flock.	A. Bread of Life
__G__	2. Jesus is YAHWEH.	B. Light of the World
__A__	3. Jesus is the source of eternal life; we can receive him in the Eucharist.	C. Word of God
		D. Good Shepherd
__C__	4. Jesus reveals God and is God revealed.	E. Vine
__B__	5. Jesus is the beacon who points us to the Father	F. Resurrection and Life
		G. "I AM"

Part 2: Multiple Choice. Write the letter of the best choice in the space provided.

__B__ 6. Which miracle shows that Jesus, like God, is master of the Sabbath?
   A. Miracle of the wine at Cana
   B. Cure of the paralytic at the pool
   C. Feeding of the 5,000
   D. Walking on water

__C__ 7. Which miracle points to Moses' miracle during the Exodus?
   A. Miracle of the wine at Cana
   B. Cure of the paralytic at the pool
   C. Feeding of the 5,000
   D. Raising of Lazarus from the dead

__E__ 8. Which miracle reveals God at work in Jesus?
   A. Miracle of the wine at Cana
   B. Cure of the official's son
   C. Feeding of the 5,000
   D. Raising of Lazarus from the dead
   E. All of the above

__B__ 9. Jesus tells which person that he must be born again of water and the Spirit?
   A. Joseph of Arimathea
   B. Nicodemus
   C. Nathaniel
   D. all of the above
   E. none of the above

__A__ 10. John has all the following in common with the synoptic gospels *except*
   A. an infancy narrative.
   B. the multiplication of loaves and fishes.
   C. a passion narrative.
   D. a definite audience for whom the gospel is directed.

Part 3: True or False. Mark **+** if the statement is true and **0** if the statement is false.

__0__ 11. John's Gospel was written around A.D. 80.

__+__ 12. John's Gospel was written to bolster the faith of Jewish-Christians expelled from synagogues.

__+__ 13. John's Gospel is the most theologically advanced of the four gospels.

__+__ 14. "The glory of God" refers to the visible revelation of the power of the invisible God.

__0__ 15. There is very clear proof in the gospel of John that the Beloved Disciple refers to John Zebedee.

__+__ 16. St. Thomas gives the loftiest profession of faith in the gospel of John when he proclaims, "My Lord and my God."

__0__ 17. Because Jesus calls us his friends, he does not require anything of us except to accept his friendship.

Part 3: Short Fill-ins.

__Christology__ 18. That branch of theology that studies the meaning of the person of Christ is __?__ .

__Paraclete__ 19. A name for the Holy Spirit, an advocate, a helper, promised by Jesus in John 14:6 __?__ .

__might not perish but__ __have eternal life."__ 20. Finish this quote: "God so loved the world that he gave his only Son so that everyone who believes in him __?__ ."

Part 4: Short Response

Please list three facts about the resurrection narrative on which *all* the gospels agree:

21-23. *Possible answers include: It took place in the morning. Women were present, most probably Mary Magdalene. The stone had been rolled away. The tomb was empty. A messenger was at the tomb. Jesus appears to his disciples. Jesus prepares his disciples for the Ascension and descent of the Holy Spirit.*

Briefly discuss two major consequences for us because Jesus rose from the dead:

24-25. *Possible answers include: It proves Jesus' claim to divinity. It accomplishes our salvation. It frees us from sin, gives us new life, justifies us in God's grace, and adopts us into God's family. It unleashes the power of the Holy Spirit who allows us to participate in the Lord's Paschal mystery. It gives new and profound meaning to our lives. It makes us a fundamentally joyful people.*

Prayer Lesson

•◆ Call on the students to write a private journal entry that speaks to a person and situation that needs their forgiveness, including practical steps that can be taken to express the forgiveness.

•◆ Review the meaning of the Jesus Prayer (page 231).

•◆ Provide a quiet setting for the students to pray the Jesus Prayer twenty times as suggested in the Resolution (page 231).

eight

Paul's Letters: Jesus the Universal Lord

Introducing the Chapter

A study of the New Testament and Christology must include a study of the Pauline letters.

St. Paul is known as the "Apostle to the Gentiles" and many details about his life, conversion, and missionary journeys are described in the Acts of the Apostles. The chapter begins with a short study of Paul's life and a brief description of his three missionary journeys, accompanied by references to a map.

The letters attributed to Paul follow a general style. These letters contain four sections: an opening address, thanksgiving, body, and final salutation.

Most of the remaining parts of the chapter investigate major themes of these letters. The letters written by Paul are discussed first. Students are asked to read the introduction to each letter in their Bible to accompany each section. Each of these letters expresses a unique teaching about Christ. These teachings are highlighted through separate material beginning with the heading "Teaching on Jesus Christ."

Additionally, special focus is paid to the letter to Philippians, allowing the students to examine one Pauline letter in more depth.

155

The chapter explains to the students that not all the letters traditionally attributed to Paul were likely written by him. The six "deuteropauline" letters—1 Thessalonians, Ephesians, Colossians, 1 and 2 Timothy, and Titus—might have been written by a close disciple of Paul. Background, theme, and important Christological themes on these letters cover the section from pages 249-254.

Bibliography

● ● ● ● ● ● ● ● ●

Achtemeier, Paul. *Romans*. Atlanta: John Knox, 1985.
    A substantial work on the letter to the Romans.

Barrett, C.K. *A Commentary on the First Epistle to the Corinthians*. Harper's New Testament Commentaries. New York: Harper & Row, 1968.

Bornkamm, G. *Paul*. New York: Harper & Row, 1971.

Bruce, F.F. *1 and 2 Thessalonians*. Waco, TX: Word, 1982.
    A masterful work by a leading Pauline scholar.

Byrne, B. *Romans*. Collegeville, MN: Liturgical Press, 1996.

Dunn, J.D.G. *The Theology of Paul the Apostle*. Grand Rapids, MI: Eerdmans, 1997.

Fitzmyer, Joseph A. *According to Paul: Studies in the Theology of the Apostle*. New York: Paulist Press, 1993.

_____. *Romans*, Anchor Bible, 33. New York: Doubleday, 1993.

_____. "The Letter to the Romans," in *The New Jerome Biblical Commentary*. Englewood Cliffs, NJ: Prentice-Hall, 1990.

_____. "Paul," in *The New Jerome Biblical Commentary*, pp. 1329-1337. Englewood Cliffs, NJ: Prentice-Hall, 1990.

Furnish, Victor Paul. *Jesus According to Paul*. Understanding Jesus Today Series. Cambridge: Cambridge University Press, 1993.

Johnson, Luke Timothy. *Letters to Paul's Delegates: 1 Timothy, 2 Timothy, Titus*. Valley Forge, PA: Trinity Press International, 1996.

Kilgallen, J.J. *First Corinthians: An Introduction and Study Guide*. New York/Mahwah, NJ: Paulist Press, 1987.
    A readable commentary by a Catholic scholar.

Koperski, Veronica. *What Are They Saying about Paul and the Law?* New York/Mahwah, NJ: Paulist Press, 2001.

Marrow, Stanley. *Paul: His Letters and His Theology: An Introduction to Paul's Epistles*. New York: Paulist Press, 1986.

Murphy-O'Connor, Jerome. *Paul: A Critical Life*. New York: Oxford University Press, 1996.

Penna, Romano. *Paul the Apostle*. two volumes. Translated by Thomas P. Wahl. Collegeville: Liturgical Press, 1996.

Puskas, C.B., Jr. *The Letters of Paul: An Introduction*. Collegeville: Liturgical, 1993.

Roetzel, Calvin J. *Paul, The Man and the Myth*. Personalities of the New Testament Series. Minneapolis: Fortress Press, 1999.

Schnackenburg, Rudolf. *The Epistle to the Ephesians*. Translated by Helen Huron. Edinburgh: Clark, 1991.

Videos
• • • • •

Paul: Apostle of Grace

Uses archaeological sites to creatively tell the story of Christianity's birth (63-minute video, Videos with Values).

Paul the Emissary

English actor Garry Cooper follows the footsteps of Saul who becomes Paul, the greatest Christian missionary ever (54-minute video, Ignatius Press).

Peter and Paul

The acclaimed three-hour, fifteen-minute film that traces the adventures of these two towering figures. Study guide is available (Christian Book Distributors).

The Story of the Twelve Apostles

Follows the lives of the twelve and their witness after the resurrection (100-minute video produced by the History Channel, Ignatius).

Resources
• • • • • • • •

As Paul Tells It

"A letters based study of what the apostle Paul tells us about his work, his teaching, and himself."
http://www.paulonpaul.org/

Journeys of Paul

An outstanding website that features many pictures of places that figured in Paul's ministry. A must-see.
http://www.luthersem.edu/ckoester/Paul/Main.htm

Paul

A source for great links on St. Paul.
http://www.textweek.com/pauline/paul.htm

Saint Paul the Apostle

Many short articles on various aspects of the life of St. Paul.
http://www.thirdmill.org/paul_frameset.asp

SECTION 1: Zealous for Christ and The Life of St. Paul (pages 233-238)

Objectives
• • • • • • • •

The goals of this section are to enable the students to:
- note the corpus of epistles written by or attributed to St. Paul;
- learn some details of Paul's life, including his three missionary journeys described in Acts;
- overview the common style of letter writing used in Paul's letters.

Summary and Background Information

The chapter focuses on the Pauline and deuteropauline epistles. This section introduces the subject by focusing on the life of St. Paul, his missionary journeys described in the Acts of the Apostles, and noting a general style used in all of these epistles.

Saul of Tarsus, originally a devout Pharisee and persecutor of Christians, became after his conversion the great Apostle to the Gentiles. His conversion occurred approximately A.D. 36 when the glorified Lord spoke to Paul in a blinding light. Paul was baptized shortly afterwards. His three missionary trips stretched over the years from 46 to 58. The Acts of the Apostles concludes in A.D. 63 with Paul preaching in Rome while living there under house arrest.

A separate feature lists the traditional grouping of the Pauline letters as early letter, "great" letters, "prison" letters, and pastoral letters. The section begins by explaining that six of these thirteen letters were likely penned by close disciples of Paul or by other admirers. Later in the chapter these six letters will be examined in a separate section.

Finally, the entire corpus of thirteen letters follows the common style of letter writing in the Greco-Roman world with four sections: opening address, thanksgiving, body of the letter, and salutation. Knowing this pattern will aid the students as they begin a more detailed study of the individual letters in the succeeding sections.

Warm Up

a) Practice the art of letter-writing with the students. Ask them to write a thank-you letter to someone who deserves their gratitude. For example, a teacher, coworker, family member, friend, neighbor, merchant, public official, teacher, Church minister, or acquaintance. Arrange for the letters to be placed in envelopes, addressed, and mailed.

b) Have the students read the letters in advice columns of recent newspapers. Choose one or more of the issues addressed in the letter and ask the students to write alternate responses. Allow time for them to share their responses with a partner. Call on several volunteers to get a sampling of the responses.

Using the Section

a) Preview the chapter and section by reading the text and objectives under the heading "Zealous for Christ" (pages 233-234).

b) Present a brief summary of the life of St. Paul. Show how he was a man of three worlds. Write on the board:

> Paul was a Jew, a student of Gamaliel and a Pharisee
>
> Paul was a Roman citizen
>
> Paul was a Christian, becoming known as the "Apostle to the Gentiles"

c) Assign the text section "The Life of St. Paul" (pages 234-238). Use the map on page 236 to trace Paul's missionary journeys.

d) Emphasize the body of Paul's work in the New Testament: thirteen of twenty-seven New Testament books are attributed to him. Familiarize the students with the term "Deuteropauline" and why these are known as "secondary" letters of Paul. Use the chart on page 238 "Arrangement, Organization, and Style of Paul's Letters" to help the students understand the grouping.

e) Continue within the feature to point out the style of letter writing common to the Greco-Roman world and to Paul's letters. Assign both of the exercises listed on page 238.

Extending the Section

a) Have the students note from Acts of the Apostles how Paul reaches out to Roman citizens in his ministry. For example:
- ➡ Paul points out his Roman citizenship (22:25-28);
- ➡ Paul's arrests are for religious reasons with no bearing on Roman law (18:14-15);
- ➡ Paul preaches the gospel to Romans (24:24-26);
- ➡ Paul, under house arrest in Rome, continues to preach the gospel without hindrance (28:31).

b) Ask the students the following questions. Provide the accompanying scripture references to help them locate the answers.

Questions:

1. Who was the travelling companion of Barnabas and Paul on their first missionary trip (Acts 13:2-5)?

2. How does Paul explain that Christians are buried with Christ (Romans 6:3-4)?

3. According to Paul, no one can say "Jesus is Lord" except under what circumstances (1 Corinthians 12:3)?

4. Before sharing Eucharist, where does Paul say Christians should eat their own meals (1 Corinthians 11:34)?

5. Paul says a Christian's faith is empty unless he or she believes in a central mystery. What is the central mystery (1 Corinthians 15:12-14)?

6. Where was Paul when he wrote the letter to Philemon? (Philemon 1:1)

c) Have the students compare and contrast the accounts of Paul's conversion from Acts (9:1-9, 22:3-21, 26:2-23) with Paul's own recounting of his conversion from Galatians 1:11-18.

Creative Learning

a) Have the students form small groups to develop pantomimes of the following scenes from Paul's life. In a pantomime, one person serves as a narrator and reads the scripture while the characters enact the scene without speaking parts:

Scene 1:   Paul's First Missionary Journey (Acts 13:4-5; 44-47; 18:1-11)
          Characters: Paul, Barnabas, Jewish people in synagogue, Gentiles on street corner

Scene 2:   Paul's Imprisonment at Philippi (Acts 16:16-34)
          Characters: Paul, Silas, slave fortune-teller, slave's owners, Roman authorities, jailers, a person holding a flashlight

Scene 3:   Paul in Rome (Acts 27; 28:11-30)

Characters: Paul, other prisoners, sailor, jailers in Rome, citizens of Rome

Allow opportunity for the groups to present their pantomimes before the entire class.

b) Similar to the letter writing suggestion in Warm Up "A" have the students write at least one letter on the following topics. As possible, arrange for the letters to be mailed to the appropriate person:

➥ the president of the United States on the topic of Christian leadership

➥ a terminally ill patient on the topic of resurrection

➥ a media personality who attacks Christian values

➥ a legislator on the issue of abortion

➥ a parent with advice on how to teach a teenager upstanding moral values.

Section 2: Letters Written by St. Paul (pages 239-249)

Objectives

The goals of this section are to enable the students to:

➥ survey the seven letters attributed to Paul, including the approximate dates of composition;

➥ highlight the major themes of Paul's letters;

➥ examine Paul's teaching on Christ revealed in these letters.

Summary and Background Information

This section covers the New Testament letters scholars believe can likely be traced directly to Paul. These letters are 1 Thessalonians, Galatians, Philippians, Philemon, 1 and 2 Corinthians, and Romans. The students are asked to read the introductions to each letter in the Bible. Also, the letter of Philippians is reviewed in depth on pages 241-243.

Besides the main themes of these letters, Paul's Christology is also highlighted from each letter. By examining the entire background and context of the letters, students get a feel for the issues that faced the early Church, the witness of Paul and the disciples of the good news, and an understanding of how the Church came to understand Christ's divinity in relation to his humanity.

Warm Up

a) As a transition from the previous section, have the students read the letter to Philemon in its entirety and note the four-part organization style explained on page 238.

b) Print the names of the letters that will be surveyed in this section (**1 Thessalonians, Galatians, Philippians, Philemon, 1 and 2 Corinthians, and Romans**) on the board. For homework, assign the students to read the introductions of each letter and write at least two important facts they gleaned about each letter in their notebooks. Allow time for the students to compare their notes with classmates.

Using the Section

● ● ● ● ● ● ● ● ● ● ● ● ●

a) Begin with the in-depth treatment of Philippians (pages 241-243) first. Have the students read the complete text. Highlight the following themes (write on the board):

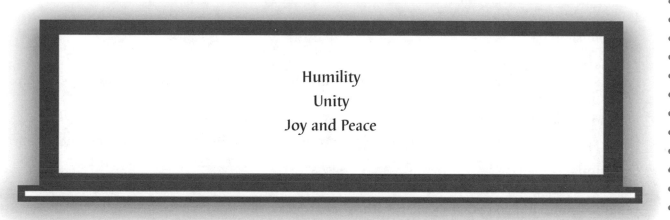

Humility

Unity

Joy and Peace

Then, highlight these themes in more depth. For example, explain that:

● Humility is not the same is humiliation. Christ's self-emptying is our model for humility. In this emptying of ourselves, we find our true life in God.

● Unity, a second theme, does not equate with uniformity. Rather, it is often a reaction against the "false teachers" Paul describes and a grasping for the truth.

● Joy, like happiness, is not synonymous with pleasure. One can be joyful and filled with peace, even in the midst of personal struggles. Christians emanate a peacefulness and joy that lead others to question their origin—that is, faith in Jesus Christ.

b) Summarize the other six texts under the heading "Letters Written by St. Paul" (pages 239-240 and pages 244-250). Use the following themes and questions as part of your presentation on each letter.

1 Thessalonians

Themes:
Jesus offers salvation to all people.
Jesus dies for us that we might live.

Questions:
Why is Paul thankful for the Thessalonians? (1:2-10)
What is Paul's ministry among the Thessalonians? (2:1-12)

Galatians

Themes:
Paul develops the theme of "justification by faith" to defend the Gentiles.
Paul uses the Hebrew scriptures to defend himself.

Questions:
Can salvation be earned?
Why would Judaizers want Christians to first become Jews?
Explain what is meant by "justification by faith."

Philemon

Theme:
Paul addresses the issue of slavery, based on the example of what Philemon should do with his runaway slave.

Question:
What is the solution Paul offers Philemon vis-à-vis slavery?

1 Corinthians

Themes:
Paul addresses Baptism, contrasting Corinthians' belief in magical powers associated with Baptism.

Paul addresses sexual problems in the context of the imminent end of the world.

Paul expresses the belief in the primacy of love connected with the celebration of the Eucharist.

Questions:
How do Paul's views on sexual morality apply today?

What are some things you associated with "proper" behavior at Mass?

2 Corinthians

Themes:
Paul makes peace with the Corinthians over previous abuses.

Paul emphasizes that Jesus was crucified in weakness and that he is our comfort, victory, freedom, light, judge, reconciler, gift, owner, and power.

Question:
Describe a workable strategy for correcting the fault of another without alienating the person.

Romans

Themes:
Salvation takes place through Jesus Christ, the Lord of the universe.

The heart of the gospel is the death and resurrection of Jesus.

Christians will participate in the resurrection of Christ.

Salvation is a free gift of God that demands faith.

Christians are bound together in unity.

The Holy Spirit is the life of the Church.

We should treat each other with dignity.

We should be willing to die for Christ.

Assignment (also on page 249):

Have the students read Romans 12–15 and write what they consider to be the ten best rules for Christian living that Paul shares.

Extending the Section

• • • • • • • • • • • • • •

a) In the letter to the Philippians, have the students note passages that depict the Christological themes of Christ's preexistence, incarnation, and saving Paschal mystery.

b) Have the students write a 750-word report that offers commentary on a particular passage from one of the letters of Paul. Explain the assignment from the resource "Passage Commentary Paper—Paul's Letters" (page 230 of this Manual). Have the students share their scholarship by giving class presentations on what they have written.

c) Assign the margin exercise "Building Community" based on 1 Corinthians 13 (page 246).

Creative Learning

• • • • • • • • • • • •

a) Have the students survey the letters discussed in this section and choose one verse that speaks a relevant and meaningful message to them. Call on volunteers to share their passage and explanation of it with others. Or, provide art media and have the students creatively print their verse on poster board for display in the classroom.

b) Following the format of the surprising profile statements of St. Paul on page 233, have the students write a similar profile of an assigned classmate without revealing who it is. Then have the students read their profiles with the rest of the class trying to guess who are being described.

SECTION 3: Deuteropauline Letters (pages 249-254)

Objectives

• • • • • • • •

The goals of this section are to enable the students to:

•◆ recognize how the deuteropauline letters differ from the epistles scholars are sure Paul wrote himself;

•◆ survey the background and content of the deuteropauline letters;

•◆ uncover more of the Church's belief about Jesus Christ from these letters.

Summary and Background Information

• •

Since the nineteenth century, biblical scholarship has identified six letters traditionally attributed to St. Paul as actually written by a disciple of Paul or perhaps by his secretary. Methods of scholarship included comparing the letter's style, use of words, concept of Church, and other doctrinal issues as compared to earlier writings of Paul. The six deuteropauline ("secondary") letters of Paul examined in this section are 2 Thessalonians, Ephesians, Colossians, 1 and 2 Timothy, and Titus. 1 and 2 Timothy and Titus are viewed together as "pastoral letters" because they were written by one pastor (shepherd) to two other pastors, Timothy and Titus.

Each of the deuteropauline letters is rich in content and contains more insight into doctrines of faith, especially those directly related to faith in Jesus Christ.

Key teachings on Jesus Christ viewed in this section include Christ as:

•◆ the coming judge

•◆ the Lord of all creation

- ➠ author of reconciliation
- ➠ source of new life
- ➠ embodiment of God
- ➠ Savior
- ➠ source of all gifts of the Holy Spirit
- ➠ Mediator between God and mankind

Warm Up

a) Show a segment of the video *Peter and Paul* (see page 157 of this Manual) that emphasizes some of Paul's teachings.

b) Point out how the Ann Lander's daily advice columns have been extended past her death in 2002 by two of her former employees who now answer mail under a column titled "Annie's Mailbox." Compare this situation with the understanding of the deuteropauline letters.

Using the Section

a) Summarize the opening text under "Deuteropauline Letters" (pages 249-250) and assign the section on "2 Thessalonians" (page 250). Focus a majority of discussion on this letter to helping the students understand the meaning of the Parousia, and the events that must take place in connection with Jesus' return. Assign 2 Thessalonians 2:1-17 and accompanying commentary. Ask the students to list the series of events in verses 3-12 that must occur before the end will come.

b) Discuss the necessity of contributing to the community as addressed in 2 Thessalonians 3, including its relationship to fulfilling Sunday worship obligations (see the assignment on page 250).

c) Use a biblical commentary and the text on pages 250-251 to briefly cover the issue of authorship of Colossians. Focus on the Christian hymn of Colossians 1:15-20 and its teaching points of Christ as mediator of creation and redemption. (Christ is the "first born of all creation" and the "firstborn from the dead.")

d) Note that "Church" is the main subject of the letter to the Ephesians. Print the outline of Ephesians on the board:

Introduction (1:1-14)

Unity of the Church in Christ (1:15—2:22)

Worldwide Mission of the Church (1:1—4:24)

Daily Conduct of a Christian as Sign of Unity (4:25—6:20)

Conclusion (6:1-24)

In addition to reading the text on pages 251-252, divide the class into small groups of three students each. Assign each person to read one of the main sections of Ephesians (not the Introduction or Conclusion) and report to the others in the group what the section teaches about Jesus Christ.

e) Share some background information on why 1 and 2 Timothy and Titus are grouped together as Pastoral Letters. Explain that they are the only letters of the Pauline corpus of letters addressed to individuals rather than communities. Also point out that they give advice about caring for the community, much as a shepherd would care for his flock of sheep. As the key points of theme and content of 1 and 2 Timothy and Titus are covered from pages 252-254 summarize on the board or PowerPoint presentation as follows:

Severe warnings against false teachings and teachers.

Many practical instructions for Church organization and criteria for Church leaders.

Instructions for Christian worship.

Instructions for Christian living.

To summarize the final point, ask the students to do the assignment on page 253. Possible answers include ideas like temperance, reverence, integrity, chastity, and living justly.

Extending the Section

a) Assign the exercise on Ephesians on page 252 for homework to be completed in a notebook or journal.

Answers:

Ephesians 2:11-22

What has Christ broken down? How? (Christ has broken down the "wall of enmity" between Jew and Gentile through his very flesh.)

What image of the church does the author give us in vv. 19-22? (a house, Temple, or dwelling place with Christ as the capstone)

Ephesians 5:21-6:24

How are husbands to love their wives? (Husbands are to love their wives as Christ loved the Church.)

What is the reward for children who obey their parents? (a long life on earth)

What image is used in vv. 10-17 for Christians to fight the wiles of the evil ones? (a warrior dressed in armor)

b) Ask the students to respond to the statement "The love of money is the root of all evils."

c) Have the students write a brief summary of Christology as contained in the Pastoral Epistles (see page 254).

Creative Learning

a) Have the students use paint, pencil, or another art medium to offer an impressionist drawing of Christ based on one of the verses of the Christian hymn in Colossians 1:15-20.

b) In the spirit of Paul's exhortation to Christian living, encourage the students to do a good deed for someone without the person knowing it. Then ask the students to write about the experience in a journal entry that should only be read by them and you.

Conclusion

a) Allow time for the students to study the Selected Vocabulary definitions (pages 256-257). Then quiz them orally or in writing on the definitions. Include on the quiz other terms the students have recorded definitions for during the course of study for Chapter 8.

b) Assign the Summary Points and Review Questions (pages 254-256). Grade them and review them as preparation for the Chapter 8 Test.

Answers to Review Questions

1. Which are the seven letters scholars agree were penned by St. Paul?

    The seven letters likely written by Paul are 1 Thessalonians, Galatians, 1 and 2 Corinthians, Philemon, and Romans.

2. What does *deuteropauline* mean? What are the deuteropauline letters?

    Deuteropauline refers to "secondary" Pauline letters—letters likely penned by close disciples of Paul or by his admirers. These letters are 2 Thessalonians, Colossians, Ephesians, 1 and 2 Timothy, and Titus.

3. Name at least five significant biographical details of St. Paul's life.

    Answers will vary. Details of Paul's life include: he was born Jewish, he was a strict Pharisee, he was a Roman citizen, he spoke Greek, he studied to be a rabbi, he made three missionary journeys, and he likely died in Rome.

4. What significance did Antioch of Syria have in the ministry of St. Paul?

    Antioch was the base of Paul's missionary activity.

5. Name the parts of the fourfold outline typical of Pauline letters.

    The fourfold outline included: 1) opening address; 2) thanksgiving; 3) body of the letter; and 4) final salutations.

6. Discuss five major themes Paul addresses in his letters. Cite passages from Paul's letters to illustrate each theme.

    Answers will vary.

7. What is the earliest letter written by St. Paul? What is one of its key themes?

    The first letter to the Thessalonians is Paul's earliest letter. Besides addressing sexual immorality among the Thessalonians, Paul assured them that Christians who had died would rise one day and live with the Lord forever.

8. What is considered the first of Paul's "great letters"? What position does it take concerning Judaism and new Gentile converts?

Galatians is considered to be the first of Paul's great letters. The letter reiterates the conclusions reached at the Council of Jerusalem that Gentiles should be admitted to the Church without having to obey the rigors of the Old Law.

9. What does St. Paul teach about faith and justification? What does "justification before God" mean?

Justification before God equates with a right relationship with God. According to Paul, observance of the Old Law does not guarantee salvation, but only faith in the Lord Jesus Christ. Faith in Jesus teaches a person to respond to the Spirit who guides Christians to live holy lives.

10. What are the likely dates of writing and city of origin of Paul's letter to the Philippians?

The letter was written either during Paul's two-year imprisonment in Caesarea in 58-60, during Paul's house arrest in Rome spanning the years 61-63, or during Paul's three-year stay at Ephesus from 54-56. Traditionally, scholars believed Paul penned Philippians from Rome, but today a growing number think the most likely locale was when Paul was in Ephesus around A.D. 56.

11. What are some themes Paul discussed in Philippians?

Among the themes Paul discussed in Philippians are peace and joy, developing an attitude toward accepting suffering, humility, against false teachers, unity of the church.

12. What is the point of the hymn Paul quotes in Philippians 2:5-11?

The hymn praises Christ's self-emptying humility in his becoming human and dying on the cross to be raised and exalted. This plea for humility is also extended to Christ's disciples.

13. List three problems Paul addresses in 1 Corinthians. What does he teach about each?

The letter addresses divisions in the Christian community (Paul teaches them to rely on Christ alone), problems in Christian morality and living (Paul addresses each practical issue, condemning immoral behavior in each instance), and problems in Christian worship (Paul tells the Christians to eat at home before gathering for Eucharist properly in a spirit of unity and love).

14. According to the letter to the Romans, what are some benefits for us of Christ's sacrifice on the cross?

Christ's sacrificial act has brought us justification, peace with God, the gift of the Holy Spirit, reconciliation with God, salvation from the wrath of God, hope of a share in God's eternal glory, and God's superabundant love poured out on us.

15. According to St. Paul what do faith in Christ and Baptism accomplish for us?

Faith in Christ and Baptism accomplish freedom from slavery to sin, freedom from the Law, and freedom from death.

16. What problem developed in Thessalonica that Paul addressed in 2 Thessalonians? What was his teaching?

Paul addressed a misunderstanding about his teaching concerning the resurrection of the dead and Christ's Second Coming. Originally, some of the converts of Thessalonia thought Christ was returning any day so they quit working. Paul told them to do as he did, work as he preached the good news.

17. How do the pseudonymous Pauline writings differ from the letters scholars are sure Paul himself wrote?

The pseudonymous letters have different vocabulary, style, theological themes, content, and historical context than those attributed to Paul.

18. What was the problem addressed in the letter to the Colossians? What is the key theological teaching in this letter?

The letter was written to contradict the bizarre teaching that claimed that Christ's death and resurrection were not enough for salvation. The key teaching in the letter is that Jesus Christ is the preeminent spiritual being; only he can save us.

19. Which of the Pauline epistles has the most developed theology about the Church? Describe some of that theology.

   Ephesus has the most developed theology about the Church. The Church is imaged as both Body of Christ and his bride.

20. What are the three pastoral letters and how did they get their name? Discuss several of the qualities these letters say a Church leader should have.

   The three pastoral letters are 1 and 2 Timothy and Titus. They get their name because they were written by one pastor (shepherd) to two individuals (pastors).

21. List five specific teachings about Jesus Christ that we learn from reading the Pauline letters.

   Answers will vary but should include information from the "Teaching on Jesus Christ..." summaries.

Chapter 8 Test

● ● ● ● ● ● ● ●

Assign and grade the Chapter 8 Test (pages 231-232 of this Manual). The answers follow below:

Chapter 8 Test   Name:_____

Questions 1 to 22 are worth 4 points each.

Part 1: Multiple Choice. Write the letter of the best choice in the space provided.

__B__   1. Which is *not* true of St. Paul?
   A. tent-maker by profession
   B. Sadducee
   C. born in Tarsus
   D. Roman citizen

__D__   2. St. Paul was baptized by:
   A. Peter
   B. Philip
   C. Barnabas
   D. Ananias

__C__   3. All of these are one of Paul's "great letters" *except*:
   A. Galatians
   B. Romans
   C. Ephesians
   D. 1 Corinthians

__C__   4. Most scholars consider all of these as deuteropauline writings *except:*
   A. Titus
   B. 1 Timothy
   C. Philippians
   D. 2 Thessalonians

   A   5. Paul's first epistle, acknowledged to be the earliest book in the New Testament:
        A. 1 Thessalonians
        B. 1 Corinthians
        C. Philemon
        D. Romans

   E   6. Which of the following is a theological theme stressed by St. Paul?
        A. Jesus is Lord of the universe.
        B. Salvation is God's free gift.
        C. The Holy Spirit enables us to call God Abba.
        D. Christians are members of Christ's body, the Church.
        E. All of the above.

   B   7. Which of the following is *not* a theme of Paul's preaching?
        A. Being a Christian means willingness to suffer for the Lord.
        B. Good works are necessary to earn God's gift of salvation.
        C. Christians will participate in Christ's resurrection.
        D. The brothers and sisters of Jesus are required to love.
        E. None of the above.

   D   8. Paul's theme of "justification" primarily means:
        A. salvation
        B. repentance
        C. redemption
        D. right relationship with God

   A   9. Paul's companion at the time of his writing Philippians was:
        A. Timothy
        B. Peter
        C. Ananias
        D. Lydia

   D   10. This, Paul's longest letter, is acknowledged to be his masterpiece:
        A. 1 Corinthians
        B. Colossians
        C. Galatians
        D. Romans

Part 2: True or False. Mark + if the statement is true and 0 if the statement is false.

   0   11. Paul required his converts to accept the customs and laws of Judaism before receiving Christian baptism.

   0   12. "Judaizers" were strong supporters of St. Paul in his ministry.

   +   13. In his joyful letter to the Philippians, Paul teaches that we must conform ourselves to Christ's Paschal mystery as the key to living a holy life.

   0   14. Paul teaches that God's rejection of the Jewish people is final, thus paving the way for the conversion of Gentiles.

   +   15. Pseudonymous authorship was common and accepted in the ancient world.

   0   16. St. Paul teaches that Christians are obligated to feed their fellow believers, even if these believers refuse to work.

   0   17. Gnostics had a high regard for the human body.

   0   18. The Pastoral Epistles reveal that overseers of early Christian communities *had* to remain unmarried or they could not be leaders.

Part 3: Short Fill-ins.

_____love_____	19. According to St. Paul's letter to Corinthians, the greatest spiritual gift is __?__ .
_____love_____	20. For St. Paul, __?__ is the fulfillment of the Law.
can be against us	21. Finish this quote: "If God is for us, who__?__ ."
Jesus Christ	22. Who is the image of the invisible God?

Part 4: Brief Essay (worth 12 points)

Pretend that you are St. Paul writing to one of his churches in Asia Minor. A conflict has come to your attention concerning Christians who are arguing about money. Write a paragraph to instruct them how they should act. Discuss at least three points that draw on the theological insights of St. Paul.

Answers will vary. Possibilities include: be humble like Christ, share with the needy, conform to the Paschal mystery by sacrificing, the love of money is at the root of all evil.

Prayer Lesson

☞ Assign the "Reflection" journal suggestion (page 257). Allow the students to discuss their ideas with a partner or in a small group.

nine

The Early Church: Jesus, True God and True Man

Introducing the Chapter

This chapter focuses on the early Church's growing understanding of the divinity of Christ and his unique role in our salvation especially as viewed through the letter to the Hebrews, the Catholic epistles, and the Revelation to John.

The letter to the Hebrews has been ascribed to Paul. Actually, it was not written by Paul nor is it a letter. Hebrews is a polished Greek sermon that comes from a time late in the first century. The author may have been located in Alexandria. The letter to the Hebrews shows a great balance in emphasizing both the divinity and humanity of Christ. A central section of the book (chapters 5–10) presents Jesus as the eternal high priest whose sacrifice overcomes sins once and for all.

Next, the Catholic Epistles are surveyed. These include James, the first and second letters of Peter, the first, second, and third letters of John, and the letter of Jude. They are called "catholic" epistles because they are addressed to the entire Church, not just a specific, local community. For each of these letters, the text provides a brief summary of the letter's teaching on Jesus.

The last book of the Bible, the Revelation to John, is covered in some detail. It is one of the most read books, yet also one of the most misunderstood. The text covers the context of the writing, major themes in Revelation, its special apocalyptic style of writing, its symbols, Jesus' identity that is revealed, and an interpretation of Revelation for today.

A final section of the chapter deals in more detail with Christology as understood in the early Church. Through the titles for Jesus used by the early Church and teachings about Jesus expressed by Church fathers, a clearer understanding of the Messiah and Lord is offered.

Bibliography

• • • • • • • • •

Achtemeier, P.J. *1 Peter*. Minneapolis: Fortress, 1996.
> A respected commentary.

Brown, Raymond E. *An Introduction to New Testament Christology*. New York: Paulist Press, 1994.

Bruce, F.F. *The Epistles of John*. Old Tappan, NJ: Revell, 1970.

Buby, Bertrand. S.M. *A Journey Through Revelation: A Message for the Millennium*. New York: Alba House, 2000.
> An excellent, well-balanced commentary with translation provided. Balanced.

Campbell, James P., editor. *Harper's New American Bible Study Program*. San Francisco: Harper & Row, 1990.
> Worth looking at for the way it integrates themes and various books of the Bible. Some good research questions. Session 4 of Theme 10 provides a good treatment of the book of Revelation.

Bourke, Myles M. "The Epistle to the Hebrews," in *The New Jerome Biblical Commentary*. Englewood Cliffs, NJ: Prentice-Hall, 1990.

Brown, Raymond E. *The Epistles of John*. Anchor Bible, 30. Garden City, NY: Doubleday, 1982.

Dalton, William J., S.J. "The First Epistle of Peter," in *The New Jerome Biblical Commentary*. Englewood Cliffs, NJ: Prentice-Hall, 1990.

Fiorenza, Elizabeth Schüssler. *The Book of Revelation: Justice and Judgment*, 2nd ed. Philadelphia: Fortress Press, 1999.

Ford, Massyingberde, J. *Revelation: A New Translation with Introduction and Commentary*. Anchor Bible, 38. New York: Doubleday, 1975.
> Highly regarded.

Harrington, Wilfrid J. *Revelation*. Sacra Pagina, 16. Collegeville, MN: Liturgical Press, 1993.
> Fr. Harrington is an excellent commentator.

Johnson, Luke Timothy. *The Letter of James*. Anchor Bible, 37A. New York: Doubleday, 1995.

Kealy, Sean. *The Apocalypse of John*. Wilmington, DE: Michael Glazier, Inc., 1987.

Laws, S. *A Commentary on the Epistle of James*. San Francisco: Harper & Row, 1980.

Pelikan, Jaroslav. *The Illustrated Jesus Through the Centuries*. New Haven: Yale University Press, 1997.

Pfitzner, Victor. *Hebrews*. Abingdon New Testament Commentary. Nashville: Abingdon, 1997.

The Theological-Historical Commission for the Great Jubilee of the Year 2000. *Jesus Christ, Word of the Father*. Translated by Adrian Walker. New York: The Crossroad Publishing Company, 1997.

> A helpful overview of contemporary orthodox teaching about Jesus.

Witherington III, Ben. *The Many Faces of the Christ: The Christologies of the New Testament and Beyond*. New York: Crossroad, 1998.

Videos

Apocalypse: The Puzzle of Revelation

> This video explores the Bible's puzzling and powerful Book of Revelation. It shows how the book's cryptic codes, strange beasts, and apocalyptic visions of Armageddon have long intrigued both mystics and scholars, and it investigates the mysteries surrounding the seven seals, the four horsemen, and the book's possible authorship (50-minute video, Insight Media).

Revelation: The Second Coming

> A series on this difficult New Testament book given by popular author, Fr. Alfred McBride (Thirteen 30-minute programs on two tapes, Ignatius).

Resources

Apocalypse
> Great website sponsored by PBS geared to the program of the same name.
> http://www.pbs.org/wgbh/pages/frontline/shows/apocalypse/

Cities of Revelation
> Great website. Beautifully designed.
> http://www.luthersem.edu/ckoester/Revelation/main.htm

Hebrews to Jude
> Excellent links are offered from Dr. Mark Goodacre on the letters of Hebrews, James, 1-2 Peter, and Jude.
> http://www.ntgateway.com/hebrews/

Links to Revelation, Apocalyptic and Millennial Websites and Materials
> Provided by Prof. Felix Just, S.J. of Loyola Marymount University. Great website.
> http://clawww.lmu.edu/faculty/fjust/Apocalyptic_Links.htm

SECTION 1: Hidden Treasures, The Letter to the Hebrews, and The Catholic Epistles (pages 259-266)

Objectives

The goals of this section are to enable the students to:

➥ test their knowledge about the Church's major dogmatic statements about Jesus;

•❖ overview the letter to the Hebrews, including an examination of Christ as high priest and model of our faith;

•❖ survey the major themes in the catholic epistles.

Summary and Background Information

Our basic beliefs about Jesus are now familiar to us, but early Christians were given the task to clarify who Jesus was and what they believed about him. This section gives the students a taste of how this clarity was pursued in part through the writings of the New Testament.

After an exercise that quizzes the students' knowledge of the Church's major dogmatic statements about Jesus that were developed in the early Church, the letter to the Hebrews is overviewed. A journal exercise asks the students to transcribe a description of faith from Hebrews 11:1. Also, the main teaching of the letter on Jesus as supreme high priest who obediently suffered for us and offered his sacrifice on the cross is explored.

The majority of the section examines the catholic epistles—James, 1 and 2 Peter, Jude, and 1, 2, and 3 John. Many passages are cited as the students are asked to address Christological questions through these lenses.

Warm Up

a) Note the opening quote from James 1:22-25 (page 258). Ask the students to write a journal entry explaining ways they plan to be "doers" of God's word.

b) This chapter concludes the study of the New Testament. Print the following questions on the board. Allow the students the time to consider their responses to each question. Then form a panel of three or four students to discuss one or more of the questions. After they have had a chance to share, call more panels with other students as time permits.

What is one important thing you have learned from studying the New Testament?

What is your favorite book of the New Testament? Why?

What is one new insight you have about Jesus from your study?

Name a favorite passage from the New Testament and tell why you chose it.

Which book or passage from the New Testament did you find most difficult to understand? Why?

Offer a suggestion for praying with the New Testament.

How will you plan to learn more about the New Testament in the future?

Using the Section

a) Assign for individual reading the opening text under the heading "Hidden Treasure" (page 259).

b) Ask the students to complete the activity "Your Knowledge about Jesus" (page 260 and page 233 of this Manual). Go over the answers below with the students.

Answers:

0	1.	There was a time when Jesus was not God.
+	2.	As light is identical to the light from which it comes, Jesus Christ is true God.
0	3.	The Father made the Son.
+	4.	The Son of God shared in the creation of the world.
0	5.	There are two "persons" in Christ.
0	6.	It is wrong to call Mary "the Mother of God."
+	7.	Christ has two natures.
0	8.	Jesus' divine nature swallows up his human nature.
+	9.	Jesus shows us God in a human way.
0	10.	Because he was God, Jesus did not have a human intellect.

c) Summarize the material on the letter to the Hebrews (page 261), pointing out that the "letter" is really more of a homily. Explain that a main theme of Hebrews is that Jesus is the high priest who is also the sacrifice offered for our behalf.

d) Assign both journal entries on page 261. Call on volunteers to share their definitions of faith. For an example of the truth of Hebrews 4:12, suggest that the students offer an example of how a scripture passage has had a dramatic effect on their life or way of thinking.

e) Provide some background on the catholic epistles (see pages 262-266). Point out that the catholic letters address several wide-ranging and timeless issues, including the necessity of combining faith and good works, of living as good citizens despite being treated as society's outcasts, and of loving enemies and neighbors alike. Also point out that though the letters are called "catholic" because they are presumed to be written for the universal Church, the first letter to Peter is addressed to a number of local churches in Asia Minor, the second letter to John to a specific, though unnamed local church, and the third letter of John to a specific person, a priest named Gaius.

f) Divide the class into groups of four. Make one person in each group responsible for reading and reporting to the others in the group on one set of the letters: the letter of James (page 262), 1 Peter (pages 262-263), 2 Jude and 2 Peter (pages 263-265), or 1, 2, and 3 John (pages 265-266).

Extending the Section

a) Follow up to the activity "Test Your Knowledge About God" by asking the students the following questions. Call on one or more volunteers to answer. Note their puzzlement. Go through the entire list of questions before correcting any misconceptions.

Questions:
Are Jesus and God the same person?
Did Jesus die on the cross?

Is Jesus dead now?

Was God ever dead?

Do you pray to Jesus?

If Jesus is God, who did he pray to? himself?

Can you call yourself a Christian if you do not believe that Jesus is God?

Can you call yourself a Christian if you do not believe Jesus rose from the dead?

b) Assign some or all of the margin exercises on pages 262, 264, and 266 for homework.

Answers for page 262 exercises on James:

There is great power in speech and it should be used properly. The tongue is compared with fire, using it improperly can spread malice far and wide.

For James 2:14-17, make sure the students stress the importance of combining great works with their expressions of faith.

Answers for page 262 exercises on 1 Peter:

"For it is better to suffer for doing good, if that be the will of God, than for doing evil" (3:17).

Suggest the students name examples from within and outside their friendship and peer groups.

Answers for page 264 exercises on 2 Peter:

For the Lord, one day is like a thousand years and a thousand years like one day. The Lord is patient with us.

We should wait patiently, conducting ourselves in holiness and devotion.

Answers for page 266 journal exercises on 1 John:

We should love in deed and truth.

We know we have the Spirit of God in us when we acknowledge that Jesus Christ comes in the flesh.

We should love because love is of God; everyone who loves is begotten by God and knows God.

We know God lives in us when we love one another.

Creative Learning

• • • • • • • • • • • • •

a) Ask the students to write a short essay that explains the differences between a contextual and fundamentalist understanding of the Bible.

b) Assign the students to groups of five or six members each. Make sure each group includes at least two people with musical experience (instrumental and/or vocal). Ask the groups to select a favorite song that speaks of faith and love in Jesus and to practice and perform it before the rest of the class. The less musical members can fill in by singing harmony, playing a rhythm instrument, snapping fingers, or dancing in unison!

SECTION 2: The Revelation to John (A.D. 92-96) (pages 267-272)

The goals of this section are to enable the students to:

➥ put the Revelation to John in the context of its time and cultural setting;

➥ examine the major themes of Revelation and consider ways for interpreting its message today;

➥ understand the apocalyptic style of writing.

Summary and Background Information

• •

This section provides a fairly in-depth profile of the Revelation to John, one of the hardest books of the Bible to understand.

The first part of the section offers a basic explanation of the context of Revelation—some details are provided for appropriate background study. Next, the many symbols of Revelation are broken down and explained in relation to the author's intentions and not to the many misinterpretations of the book that abound today.

The central question of the section is related to revealing what the book says about Jesus' identity. This is accompanied by a complete outline of the text, in which the students are asked to read the Revelation of John in its entirety.

Warm Up

a) Provide some brief background on the book of Revelation. Explain that it is one of the most difficult books of the Bible to understand because it was written in a style of writing called apocalyptic writing which was popular from 200 B.C. to A.D. 200. In Greek, apocalypse means "unveiling." The author of Revelation, a prophet named John, is not associated with the John of the gospel or the John of the letters of the New Testament. The prophet wrote to unveil what was going to take place in the future. Allow the students a brief time to ask questions or share comments they have about the book of Revelation. (For example, they may be aware of the symbolism of Revelation, including the symbolism of certain numbers.)

b) To further familiarize the students with Revelation, ask them to browse the entire book before focusing on a specific passage. Have them use the following format:

Select a passage.

Read the passage all the way through.

Reread the passage slowly.

Write down questions you have about the passage.

Use a Bible commentary and other notes to answer the questions.

In a free flowing manner, note personal thoughts and insights you have about the passage.

Call on volunteers to share with the entire class the passage they chose and the information they gleaned about it.

Using the Section

a) Overview the text sections "The Revelation to John (A.D. 92-96)" including the subsections "The Context of the Revelation to John," "Major Themes in the Revelation to John," and "Apocalyptic Literature" (pages 267-269). Include these points in your summary (board or PowerPoint presentation):

✓ Revelation was written at time of Christian persecutions under the emperor Domitian.

✓ Author was Aramaic-speaking Jewish Christian who knew the Old Testament well, especially apocalyptic writings.

✓ Major theme of Revelation: an "unveiling" of the risen Christ. This unveiling is to encourage Christians to remain faithful and hopeful in times of persecution.

✓ Common elements of apocalyptic writings found in Revelation: visions given to human beings who take a heavenly vantage point; symbolic words, images, and numbers; and pessimism about current situation in world, but optimism over God's final triumph.

b) Assign the next three subsections "Understanding the Symbols in the Revelation to John" (pages 269-270), "Jesus' Identity in the Revelation to John" (pages 270-271), and "Interpreting Revelation Today" (page 271).

c) Check student understanding of the symbols in Revelation. Ask them to look up the following symbols and name what each symbolizes. Answers are in parenthesis:

12:3 Dragon (Satan)
12:5 Shepherd/Boy (Messiah)
12:6 Woman in Desert (Church)
13:11 Another Beast (Organizations enforcing worship of Caesar)
13:18 Beast (Nero)

d) Assign feature "Reading Revelation" (pages 271-272). In conjunction with this text section the students should read the entire Revelation to John following the organizational structure listed. Also, assign the margin exercises that accompany the reading. Answers are below:

Answers for Exercise on page 271 on Revelation 1–3:

Describe the risen Lord in 1:12-16. Using the footnotes in your Bible or a commentary, interpret the meaning of the various symbols connected with Christ's appearance. (Symbols: gold sash=Christ the king; hair=Christ is eternal; eyes were like a fiery flame=Christ as all-knowing; feet like polished brass=Christ as unchangeable; seven stars=universal domination; two-edged sword=word of God.)

Using the fourfold division of the seven letters, outline the contents of one letter. (answers will vary)

Answers for Exercise on page 272 on Revelation 4–5:

Who might the twenty-four elders represent? (twelve tribes of Israel and twelve apostles)

Since the second century, the four creatures in Revelation 4 have been used as symbols of the four evangelists. Match the creature with the correct gospel. (lion=Mark, calf=Luke, human being=Matthew, eagle=John)

List two titles given to Christ in Revelation 5. Discuss the significance of these titles (titles include, "lion of the tribe of Judah," "the root of David," and the main title: "Lamb").

Answers for Exercise on page 272 on Revelation 12:1–13:18:

One interpretation of the woman is that she represents Israel, God's people. Explain how this might be the case. (The Israel of old gave birth to the Messiah, and then became the new Israel, the Church, which suffers persecution by the dragon.)

Another traditional interpretation is that the woman symbolizes Mary, the mother of Jesus, and the Church. Explain how this might be so. (Revelation 12:5 is especially relevant to Mary: "She gave birth to a son, a male child, destined to rule all the nations with an iron rod.")

Who is the person in 12:17? Who is the offspring of the woman? (The offspring of the woman is the Church.)

What does the reign of forty-two months signify (13:5)? (Forty-two months is the same duration as the profanation of the holy city, the prophetic mission of two witnesses in 11:3, and the retreat of the woman into the desert in 12:6).

Many people thought Nero would come back to life to terrorize his subjects. At the time of Revelation's composition, who might the 666 (13:18) refer to? (Caesar Nero)

Answers for Exercise on page 273 on Revelation 21–22:

Why is there no need for a Temple in the new city? (The Temple in the new city will be Christ himself who is present in the Church.)

What is your own image of heaven? Compare it to Revelation's poetic image (see Creative Learning, below).

Extending the Section

a) Assign research reports on topics related to the book of Revelation. For example: apocalyptic literature, apocalyptic movements, eschatological teachings of other religions, "end of the world" messages preached by secular society.

b) Have the students read Daniel 7–12 and report on the similarities between this example of apocalyptic literature and the apocalyptic literature of the New Testament.

c) Assign a report on various Christian symbols, including a detailed explanation of their meaning. For example, the symbols of liturgical colors, various types of crosses, symbols for the evangelists, icons, etc.

Creative Learning

a) Encourage the students to write about, draw, or use other art medium to depict their own image of heaven (see page 273).

b) Have the students assemble a scrapbook of news articles that depict the positive aspect of humanity and give encouragement to the future of our world, not its demise.

SECTION 3: Christology of the Early Church (pages 273-279)

Objectives

The goals of this section are to enable the students to:

➡ understand various titles that reflect New Testament Christology;

➡ summarize several heretical Christological teachings accompanied by the Church's response;

➡ rate their beliefs related to the tenets of the Nicene Creed.

Summary and Background Information

The titles of Jesus contained in the scriptures reveal many unique and profound elements of his identity. Jesus' titles also help us to define our beliefs about him. This section opens with a survey of several titles of Jesus found in the New Testament.

Next, an examination of the heresies that developed in the early Church surrounding beliefs in Jesus is presented. From these heresies (false beliefs) the Church was able to respond and offer clear dogma on its belief in Christ as true God and true man. Pages 275-277 list several important truths about Jesus Christ.

Finally, the students are asked to reflect on and commit to their beliefs in the tenets of the Nicene Creed.

Warm Up

a) Discuss with the students several titles for famous people from the past and present. For example, Siddhartha Gautama ("Buddha"), Abraham Lincoln ("The Emancipator"), Muhammad Ali ("The Greatest"). Allow the students to offer some more titles. Then ask them to explain why we use titles for people. Point out that titles help us to gain an understanding of a person. They shed light on how and what we believe about someone.

b) Review some of the titles they have already studied pertaining to Jesus: Lord, Son of God, Prophet, High Priest, and King. Ask them to explain what each title reveals about Jesus.

Using the Section

a) Assign the text under the heading "Christology of the Early Church (CCC 465-467)" (pages 273-277). Informally quiz the students on the material using the following true and false questions:

Docetists held that God could not become truly human yet remain God. (true)

Irenaeus answered the charges of the Docetists. (false)

Heresy means "a false teaching about some point in Christian doctrine." (true)

The Church Fathers were a group of bishops, theologians, teachers, and scholars whose writings have greatly contributed to Church doctrine and practice. (true)

An "apologist" is someone who publicly disavows his or her faith. (false)

Gnosticism denied the true humanity of Jesus, his resurrection, the validity of scriptures, and the authority of the bishops to rule the Church. (true)

The Golden Age of the Church Fathers spanned the first and second centuries. (false)

Arianism was a belief that Jesus was God's greatest creature, but not God. (true)

St. Athanasius taught that if Christ was not divine he could not be our savior. (true)

The Church accepts Nestorius' belief that there are two persons in Christ—one human, the other divine. (false)

Jesus is one divine person with two natures—a divine nature and a human nature. (true)

St. Augustine of Hippo is the most famous Church Father. (true)

b) Read and summarize the "Key Dogmatic Teachings about Jesus (CCC 464-483)" (pages 275-277). Emphasize some of the practical applications these truths have for our lives. For example, the first four teachings (emphasizing Jesus' divinity) encourage our desire to follow him and his example. Also, the fact that Jesus has a human intellect and human will means that he can empathize with us and we can identify with him. Remind the students that with God's grace, we can learn to live in a Christlike way.

c) Assign the exercise "The Nicene Creed" (page 279 and page 234 of this Manual). Suggest that the students write one paragraph for a statement they were most firm about and another paragraph for a statement they were least sure about. Allow opportunity for sharing and the dialogue.

Extending the Section

· · · · · · · · · · · · · · · ·

a) Assign the students to do a three-page report on the Church Fathers or Apostolic Fathers collectively or one of the individuals in either of these groups, focusing especially on how they helped to clarify Church belief being threatened by heresy.

b) Provide copies of the *Catechism of the Catholic Church* or have the students read on-line (http://www.christusrex.org/www2/kerygma/ccc/searchcat.html) paragraphs 464-483 related to beliefs about Jesus Christ. Ask them to write a report tracing the heresies surrounding Jesus' true divinity and true humanity and how the Councils of Ephesus, Chalcedon, and the fifth ecumenical Council at Constantinople answered them.

Creative Learning

· · · · · · · · · · · ·

a) Ask the students to create a title for themselves that explains in a nutshell what they are all about. Allow an opportunity for them to share their title in class.

b) Have the students write a personal creed for their lives, beginning with "I believe" statements. Ask them to write statements for everything they believe in firmly. Offer reflection on how each of their belief statements also reflect their Christian beliefs.

Conclusion

a) Allow time for the students to study the Selected Vocabulary definitions (page 282). Then quiz them orally or in writing on the definitions. Include on the quiz other terms the students have recorded definitions for in their notebooks or journals.

b) Assign the Summary Points and Review Questions (pages 280-282). Grade them and review them as preparation for the Chapter 9 Test.

Answers to Review Questions

1. What is the main theme of the letter to the Hebrews?

   Hebrews develops the theme of Christ as high priest, the model of our faith.

2. What are the seven "Catholic Epistles" and how did they get their name?

   The seven Catholic epistles are James, 1 and 2 Peter, 1, 2, and 3 John, and Jude. They are called "catholic" because they contain advice helpful for all churches (catholic means "universal"), they were accepted eventually by both Eastern and Western churches, and these letters help to explain how the worldwide Catholic Church developed.

3. What are two ways the letter of James serves as a foundation for the Church's social teaching?

   One of the letter's key themes is God's preferential love for the poor and the need for rich people to care for the poor.

4. Why did the author of the letter of James emphasize good works in addition to faith?

   The author probably emphasized this point because some Christians may have misunderstood St. Paul's teaching about the necessity of faith in Jesus alone as the way to share in Christ's saving Paschal mystery.

5. What does the first letter of Peter say about the role of suffering in the life of Christians?

   It teaches that Christians should not return evil for evil; rather they should return abuse with a blessing. Christians should keep doing good despite the attacks of others; their good example will eventually help people recognize the truth and put detractors to shame. Finally, Christians should look on their sufferings as a test of their faith and see them as a share in Christ's own sufferings.

6. What is the relationship between Jude and the second letter of Peter?

   2 Peter borrows heavily from Jude 4-16.

7. How does the second letter of Peter deal with the delayed return of the Lord?

   The second letter of Peter looks at the "delay" as a matter of perspective: "With the Lord one day is like a thousand years" (3:8) the letter explains. Christ is giving people the time to repent their sins.

8. According to the second letter of John, who is the Antichrist?

   According to the second letter of John, anyone who denies the Incarnation is the Antichrist.

9. Identify the term *Docetism*.

   Docetism comes from the Greek word meaning "to seem." Those teaching it boasted special knowledge about Jesus and Christian life that they claimed they received from mystical experiences with Christ.

10. What does the first letter of John say about love?

    The first letter of John says that true belief in Jesus must show forth in concrete acts of love, imitating the love of Christ.

11. Why shouldn't we look to the book of Revelation for answers about the end of the world?

    The book was written in an apocalyptic style with symbols applicable to Christians living under the rule of Roman persecutions of the day.

12. Who wrote Revelation and why?

John of Patmos wrote the book of Revelation to wavering Christians to encourage them to remain faithful during times of persecution, false teaching, and complacency.

13. What is *apocalyptic writing*? What purpose does it serve?

Apocalyptic writing contains visions, symbolic words, images, numbers, and pessimism about the world, but optimism about God's final triumph. Apocalypses were written in times of crisis to bolster the faith of believers and to help give them hope about the future, a time when God will establish his heavenly kingdom on earth.

14. What is the theme of the book of Revelation? What are some of its views of Jesus?

The theme of the book of Revelation is encouragement to remain faithful in the midst of persecution Answers will vary for second question.

15. Discuss the meaning of any three symbols in the book of Revelation.

Answers will vary.

16. What is *Christology*? List at least three titles of Jesus that reflect a New Testament Christology.

Christology deals with who the person of Jesus Christ is. Titles of Jesus cited will vary.

17. Define *Church Fathers*. List four important Church Fathers that defended orthodox belief in Jesus.

Church Fathers were a group of bishops, theologians, teachers, and scholars whose writings have greatly contributed to Church doctrine and practice. Church Fathers included St. Justin Martyr, St. Irenaeus, Tertullian, and Origen.

18. What did each of the following heresies teach: Arianism, Nestorianism, and Monophysitism?

Arianism denied Christ's divinity. Nestorianism taught that there were two persons in Jesus—one divine, the other only human. Monophysitism denied the true humanity of Jesus.

19. List and explain two principal teachings of the Church about Jesus Christ.

Examples are: Jesus is the only Son of God. Jesus is true God. Jesus is God from God, Light from Light, Jesus is begotten, not made, one in Being with the Father, all things were made through Jesus, there is only one person in Christ, the divine person, Mary is the Mother of God, there are two distinct natures in the one person of Christ, Jesus embodies the divine ways of God in a human way, Jesus has a human intellect and a human will, and Jesus is our Savior.

20. What is the Chalcedon formula?

"Jesus is one divine person with two natures—a divine nature and a human nature."

Chapter 9 Test

• • • • • • • • •

Assign and grade the Chapter 9 Test (pages 235-236 of this Manual). The answers follow below:

Chapter 9 Test   Name:_____

All items are worth 4 points each.

Part 1: Multiple Choice. Write the letter of the best choice in the space provided.

__B__ 1. The central theological point of the epistle of the Hebrews is that:
   A. Jesus will soon come in glory.
   B. Jesus is the High Priest, our model of faith.
   C. Jesus is the Suffering Servant.
   D. Jesus is the Son of God.

__C__ 2. Which of the following is *not* a "Catholic" epistle?
   A. 1 Peter
   B. 3 John
   C. Titus
   D. James

__D__ 3. The Catholic Epistles are so named because:
   A. They give general advice for all the churches.
   B. They were eventually accepted by Eastern and Western churches.
   C. They help reveal how the universal church grew.
   D. All of these.
   E. None of these.

__A__ 4. Which epistle stresses social justice themes that are widely admired today?
   A. James
   B. 2 Peter
   C. 1 John
   D. Hebrews

__D__ 5. The first letter of Peter teaches all of the following about suffering *except*:
   A. Christians should bless their persecutors.
   B. Christians should persist in doing good despite hardships.
   C. Christians should see suffering as a share in Christ's cross.
   D. Christians should interpret personal suffering as a punishment from God.

__A__ 6. The latest New Testament writing is generally believed to be:
   A. 2 Peter
   B. Revelation
   C. 3 John
   D. Jude

__D__   7. The number **7** in the book of Revelation signifies:
       A. imperfection
       B. the Church
       C. the world
       D. wholeness

__A__   8. Babylon in Revelation is a symbol for:
       A. Rome
       B. Antioch
       C. Jerusalem
       D. Damascus

__C__   9. The greatest Father of the church was:
       A. St. Cyril
       B. St. Jerome
       C. St. Augustine of Hippo
       D. St. Athanasius

__B__   10. Which heresy claimed that Jesus, God's Son, was the Father's greatest creature, but not divine?
       A. Monophysitism
       B. Arianism
       C. Docetism
       D. Nestorianism

Part 2: True or False. Mark **+** if the statement is true and **0** if the statement is false.

__0__   11. The letter of Jude teaches that we need an objective standard of Christian faith and morality, namely, the teaching of the apostles.

__+__   12. The Catholic Church teaches that we should not use the symbols of the book of Revelation to identify *specific* political leaders living today.

__+__   13. The Revelation to John teaches that we must at all times worship the one true God and him alone.

__+__   14. *Apologists* were defenders of the faith.

__0__   15. *Docetism* taught that Jesus only seemed to be God.

__0__   16. God the Father *created* God the Son.

__+__   17. When we call Mary *Theotokos* we are affirming that she is the "Mother of God."

Part 3: Fill-ins.

____works____   18. According to the letter of James, faith without __?__ is dead.

__Nero (or emperor)__   19. The number 666 in the Book of Revelation refers to __?__ .

__two natures__   20. The Council of Chalcedon taught that Jesus is one divine person with __?__ .

Part 4: Brief Essay
List and briefly discuss the meaning of five of your favorite titles of Jesus. Mention why you like each of your choices.

There are many possible answers. Assign one point for each title, another point for the reason it was chosen, and two points for a correct theological explanation of a particular title.

Prayer Lesson

- ➠ Provide some brief background on the life of St. Teresa of Avila (see http://www.newadvent.org/cathen/14515b.htm).
- ➠ Pray the prayer of St. Teresa (page 283) with the class, dividing the students on two sides of the room and alternating each line of the prayer.
- ➠ In their journals, ask the students to write some of the things that disturb them.

ten

The Living Jesus Today: Constant Friend and Companion

Introducing the Chapter

This final chapter may be the most important one of the text. It takes up the issue of how a believer in Christ can meet and respond to the living Lord.

The chapter begins with a review of some of the people from the New Testament who met and recognized Jesus. It continues by showing how Jesus remains present and continues his saving mission in the Church. The Church is the Body of Christ. Baptism incorporates us into that Body. The Church is also a sacrament, the visible sign and instrument of the hidden mystery and reality of salvation in Jesus Christ. An opening story on pages 285-287 illustrates this point. The text points out that while we are the presence of Christ in our world, so too is every person that we meet, especially the poor.

Specifically, Jesus meets us in the sacraments of the Church. The chapter points out that the seven sacraments are efficacious signs, that is, they bring about what they point to. Christ is always present in and working through them. Jesus also meets us in scriptures. They are the word of God. They hand on the truth of God's revelation. Their central object is Jesus Christ. The text presents a process for reading and living the scriptures.

Connected with our participation in the sacraments and the reading of the scriptures is prayer. Prayer is the way to talk with and listen to Jesus Christ. The text presents several prayer forms and names expected results of how our prayer can bring us closer to Christ.

Finally, the chapter examines several ways contemporary media has depicted Christ, especially in documentaries and full-length films. A synopsis of four recommended films about Jesus is offered.

Bibliography

Baugh, Lloyd. *Imaging the Divine: Jesus & Christ Figures in Film.* Kansas City: Sheed & Ward, 1997.

Barry, William A., S.J. *Who Do You Say I Am? Meeting the Historical Jesus in Prayer.* Notre Dame, IN: Ave Maria Press, 1996.
    Uses John Meier's *The Marginal Jew* to help readers encounter the risen Lord in prayer. Good reading.

Green, Thomas H., S.J. *Opening to God: A Guide to Prayer.* Notre Dame, IN: Ave Maria Press, 1977.
    A time-tested introduction to prayer used successfully by high-school students for many years.

Hutchinson, Gloria. *Six Ways to Pray from Six Great Saints.* Cincinnati, OH: St. Anthony Messenger Press, 1982.
    Looks to spiritual masters—Francis and Clare of Assisi, Ignatius Loyola, Thérèse Lisieux, Teresa of Avila, and John of the Cross—for guidance on how to pray.

Kinnard, Roy and Davis, Tim. *Divine Images: A History of Jesus on the Screen.* Secaucus, NJ: Citadel Press, 1992.

Mother Teresa. *A Simple Life.* Lucinda Vardey, compiler. New York: Ballantine Books, 1995.
    Inspirational reading for all.

O'Collins, Gerald, S.J. *Following the Way: Jesus, Our Spiritual Director.* New York/Mahwah, NJ: Paulist Press, 1999, 2001.
    Insightful reflections on some key parables and how they relate to living the gospel in daily life.

Stern, Richard C., Clayton Jefford, and Guerric Debona. *Savior on the Silver Screen.* New York: Paulist Press, 1999.
    Looks at how nine films reflect the time and culture in which the film was produced.

Videos

Jesus of Montreal
    A French Canadian allegory about an acting troupe that puts on a passion play and begins to take on the stories of the characters they play (1989; 119-minute feature film, French with English subtitles, Amazon.com).

(Other videos are suggested throughout this chapter.)

Resources

"Another Hundred Years of Jesus Christ on Film"
    Website by Pete Aiken.
    http://www.postfun.com/pfp/features/98/mar/filmography.html

Bibleinfo.com
What the Bible says about a host of topics. Good research aid on Christian living.
http://www.bibleinfo.com/

Biblical evidence for Catholicism
Many students have used some of the links provided here to help explain the Catholic faith to their Protestant friends at school.
http://ic.net/~erasmus/erasmus.htm

The Face of Jesus in Art
http://www.hollywoodjesus.com/jesus_in_art.htm

Hollywood Jesus
Film reviews from a minister of the gospel. Check this site out.
http://www.hollywoodjesus.com/

Images of Jesus Through Two Millennia
http://www.beliefnet.com/story/22/story_2283_1.html

Interview with God
Words and fantastic photos with a good reminder of eternal truths for living.
http://www.reata.org/interview.html

Jesus Real to Reel: Bibliography and Web Resources for Religion/Theology and Film
Bibliography and links provided by Richard Ascough and Peter Gilmour who offered a course on "Jesus in the Media" at Loyola University, Chicago. Worth checking out.
http://post.queensu.ca/~rsa/realreel.htm

McNulty, Rev. Ed. "Jesus Goes to Hollywood: A Bibliography."
http://www.pcusa.org/cga/hollywood.html

SECTION 1:
Are *You* Jesus?, Jesus Is Present in the Church, and Jesus Is Present in Others, Especially the Poor and Suffering (pages 285-291)

Objectives

The goals of this section are to enable the students to:
- recognize how they can be Jesus to others and others can Jesus for them, especially the poor;
- understand that the Church is the Body of Christ, and that each of us are members of this Body as a result of our Baptisms;
- find concrete ways they can be a sign and instrument of Christ's continuing work of salvation.

Summary and Background Information

Having studied Jesus in the New Testament, the students are now reminded of all the ways Christ is present in our world today. The course comes full circle, ending by focusing on ways the students can continue to develop their relationships with Jesus.

The section begins with a short story reminding the students that Jesus lives in them. The popular question "What would Jesus do?" is re-worked to the more essential "What *is* Jesus doing through me?" As a review, the students are asked to complete a short exercise to name some of the people in the New Testament who met and recognized Jesus.

As he taught, Jesus had a special regard for the poor. Similarly, Jesus is especially recognized in the poor. By being mindful of Jesus' presence in others—especially the poor—the students become cognizant of ways they can continue to meet Christ and grow closer to him.

Warm Up

• • • • • • •

a) Read the passage from Matthew 18:20—"For where two or three are gathered together in my name, there am I in the midst of them"—on page 284 of the text. Discuss the unity of Christians with Jesus implied by these words of Christ. Ask the students how they envision Christ being "in the midst of them" when they pray with other believers.

b) Read or summarize the opening story about the salesmen and girl selling fruit in the airport under the heading "Are *You* Jesus?" Address the questions on page 285 to the class: Where can we find the Risen Jesus in our world today? Where can we meet him? Allow the students to brainstorm responses. Record these on the board.

c) Assign the exercise "Recognizing Christ" (pages 287-288 and page 237 of this Manual). Remind the students to first guess the name of the person described, then check the answer by reading the scripture reference. Allow an opportunity for the students to share what they would say to Jesus.

Answers:
1. Samaritan woman at the well
2. Saul (Paul)
3. Two disciples on the road to Emmaus
4. Peter
5. Nathanael
6. The magi
7. John the Baptist
8. Thomas
9. Man possessed by demons
10. The devil

Using the Section

• • • • • • • • • • • •

a) Summarize the remaining paragraphs in the text section, "Are *You* Jesus?" (pages 285-287). Point out:

✓ Christ has chosen us to be his ambassadors in the world for others.

✓ Baptism incorporates us into the Church.

✓ Faith is the God-given virtue that enables us to see the reality of who Christ is.

✓ We enter into the Paschal mystery when we accept our sufferings and join them to Christ.

b) Assign the text section "Jesus Is Present in the Church" (pages 288-289). To follow up the reading, call on students to name many different ways Catholic teens can be a sign and instrument of Christ.

c) Prior to covering the text section "Jesus Is Present in Others, Especially the Poor and Suffering" (pages 289-291), read to the students the parable of the Good Samaritan (Lk 10:29-37). Ask the students to create alternate characters for the parable from their own lives (e.g., naming groups of people who are meant to be holy, as well as those who are often thought of as enemies.) For discussion, ask: "What are some practical things you can do to treat even your enemies as neighbors?"

d) Assign for reading "Jesus Is Present in Others, Especially the Poor and Suffering" (pages 289-291) and the margin feature "Responding to Christ in Others" (page 291). Assign the discussion as a journal entry. Also, have the students comment on this Gandhi quote: "The world holds enough for every man's need, but not enough for every man's greed."

Extending the Section

a) Assign paragraphs 48-51 of *Lumen Gentium*, the Second Vatican Council document on the Church. Have the students write a summary report, naming how the document explains how Christ is present in the Church and how they, in turn, are connected to Christ and the Church.

b) Extend the margin exercise on page 289. Ask the students to compose five ways teenagers can accomplish each of the tasks listed on page 289: to program Christ's message of love and forgiveness, to build community among believers, to serve others, especially those most in need, and to worship God in truth and love.

Creative Learning

a) Have the students work with the images for disciples described by Jesus in the Sermon on the Mount—"light of the world" and "salt of the earth"—to develop a poster montage that represents either or both images.

b) Have the students organize a hunger fast among their peers. Collect pledges in exchange for a one-day fast. Donate the proceeds to a world hunger agency.

SECTION 2: Jesus Meets Us in the Sacraments, Jesus Meets Us in Scripture, and Meeting Jesus in Prayer (pages 291-298)

Objectives

The goals of this section are to enable the students to:

➦ know that Jesus is always present in and works through the seven sacraments; and especially understand the effects of the sacraments of Penance and Eucharist;

➦ recall that Jesus Christ is the central object of the New Testament and reading the scriptures is another way to meet the Lord;

➦ understand that Jesus will meet them and be with them when they pray.

Summary and Background Information

The section touches on the seven sacraments, naming them as efficacious signs, that is, bringing about what they point to. Christ institutes the sacraments and is present in them. The text touches on all seven sacraments and covers in more depth Penance and Eucharist—two sacraments that have a direct impact on the daily lives of teens. The students are reminded of how Jesus meets them in his mercy, reconciliation, and forgiveness in the sacrament of Penance and how he meets us in a preeminent way in the sacrament of Eucharist.

The next part of the section (pages 295-297) offers ways for meeting the Lord by regularly reading the scriptures. This is a point that has been emphasized through direct study of the New Testament in the previous chapters, but is now combined with a focused discussion of how to pray with the Bible.

Finally, the section focuses on meeting Jesus in prayer, whether traditional vocal prayer, meditation, affective prayer, or contemplation. The students are reminded over and over that Jesus will meet them if they continue to pray.

Warm Up

a) Briefly review the names of the sacraments. In an informal quiz, have the students write the names of the sacraments on scrap paper. Collect. Read aloud (anonymously and in a light-hearted way) any incorrect answers before verifying the names of all seven sacraments.

b) Write the following sentence starters on the board:

> Name is missed because . . .
>
> Name contributes to these classes by . . .
>
> What I like about Name is . . .
>
> I wish Name were here because . . .

Choose someone known to be well liked by most of the students to be "absent" from the group. Absent means sitting in the corner of the class, facing the wall. When the person is placed go around the group and hear volunteers finish the sentences about the absent person. When the discussion ends, point out that if the person really were absent he or she *would* have been missed. In the same way, fellow Christians and the Lord himself miss us when we fail to participate in the life of the Church and fail to pray. Relate this activity to the exercise (why or why not students go to Mass) on page 295.

Using the Section

• • • • • • • • • • • • •

a) Assign the text section "Jesus Meets Us in the Sacraments" (pages 291-295). Make a chart on the board or with a PowerPoint presentation that summarizes how Jesus is with us in the sacraments.

JESUS IS PRESENT IN . . .

Baptism as a companion on life's journey in Church

Confirmation as an advocate sending his Spirit to help us be his witness

Eucharist as a friend who shares life with us on a daily basis

Penance as a forgiving friend who heals guilt and alienation

Anointing of the Sick as a healer in times of suffering

Matrimony as a companion in marriage and family life

Holy Orders as a minister to the faithful

b) The *Catechism of the Catholic Church* lists several ways that Jesus is present in the Eucharist. Make sure the students take notes of these ways in their notebooks.

Jesus is present in the heart of the individual Christian.

Jesus is present in the community gathered in his name.

Jesus is present in the words from scripture that are read at Mass.

Jesus is present in his priest, his official representative.

Jesus is MOST present in the consecrated bread and wine—the eucharistic species.

Emphasize the quotation from *The Constitution of the Sacred Liturgy* on pages 294-295 of the text.

c) The students have spent a great deal of time *studying* the New Testament. The text section "Jesus Meets Us in Scripture" (pages 295-297) reminds them that the Bible is primarily a book of prayer. Set aside ten minutes of class time to conduct the process for reading scripture suggested on pages 296-297. Allow the students to choose one technique out of the three. If possible, conduct the exercise in a church, chapel, or outdoors.

d) In covering the section "Meeting Jesus in Prayer" (pages 297-298), write the four forms of prayer described on the board.

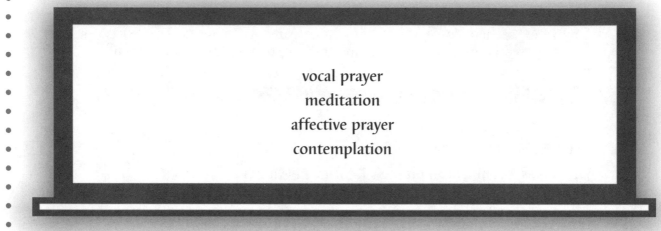

vocal prayer

meditation

affective prayer

contemplation

Define each form of prayer. Ask the students to discuss what they like and don't like about each form of prayer. Ask them to tell about times they pray and when they feel their prayer is most effective.

Extending the Section

a) Arrange for the students to participate in the sacrament of Penance. One way to do this is to have the students meet at a local parish at a regularly scheduled time for confessions (e.g., on a Saturday afternoon). After the students have celebrated the sacrament of Penance, have them attend Mass and/or go out for supper together if possible.

b) Assign the students to write a report on Christ's presence in the Eucharist using paragraphs 1373-1381 of the *Catechism of the Catholic Church* as a starting point. The report may be titled "How Christ is truly present in the Eucharistic Species." If the students have not commented on their participation at Mass (page 295), have them include this issue as a second part of the report.

c) Extend the margin exercise on page 297. Invite two people who can be considered "close to Jesus." These people may be teens or adults, but the presentation may carry more weight with the students if at least one of the people is a teenager. Have them talk about their prayer life, including how and why they pray. Have the students compose questions to ask the presenters. Allow a brief question and answer period.

Creative Learning

a) Select several quotes of Jesus (see samples below). Read the first part of the quote. Call on students to complete the second part of the quote. To play as a game, divide the class into two teams. Choose a representative from Team 1 to try to finish the quote. If correct, award a point.

If incorrect, call on a representative from Team 2. Continue in the same way until the quote is finished. For the next quote, start with Team 2.

Samples

"My Father, if it is possible, *let this cup pass from me.*" (Mt 6:39)

"Whoever eats my flesh and drinks my blood *has eternal life.*" (Jn 6:54)

"For behold, some are last who will be first *and some are first who will be last*" (Lk 13:30)

"Whose sins you forgive are forgiven them, *and whose sins you retain are retained.*" (Jn 20:23)

b) Have the students form a scripture group as suggested on page 297. If the group is to meet at school, help to provide space for a study hall time, lunch hour, or before school.

c) Use this form of centering prayer as part of a class session. Say to the students: "Close your eyes. Quiet yourself and keep your back straight. Become aware of God's presence. Express your faith in words such as these: 'Lord, I believe that you are present in me, at the very center of my existence, keeping me alive in your love. For my prayer now, I just want to be with you. Draw me close to you, Lord, Let me experience your presence and your love." Pause for about 30 seconds. Then, conclude. Say: "Select a word that makes you think of God and his love for you. Choose a name, quality, or title that carries deep meaning for you, for example (pause between each): Jesus, Father, Spirit, Lord, Abba, Wisdom, Love, Truth, Life, Way, Savior, Yahweh, Protector. Recite the word over and over to yourself, quietly enough so that it does not become a distraction." Conclude the centering prayer by having the students recite an Our Father.

SECTION 3: Jesus and Contemporary Cinema (pages 299-302)

Objectives

The goals of this section are to enable the students to:
- reflect on the effectiveness of contemporary films about Jesus as ways to meet the Lord;
- critique some popular feature-length films about Jesus;
- consider the necessary elements that make up an authentic presentation on the life of Jesus.

Summary and Background Information

The chapter and text concludes with an overview of several contemporary media presentations of the life of Jesus.

The main point made in the section is that no film can possible capture who Jesus is or what he was *really* like in his earthly ministry. However, a strength of films about Jesus is they get people thinking about who Jesus is and what his message is all about.

A criteria for judging films about Jesus is presented on page 299. These points will help the students as they critique some of the popular films often shown on television around the Christmas and Easter seasons as well as serve them as new films about Jesus are released.

It is recommended that after the students learn to be critically reflective of these films that you provide an opportunity to view all of one film or main parts of several of these in class.

Warm Up

a) Display several images of Jesus. Ask the students to look at the images and name things they find appealing and not appealing about the images and tell why.

b) Brainstorm a list with the students of several films about Jesus they have seen on television or on video. Collect as much information on the film as possible, including names of actors, approximate year the film was made, and general plot or theme.

Using the Section

a) Read or summarize the text under "Jesus and Contemporary Cinema" up to the paragraphs that offer synopses of the specific films about Jesus (page 299). Expand on the points for critiquing these films listed on the bottom of page 299.

> Judge whether certain characters or events depicted in these films appear in the gospel record or not;
>
> recognize whether Jesus said or did something the film claims he did;
>
> evaluate the validity of the actor's portrayal of Jesus against the Jesus you met in the gospels;
>
> discover the agenda of the producer—for example, a Jesus who preaches political violence.

b) Offer a brief synopses of the films listed on pages 300-302, sharing more information about films you may have personally seen and drawing on the students' comments as well. As you are able, show brief portions of these films on video to the class.

c) Reserve two or more class periods to show one of the films suggested in this chapter. Have the students write a review of the film based on the criteria listed above and on page 299.

Extending the Section

a) On the Internet, have the students look up one or more of the films listed in the text and write a report summarizing the various reviews the films have received over the years.

b) Assign one or more of the activities listed on page 301. If the students did not have the opportunity to view one of these films in entirety in class, make sure they are assigned the first activity as homework.

Creative Learning

• • • • • • • • • • • •

a) Have the students create a notebook of favorite images of Jesus they discover on the Internet. In the notebook, have them include a copy of the image itself or a link to its Web address. Also included should be a brief explanation of the image, including its history, creator, and a personal opinion of the image offered by the student. (See http://home.nyc.rr.com/mysticalrose/jesusart.html as a source to several sites with images of Christ.) You may want to combine this assignment with the third activity listed on page 301.

b) Divide the class into small groups of four students each. Assign each group to enact the Transfiguration of Jesus (e.g., Mt 17:1-8), depicting the scene in any way they chose. Allow an opportunity for the groups to present their scenes to the class. Ask the rest of the students to critique the scene based on the criteria of creativity, authenticity, and agenda.

Conclusion

• • • • • • • •

Assign the Summary Points and Review Questions (pages 302-304). Grade them and review them as preparation for the Chapter 10 Test.

Answers to Review Questions

1. How are you a presence of Christ in the world?

   Answers will vary. See the opening story on page 285 for an example.

2. Give some personal examples of how you can be light of the world and salt of the earth for others.

   Answers will vary. Look for examples that center on how the person enters into the Paschal mystery that comes when we accept the sufferings that come into our lives.

3. In what way is the Church the Body of Christ?

   Jesus is the head of the Body, we are the members. Baptism incorporates us into the Body.

4. What does it mean to call the Church the Sacrament of Christ?

   The Church is a visible sign and instrument of the hidden mystery and reality of salvation in Jesus Christ.

5. Name four activities that help carry on the work of Christ's saving acts.

   Four activities that help carry on the work of Christ's saving acts are: proclaim his message of love and forgiveness; build community among our fellow believers; serve others, especially the most needy; and worship God in truth and love.

6. Why should Christians have a preferential love for the poor, lonely, and suffering?

   Christians should have a preferential love for the poor, lonely, and suffering because Jesus identified with the lowly, the outcast, and those who were not accepted by the well-established.

7. Why did Christ institute the sacraments?

   Christ instituted the sacraments so that he can "stay in touch" with us. Through the sacraments we remain in touch with the real presence of the Lord.

8. Define *sacramental character*. Which sacraments convey a sacramental character?

   Sacramental character is an indelible spiritual mark that permanently configures a person to Christ and gives him or her a special standing in the Church. Baptism, Confirmation, and Holy Orders are the sacraments that confer a special sacramental character.

9. List several effects of meeting Christ in the Sacrament of Penance.

   Effects of the sacrament include reconciliation with the Church, remission of the eternal punishment incurred by mortal sins, remission, at least in part, of the temporal punishments from sin, peace of conscience, and spiritual strength to live the Christian life.

10. What does the word *Eucharist* mean? What are some of the effects of receiving the Lord in Holy Communion?

    Eucharist means "thanksgiving." Reception of Holy Communion unites us more closely with Jesus, forgives our venial sins, keeps us from mortal sin, and strengthens our unity with other members of the Church.

11. Define prayer. List four types of prayer.

    Prayer is "the living relationship of the children of God with their Father, who is good beyond measure, with his Son Jesus Christ and with the Holy Spirit" (CCC, 2565). Four types of prayer are vocal prayer, meditation, affective prayer, and contemplation.

12. List two important feature films made about Jesus. Discuss at least two ways for watching Jesus films in an intelligent, critical way.

    Answers will vary on specific films. Ways to watch films critically include judging conformity with the gospel, recognizing whether Jesus said or did something included in the film, evaluating the validity of the actor's performance in comparison with the Jesus of the gospels, and discovering the agenda of the film's producer.

Chapter 10 Test

● ● ● ● ● ● ● ● ●

Assign and grade the Chapter 10 Test (pages 238-239 of this Manual). The answers follow below:

Chapter 10 Test   Name:_____

All questions are worth 4 points each.

Part 1: Matching. Please match the sacrament in Column B with its description in Column A.

Column A		Column B
__E__	1. Strength to endure sufferings of old age	A. Holy Orders
__F__	2. Creates and celebrates Christian community	B. Confirmation
__G__	3. Forgives original sin	C. Matrimony
__D__	4. Renewal and healing of friendship with God and the Christian community	D. Reconciliation
		E. Anointing of the Sick
__B__	5. Strengthens faith commitment by showering the gifts of the Holy Spirit	F. Eucharist
		G. Baptism

Part 2: True or False. Mark **+** if the statement is true and **0** if the statement is false.

___+___ 6. A concordance will help you locate where a particular word appears in your Bible.

___+___ 7. *Affective* prayer involves one's feelings and imagination.

___0___ 8. In *meditative* prayer, we empty our minds of thoughts about everything and just sit in God's presence.

___0___ 9. We should always trust contemporary television documentaries to be objective when they portray Jesus' life.

___+___ 10. We cannot say we love Jesus if we do not find him in the hurting, lonely, poor, and suffering people in our world.

Part 3: Fill-ins.

___faith___ 11. This virtue enables us to see the reality of who Jesus Christ truly is.

___thanksgiving___ 12. The word Eucharist means ___?___.

___sacrament___ 13. The Church is like a ___?___, that is, a visible sign and instrument of the hidden mystery and reality of salvation in Jesus Christ.

___St. Teresa of Avila___ 14. Which saint said that we are the hands, feet, eyes, and voice of Christ responding to the needy in our midst?

___Holy Spirit___ 15. The church is the Body of Christ and the Temple of the ___?___.

Part 4: Essay

16-25. Suppose an extremely wealthy producer came to you to write a movie script on the life of Jesus. Based on your knowledge of Jesus and the New Testament, list ten events or specific teachings of Jesus that you absolutely want to include in your film. Then give a reason why you picked each particular event or teaching.

Be generous in assigning points to this open-ended question. Assign two points for each event/teaching; two points for a cogent reason given.

Prayer Lesson

➼ Allow quiet time for the personal prayer called for on page 305.

Reproducible Pages

Name ....

Learning More About Peter

Peter was the apostle who acknowledged Jesus to be the Messiah and the Son of God. But Peter was not always the steadfast and dependable friend of Jesus. At times, he was weak and all-too-human. Learn more about Peter by checking these passages and answering the questions that follow.

Matthew 4:18-22

What was Peter's profession? _____

Who was his brother? _____

Who else were among Jesus' first apostles? _____

Matthew 8:5; 14

Where was Peter's home? _____

Luke 9:28-36

Which other apostles were at Jesus' Transfiguration? _____

Who did the apostles see with Jesus? _____

What did Peter propose to do? _____

Mark 14:27-31; 66-72

What did Peter say he would do rather than deny Christ? _____

Why did the woman think Peter was Jesus' companion? _____

What did Peter do when he realized he had betrayed Christ? _____

John 21:1-19

What did Peter do once he saw Jesus? _____

How many times did Jesus ask Peter to profess his love? _____

How will Peter die? _____

Name ....

New Testament Names

Use a dictionary or book of names to match the meaning of these New Testament names with the description that fits from the right column.

_____   1. Joseph   a. "let God protect"

_____   2. Mary   b. "virile one, manly"

_____   3. John   c. "bitter" or "grieved"

_____   4. Elizabeth   d. "lily"

_____   5. James   e. "God is fullness"

_____   6. Matthew   f. "may God add"

_____   7. Martha   g. "friend of horses"

_____   8. Andrew   h. "lady or mistress of the house"

_____   9. Susanna   i. "God has shown favor"

_____   10. Philip   j. "gift of God"

Name ....

Test on the Introduction

Part 1: True or False: Mark **+** if the item is true and **0** if the item is false. (4 points each)

_____ 1.   A.D. stands for "in the year of the Lord."

_____ 2.   There is little or no connection between the historical Jesus and the living Christ of faith.

_____ 3.   God becoming human makes it possible for humans to share in the divine nature.

_____ 4.   Christian faith in Jesus as God's Son depends on apostolic testimony about him.

_____ 5.   Caesar Tiberius was the Roman Emperor at the time of Jesus' birth.

_____ 6.   The "real Jesus" of Christian faith is the resurrected Jesus.

_____ 7.   The name Jesus means "savior."

_____ 8.   By the end of the first century, the name Jesus was used often by Jewish fathers to name their boys.

_____ 9.   When Christians proclaim that Jesus is the "Son of God," they are professing that Jesus has the same divine nature as God the Father.

_____ 10. _Adonai=Yahweh=Kyrios_=Lord!

Part 2: Multiple Choice. Write the letter of the best choice in the space provided. (4 points each)

_____ 11. Which title of Jesus means "anointed one"?
A. Lord   B. Good Shepherd   C. Christ   D. Son of God

_____ 12. Which title definitively proclaims the divinity of Jesus?
A. Lord   B. Christ   C. Judge   D. Prophet

_____ 13. The essential teaching about salvation accomplished in the life, death, and resurrection of Jesus is known as:
A. _diakonia_   B. _kerygma_   C. _leitourgeia_   D. _koinonia_

_____ 14. This heresy held that Jesus only "seemed" to be human:
A. Arianism   B. Nestorianism   C. Fideism   D. Docetism

_____ 15. The title that translates the Hebrew word for Messiah:
A. Christ   B. Lord   C. Jesus   D. Alpha

Part 3: Short Fill-ins: (4 points each)

_____ 16. Term: "a doctrine taught with the highest authority"

_____ 17. Term: "the central teaching that God's Son became man in the person of Jesus Christ."

_____ 18. Give a possible "surname" for Jesus.

_____ 19. What year was Jesus born?

_____ 20. This person proclaimed Jesus' true identity on the road to Caesarea Philippi.

Part 4: Short Answers: (4 points each)

21. Write out the "Jesus Prayer."

_____

_____

List and discuss four ways you can meet the living Lord today:

22.

_____

23.

_____

24.

_____

25.

_____

Name ....

Rate Your Relationship

Rate your relationship with Jesus. Write your initials on the point on the dotted line which best represents your relationship with him right now.

active .... passive

exciting .... dull

close .... distant

friendly .... estranged

personal .... shallow

▶ If Jesus were to appear physically to you, name one question you would like to ask him.

▶ List several of the questions you and your classmates would like to ask Jesus. Write answers for how you think he might answer them.

Name ....

Form Criticism

Read the following passages. Match the name of one of the literary forms discussed in this section with the passage. Be able to defend your choice in a discussion.

1. Mk 8:1-9 _____

2. Mt 17:19-20 _____

3. Lk 1:46-55 _____

4. Jn 6:51 _____

5. Mk 1:23-26 _____

6. Lk 12:49 _____

7. Lk 10:29-37 _____

8. Mt 10:1-12 _____

9. Mk 7:24-30 _____

Name ....

Chapter 1 Test

▶ All questions worth 4 points each.

Part 1: Matching. Please match the person or type of biblical criticism in Column B with the descriptions in Column A.

Column A

_____ 1. wrote of a riot in Rome caused by "Chrestus"

_____ 2. Jewish historian who referred to Jesus

_____ 3. masterful letter writer who wrote to Emperor Trajan about Christians

_____ 4. tries to discover what comes from Jesus in the gospel texts

_____ 5. studies literary differences in the biblical texts

_____ 6. analyzes how gospel writers edited their works for their particular audiences

Column B

A. Pliny the Younger

B. Suetonius

C. Josephus

D. Tacitus

E. Lucian of Samosota

F. source criticism

G. historical criticism

H. form criticism

I. redaction criticism

Part 2: True or False. Mark + if the statement is true and **0** if the statement is false.

_____ 7. There are a total of twenty-three books in the New Testament.

_____ 8. *Gospel* refers to Jesus himself, the preaching about him, and the four written accounts.

_____ 9. A New Testament book was not considered inspired unless it had roots in the apostolic witnesses.

_____ 10. The gospel of Thomas is an inspired biblical work.

_____ 11. Early apostolic preaching involved *catechesis*, that is, further instructions for new converts.

_____ 12. *Q* was a source for the gospels of Matthew and John.

_____ 13. *M* was a unique source for Matthew's gospel.

Part 3: Short Fill-ins.

_____ 14. What is our primary source of knowledge about the historical Jesus?

_____ 15. A ___?___ is a special kind of contract marked by *hesed* (loving-kindness).

_____ 16. Biblical ___?___ refers to the Holy Spirit teaching truth without destroying the free and personal activity of the human author.

_____ 17. Term for a gospel writer: ___?___ .

_____ 18. The official list of books considered inspired is known as the ___?___ of the Bible.

_____ 19. The three stages in the formation of the gospels are the historical Jesus, the New Testament writings, and ___?___ .

_____ 20. Matthew, Mark, and ___?___ are known as the synoptic gospels.

_____ 21. Name a good English translation of the Bible done by *Catholic* scholars.

_____ 22. Give an acceptable date for when the first gospel was written.

Part 4: Short Answers

23. Why did it take so long before the gospels were written?

24.-25. Discuss two reasons why the gospels were eventually written:

Name ....

Map of the Holy Land

Check the following New Testament references. Then write the number of the correct location of where each event took place.

_____ Where did the resurrected Jesus eat a meal with two disciples? (Lk 24:13)

_____ To which city was the traveler in the parable of the Good Samaritan going? (Lk 10:30)

_____ To what did Jesus compare Chorazin and Bethsaida? (Mt 11:20-22)

_____ Where was the birthplace of Peter, Andrew, and Phillip? (Jn 1:44)

_____ Where did the resurrected Jesus appear to the apostles in John's gospel? (Jn 21)

_____ Where did Jesus give sight to a blind man (Lk 18:35-43) and dine with Zaccheus (Lk 19:1-10)?

A map of the Holy Land with numbered locations:

1 Sidon
Sarepta
ABILENE
Damascus
Mt. Hermon 2
SYRIA
PHOENICIA
GREAT SEA (Mediterranean Sea)
1 Tyre
Caesarea Philippi 3
Hulch Valley
GALILEE 4
Mt. Meron
Ptolemais (Accho)
Chorazin
7 Capernaum
Bethsaida 6
9 Cana
Magdala 8
Sea of Galilee 5
Tiberias
10 Nazareth
Mt. Tabor 2
Nain
Yarmuk
Gadara
Megiddo
Caesarea
DECAPOLIS
SAMARIA
Samaria
Sychar
Amathus
Jabbok River
Jordan River
Plain of Sharon
Arimathaea
Gadara
Joppa
Bethel
Philadelphia
Aj
14 Emmaus
Gibeah
Jericho 11
Jerusalem
Bethabara 12
15 Bethphage
Bethany 16
17 Bethlehem
Wilderness of Judea
Azotus
Dead Sea
Ascalon
JUDAEA
Hebron
Machaerus
Gaza
R. Arnon
NABATEA
IDUMEA
Hormah
Beersheba
13
N

Name ....

Jesus the Messiah

Read the following references to a messiah from the Old Testament prophets. Describe what type of messiah is prophesied.

Isaiah 9:5-7   **Isaiah 40:10-11**   **Isaiah 52:13**

Isaiah 53:6-7   **Micah 5:1-4**   **Malachi 3:1-5**

_____

_____

_____

_____

_____

_____

_____

_____

Read the following passage from Mark's gospel. How does this description of Jesus compare with the Old Testament expectations of a messiah?

**For the Son of Man did not come to be served but to
serve and to give his life as a ransom for many (10:45).**

_____

_____

_____

_____

_____

_____

_____

Name ....

Chapter 2 Test

▶ All questions worth 4 points each.

Part 1: Matching. Please match the group of Jesus' Jewish contemporaries with the descriptions given below.

Groups

A. Samaritans   B. Essenes   C. Pharisees   D. Zealots   E. Sadducees

Descriptions

———— 1. many were scribes who valued oral interpretation of the Law

———— 2. centered their power in Jerusalem and collaborated with the Romans

———— 3. founded by the Teacher of Righteousness

———— 4. descended from foreigners who intermarried with northern tribes of the Chosen People

———— 5. one of Jesus' disciples belonged to this group

———— 6. Jesus was closest to them in belief and spiritual practice

———— 7. despised Roman rule and worked to overthrow it

———— 8. believed Mount Gerazim was the God-chosen proper place for worship

———— 9. a priestly, conservative, aristocratic group

———— 10. associated with Qumran and the Dead Sea scrolls

Part 2: True or False. Mark **+** if the statement is true and **0** if the statement is false.

———— 11. Jesus chose Cana in Galilee to be his headquarters during his public ministry.

———— 12. In Jesus' day, the feast of Pentecost celebrated Yahweh's giving of the Law to Moses.

———— 13. The Roman general Pompey conquered Palestine in 63 B.C.

———— 14. Pious Jews were happy to cooperate with the adoption of Hellenism in Palestine.

———— 15. Jewish contemporaries of Jesus saw Messiahship in terms of political power.

———— 16. Common people in our Lord's day were surprisingly knowledgeable about the Law.

———— 17. Jesus and early Christians preached for the abolishment of the institution of slavery.

Part 3: Short Fill-ins.

————————————— 18. What is the meaning of the term *angel*?

————————————— 19. What is the term for the Jewish Law found in the first five books of the Bible (Pentateuch)?

————————————— 20. The 71-member supreme legislative and judicial body of the Jewish people was known as ___?___ .

————————————— 21. The three major regions of the Holy Land in our Lord's day were Galilee, Samaria, and ___?___ .

————————————— 22. The language Jesus spoke on a daily basis was ___?___ .

————————————— 23. This Herod was ruler in Galilee for most of Jesus' life: ___?___ .

Part 4: Short Essay.

24.-25. List and discuss two of the most interesting things you learned about Jesus from your study of Chapter 2.

Name ....

Old Testament Search—The Kingdom of God

Look up and summarize what each of the following passages has to do with the kingdom of God.

▶ **Micah 2:13**

▶ **Zephaniah 3:15**

▶ **Obadiah 1:21**

▶ **Zechariah 14:9**

▶ **Isaiah 24:23**

▶ **Jeremiah 31:31**

Name ....

Chapter 3 Test

▶ All questions worth 4 points each.

Part 1: Matching. Please match the mystery from Jesus' life in Column B with its description in Column A.

Column A	Column B
_____ 1. Simeon and Anna recognize the Messiah	A. Transfiguration
_____ 2. serves as a model for our baptism	B. circumcision of Jesus
_____ 3. Jesus' full glory is manifested during his earthly ministry	C. presentation in the Temple
_____ 4. signified Jesus' incorporation into Abraham's descendents	D. hidden life of Jesus
	E. baptism of Jesus
_____ 5. Jesus learns obedience from his parents	F. temptations of Jesus

Part 2: True or False. Mark **+** if the statement is true and **0** if the statement is false.

_____ 6. A key purpose of Matthew's infancy narrative is to show how Jesus fulfilled Old Testament prophecies about the Messiah.

_____ 7. Luke traces Jesus' genealogy to Adam to show how Jesus is the father of all Jews.

_____ 8. Luke's infancy narrative stresses the relationship between John the Baptist and Jesus.

_____ 9. The Lucan infancy narrative highlights Jesus' coming for the downtrodden.

_____ 10. According to the strictest methods of historical scholarship, scholars conclude that Jesus' baptism was a story made up to inspire early Christians to get baptized.

_____ 11. The Temptations of Jesus in the desert show how Jesus, like all humans, was a sinner.

_____ 12. When he taught, Jesus often quoted famous Jewish teachers of his day.

_____ 13. Jesus revealed himself to be an outstanding debater in his attempts to win over his opponents.

_____ 14. Jesus worked miracles primarily to force people to believe in him.

_____ 15. Jesus' miracles prove his mastery over Satan and the forces of darkness.

Part 3: Short Fill-ins.

_____ 16. What is the term for a literary form that relates past scriptural events to help explain and interpret present events?

_____ 17. ___?___ are vivid picture stories told by Jesus to convey religious truth.

_____ 18. The term ___?___ refers to God's infinite incomprehensibility and his plan for salvation and redemption in Christ Jesus.

_____ 19. The term ___?___ describes God's process of reconciling and renewing all things through his Son. It was proclaimed by Jesus and begun by his life, death, and resurrection.

_____ 20. Hebrew word that means "certainly."

Part 4: Short Answers with Discussion. List and briefly discuss five major points in the teaching of Jesus.

1. _____
2. _____
3. _____
4. _____
5. _____

Name ....

Scripture Search

What is happening in the following passages in Mark's Gospel?

1. 8:27   9:30   10:32   _____

2. 8:31   9:31   10:33-34   _____

3. 8:32-33   9:32-34   10:35-41   _____

4. 8:34-9:1   9:35-37   10:42-45   _____

5. What do 5:43, 7:36, 8:30, and 9:9 have in common?

6. List three parables found in Mark 4.

7. Write out the first saying of Jesus in Mark's Gospel (1:14).

8. What term does Jesus use for God in 14:36?

Name ....

Chapter 4 Test

▶ All questions worth 4 points each.

Part 1: Multiple Choice. Write the letter of the best choice in the space provided.

_____ 1. Mark's Gospel was probably written around:

   A. A.D. 70   B. A.D. 76   C. A.D. 80   D. A.D. 85

_____ 2. The symbol for the evangelist Mark is:

   A. an eagle   B. a man   C. a lion   D. a bull

_____ 3. Mark compares John the Baptist to which prophet?

   A. Elijah   B. Jeremiah   C. Ezekiel   D. Amos

_____ 4. Jesus' miracles included all of these *except*:

   A. exorcisms   B. healings   C. raisings from the dead   D. legerdemain

_____ 5. Jesus was seen as a threat by the authorities because of his:

   A. forgiveness of sin   D. his cleansing of the Temple

   B. disregard of cleanliness laws   E. all of these

   C. association with sinners

_____ 6. The high priest at the time of Jesus' crucifixion was:

   A. Joseph of Arimathea   B. Joseph Caiaphas   C. Nicodemus   D. Annas

Part 2—True or False: Mark **+** if the item is true and **0** if the item is false.

_____ 7. Jesus was a teacher of authority in the sense that he had original teachings.

_____ 8. Because he respected the Torah, Jesus forbade healing on the Sabbath.

_____ 9. Mark emphasizes Jesus' miracles as demonstrations of God's power (*dynamis*) breaking into human history.

_____ 10. For Jesus, repentance and faith are intimately linked.

_____ 11. By cursing a fig tree, Jesus symbolically reprimanded *Gentiles* for their lack of faith.

_____ 12. The title *Son of Man* emphasizes both Jesus' human and supernatural natures.

_____ 13. Jesus requires his followers to give up their wealth to follow him.

Part 3: Short Fill-ins

_____ 14. The term *disciple* means ___?___.

_____ 15. By claiming to forgive sin, Jesus' opponents accused him of ___?___ [name of sin].

_____ 16. Complete this quote: "Those who are well do not need a physician, but the sick do. I did not come to call the righteous but ___?___."

_____ 17. What literary term fits this definition: "A story in which people, things, and events have symbolic meanings that represent something else."

_____ 18. For Jesus, the Messiah is a ___?___ ___?___.

Name ....

_____ 19. Complete this quote: "Whoever wishes to come after me must deny himself, take up a __?__ , and follow me."

_____ 20. Complete this quote: "Amen, I say to you, whoever does not accept the kingdom of God like a __?__ will not enter it."

Part 4: Short Answers (4 points each)

Give one reason why Jesus instructed people not to reveal his identity.

_____

_____

_____

_____

Analysis: "It is like a mustard seed that, when it is sown in the ground, is the smallest of all the seeds on the earth. But once it is sown, it springs up and becomes the largest of plants and puts forth large branches, so that the birds of the sky can dwell in its shade" (Mk 4:31-32).

_____ 22. Who is the speaker?

_____ 23. What literary form is this an example of?

_____ 24. To what is the mustard seed compared?

25. What is the meaning of this story?

_____

_____

_____

_____

Name ....

Characters and Events of Matthew

The Kingdom of God Proclaimed (Mt 3–7)

▶ **major characters:**

▶ **key events:**

Christian Discipleship Proclaimed in Galilee (Mt 8–10)

▶ **major characters:**

▶ **key events:**

Opposition to Jesus Grows (Mt 11–13)

▶ **major characters:**

▶ **key events:**

Jesus the Christ and His Church (Mt 14–18)

▶ **major characters:**

▶ **key events:**

Journey to and Ministry in Jerusalem (Mt 19–25)

▶ **major characters:**

▶ **key events:**

Name ....

Jesus' Teachings

Examine your own progress on living Jesus' law of love. Check the appropriate column: **1**-means making excellent progress; **5** means having a very long way to go.

	1	2	3	4	5
Anger: I easily and properly deal with anger by not letting it fester within.					
Sexuality: I respect my own sexuality and that of others. I exercise self-discipline in thought and action.					
Oaths: I am a truthful person.					
Forgiveness: I forgive others. I don't seek revenge.					
Enemies: I am courteous to all people. I try to love people I may not particularly like.					

Name ....

The Church

Rate your own parish or school community to see if it lives up to the description of the Church given. Mark according to this scale: **+** if the description fits; **-** if it does not fit; **?** if you are not sure.

_____ 1. A community that reaches out to other people. (Mt 28:19-20)

_____ 2. A community of believers. (Rom 12:4-8)

_____ 3. A forgiving community. (Lk 19:10)

_____ 4. A community founded by Christ on Peter and the apostles. (Mt 16:15-19)

_____ 5. A loving community. (Mt 25:31-46)

_____ 6. A Eucharistic community. (1 Cor 10:15-17)

_____ 7. A community willing to suffer. (Mt 5:10-12)

_____ 8. A community of faith as taught by the apostles. (Acts 4:1-4, 33)

▶ What standards should the Church have for membership? How would Jesus answer this question?

Name ....

Chapter 5 Test

▶ All questions are worth 4 points each.

Part 1: Matching. Please match the theme of the parable in Column A with the parable listed in Column B.

Column A	Column B: Parable
_____ 1. Always be ready for Christ's return.	A. Yeast
_____ 2. Despite being opposed, God's kingdom. will grow immensely.	B. Pearl of great price
_____ 3. God's kingdom grows mysteriously.	C. Weeds among the wheat
_____ 4. Sacrifice all for God's kingdom.	D. Sower
	E. Judgment at end of time
	F. Wise virgins

Part 2: True or False. Mark **+** if the statement is true and **0** if the statement is false.

_____ 5. Matthew's gospel is listed first in the New Testament because it links well the Old Testament to the New Testament.

_____ 6. Matthew includes a number of women in his genealogy of Jesus to show that the gospel will be preached to all people.

_____ 7. Matthew tends to paint a *harsher* view of the apostles than does Mark.

_____ 8. Jesus endorses a concept of *lex talionis*, that is, reasonable retaliation.

_____ 9. The Sermon on the Mount permits divorce in the case of physical abuse.

_____ 10. Matthew's gospel stresses how Jesus fulfills Old Testament prophecies about the Messiah.

_____ 11. Apocalypse means "revelation."

_____ 12. "Eschatological" has to do with death and the end of the world.

_____ 13. To be anti-Semitic is to be anti-Christian.

Part 3: Multiple Choice. Write the letter of the best choice in the space provided.

_____ 14. Which is the Hebrew word for "hell"?

A. Talitha koum   B. Gehenna   C. Golgotha   D. Beelzebul

_____ 15. Matthew has as one of its sources all of the following *except*:

A. Luke   B. *Q*   C. *M*   D. Mark

_____ 16. This title means "God is with us":

A. Emmanuel   B. Son of Man   C. Son of David   D. Yahweh

_____ 17. The title "Son of David" in Matthew especially emphasizes that Jesus is:

A. God's Son   B. the Lord   C. the Messiah   D. the Son of Man

_____ 18. The quote, "You are Peter, and upon this rock I will build my church . . . . I will give you keys to the kingdom of heaven . . ."

A. establishes Peter as the earthly leader of Christ's Church.

B. shows Christ's intent to found a hierarchial church.

C. gives Peter and his successors the power to forgive sin and teach authoritatively.

D. all of these

E. none of these

Name ....

Part 4: Short Fill-ins.

_____ 19. Who is the founder of the Christian church?

_____ 20. Bad example that leads others to sin is __?__ .

21. "Blessed are the poor in spirit, for theirs _____ "

22. "Blessed are the merciful, for they _____ "

23. Write out the Golden Rule: _____

_____

Part 5: Short Reflection.

"You are the salt of the earth. You are the light of the world."

24. What do these words of Jesus mean?

_____

_____

_____

_____

25. Give four examples of how you can be salt and light in your world:

_____

_____

_____

_____

_____

_____

_____

_____

Name ....

Parable Themes and Reflections

Below you will find a summary of the key themes of Jesus' parables with a sample parable that illustrates that theme. Examine how you are taking to heart the message of the parables by rating yourself on the follow-up reflections. Use the following scale: **A**=I wholeheartedly believe this, and it makes a difference in my life; **B**=I am lukewarm on this; **C**=I have a long way to go to make this a reality in my life.

	A	B	C
1. God's kingdom is here. Salvation is taking place. [Mustard seed: Mk 4:30-32] **I accept that God has done and is doing marvelous things for me and for everyone.**	◯	◯	◯
2. God's kingdom is a free gift. He calls everyone to enter. [Vineyard workers: Mt 20:1-16] **I accept God's love and salvation. I thank him for all that he has given to me: my life, my talents, his friendship and love.**	◯	◯	◯
3. God loves sinners. We should be like God by forgiving those who have harmed us. [Unforgiving servant: Mt 18:23-25] **I regularly forgive those who have hurt me.**	◯	◯	◯
4. The good news demands an urgent response. We should always be ready to act on it. [Hidden treasure: Mt 13:44-46] **Every day I try to make my life an act of love by doing good for others.**	◯	◯	◯
5. God's kingdom requires repentance. We should ask for God's forgiveness when we sin. We should pray and make God our #1 priority in life by being faithful to him and by loving everyone we meet. [Wedding feast: Mt 22:1-14] **I admit I am a sinner and ask for God's forgiveness. I have a close relationship with the Lord.**	◯	◯	◯
6. God's kingdom comes with a price. It may bring suffering, but we will gain our reward. [Last judgment: Mt 25:31-46] **I am willing to suffer for my Christian beliefs.**	◯	◯	◯

Name ....

Lucan Parables

Luke's Gospel contains some of the most important of Jesus' parables. Read the following six parables. Then briefly summarize the main point of each. Finally, match its theme with one of the statements given on pages 174-175 of the Student Text.

Parable	Summary Statement	Theme Number
Lost coin and lost sheep (Lk 15:3-10)		
Places at table (Lk 14:7-14)		
Yeast (Lk 13:20-21)		
Faithful Servants (Lk 12:35-48)		
Wedding Banquet (Lk 14:16-24)		
Pharisee and tax collector (Lk 18:8-14)		

Name ....

Chapter 6 Test

▶ All questions are worth 4 points each.

Part 1: Matching. Please match the mystery from Jesus' life in Column B with its description in Column A.

Column A

_____ 1. tax collector who converted to Christ; short in stature

_____ 2. "brother of the Lord," leader of Jewish-Christians in Jerusalem

_____ 3. companion of Paul on missionary journeys

_____ 4. greatest Christian saint; prayed the Magnificat

_____ 5. first Christian martyr

_____ 6. Gospel of Luke and Acts are dedicated to him

_____ 7. Apostle to the Gentiles

_____ 8. replaced Judas as an Apostle

Column B

A. Stephen
B. Matthias
C. Cornelius
D. Good Samaritan
E. Prodigal Son
F. Barnabas
G. Paul
H. James
I. Mary
J. Theophilus
K. Demetrius
L. Zaccheus

Part 2: Multiple Choice: Write the letter of the best choice in the space provided.

_____ 9. Jesus was like Old Testament prophets. He did all of the following *except*:

A. He spoke in tongues.

B. He used attention-getting actions.

C. He warned of God's judgment on evil-doers.

D. He performed miracles.

_____ 10. Jesus' parables are important because:

A. they contain the heart of his message.

B. they show him to be a remarkable teacher.

C. they reveal how he dealt with his opponents.

D. All of the above.

E. None of the above.

_____ 11. The gospel of Luke highlights this city as a central symbol of God's salvific activity:

A. Rome   B. Antioch   C. Jerusalem   D. Capernaum

Name ....

_____ 12. According to Acts, the ideal Christian community included all of these *except*:

    A. *koinonia*

    B. excommunication of known sinners

    C. celebrating the Eucharist

    D. studying the teaching of the apostles

_____ 13. The theme of this parable is to share your gifts with poor people:

    A. Lazarus and the rich man

    B. The Lost Coin

    C. The Prodigal Son

    D. The Unjust Judge

_____ 14. The theme of this parable is God's incredible love for sinners:

    A. Lazarus and the rich man

    B. The Good Samaritan

    C. The Prodigal Son

    D. The Friend at Midnight

Part 3: True or False. Mark **+** if the statement is true and **0** if the statement is false.

_____ 15. Luke wrote primarily for a Gentile-Christian audience.

_____ 16. The author of Luke's gospel knew the historical Jesus.

_____ 17. Acts of the Apostles is properly known as the "Gospel of the Holy Spirit."

_____ 18. Unlike the gospel of Matthew, the gospel of Luke downplays the role of women in Jesus' ministry.

_____ 19. The doctrines of the Ascension and the Assumption both refer to Jesus' going to heaven.

Part 4: Short Fill-ins

_____ 20. The term *martyr* means ___?___ .

_____ 21. For Luke, the three periods of salvation history included: the age of promise; the time of Jesus; and the ___?___ .

_____ 22. The Jewish feast of ___?___ is considered the "birthday of the church."

_____ 23. This doctrine of the ___?___ of Mary holds that from the first moment of her existence, Mary was free from any alienation caused by original sin.

Part 5: Short Responses

24. What is the lesson of the parable of the Good Samaritan?

25. If Jesus were retelling the parable of the Good Samaritan today, who might he choose to be the hero of his story? Why?

Name ....

Friendship With Jesus

John's gospel expresses the great news that we, as believers, can be called friends of Jesus:

> I no longer call you slaves, because a slave does not know what his master is doing. I have called you friends, because I have told you everything I have heard from my Father. It was not you who chose me, but I who chose you and appointed you to go and bear fruit that will remain, so that whatever you ask the Father in my name he may give you. This I command you: love one another. (Jn 15:15-16)

Jesus loves each of us so much that he values our friendship. A good question, though, is what kind of friend are we to him? In a survey given to students for many years, the following qualities of friendship consistently rank as the most important ones. Judge how well this quality is in evidence in your relationships with a close friend and with your friend, Jesus.

▶ Grade according to this scale:

A=doing great;   **B**=very good;   **C**=so-so;   **D**=needs lots of work;   **E**=not present at all

Initials of your friend: _____

Quality	Friend	Jesus
1. Trust: can *always* be counted on.		
2. Honesty: truthful in relationship; holds nothing back.		
3. Loyalty: devoted and faithful.		
4. Common interests: likes the same things.		
5. Availability: makes time for the other.		
6. Caring/considerate: loving at all times.		
7. Acceptance: can be oneself without proving anything.		

Name ....

Jesus' Use of Allegory

Read John 15:1-11 to see how Jesus used allegory in his teaching. Recall that an allegory has a number of points of comparison. Answer the following questions.

▶ Who is the vine?

▶ Who is the vinegrower?

▶ What does the pruning process represent?

▶ Who are the branches?

▶ What happens if the branches remain attached to the vine?

▶ What does the fruit represent?

Name ....

Christian Leadership

Jesus upset many conventional ideas about leadership when he taught that its primary quality is service. Here are some traits of leadership modeled by Jesus. In column 1, rank these from the ones you think are **most important (1)** to **least important (10)**. In column 2, check those that you believe you possess.

Leadership quality	1	2
Service: ability to serve others		
Dynamic: powerful personality		
Warm: friendly, open, and compassionate		
Intelligent: brains to do the job		
Flexible: can change when necessary		
Authentic: practices what he or she preaches		
Courageous: will take calculated risks		
Task-oriented: focuses on outcomes		
Motivator: can get others to join in		
Confident: inspires trust in others		
Other: [add your own]		

Name ....

Chapter 7 Test

▶ All questions are worth 4 points each.

Part 1: Matching. Please match the title of Jesus from John's gospel in Column B with its description in Column A.

Column A

_____ 1. Jesus is willing to die for his flock.

_____ 2. Jesus is YAHWEH.

_____ 3. Jesus is the source of eternal life; we can receive him in the Eucharist.

_____ 4. Jesus reveals God and is God revealed.

_____ 5. Jesus is the beacon who points us to the Father.

Column B

A. Bread of Life

B. Light of the World

C. Word of God

D. Good Shepherd

E. Vine

F. Resurrection & Life

G. "I AM"

Part 2: Multiple Choice. Write the letter of the best choice in the space provided.

_____ 6. Which miracle shows that Jesus, like God, is master of the Sabbath?
      A. Miracle of the wine at Cana
      B. Cure of the paralytic at the pool
      C. Feeding of the 5,000
      D. Walking on water

_____ 7. Which miracle points to Moses' miracle during the Exodus?
      A. Miracle of the wine at Cana
      B. Cure of the paralytic at the pool
      C. Feeding of the 5,000
      D. Raising of Lazarus from the dead

_____ 8. Which miracle reveals God at work in Jesus?
      A. Miracle of the wine at Cana
      B. Cure of the official's son
      C. Feeding of the 5,000
      D. Raising of Lazarus from the dead
      E. All of the above

_____ 9. Jesus tells which person that he must be born again of water and the Spirit?
      A. Joseph of Arimathea
      B. Nicodemus
      C. Nathaniel
      D. all of the above
      E. none of the above

_____ 10. John has all the following in common with the synoptic gospels *except*
      A. an infancy narrative.
      B. the multiplication of loaves and fishes.
      C. a passion narrative.
      D. a definite audience for whom the gospel is directed.

Name ....

Part 3: True or False. Mark **+** if the statement is true and **0** if the statement is false.

_____ 11. John's Gospel was written around A.D. 80.

_____ 12. John's Gospel was written to bolster the faith of Jewish-Christians expelled from synagogues.

_____ 13. John's Gospel is the most theologically advanced of the four gospels.

_____ 14. "The glory of God" refers to the visible revelation of the power of the invisible God.

_____ 15. There is very clear proof in the gospel of John that the Beloved Disciple refers to John Zebedee.

_____ 16. St. Thomas gives the loftiest profession of faith in the gospel of John when he proclaims, "My Lord and my God."

_____ 17. Because Jesus calls us his friends, he does not require anything of us except to accept his friendship.

Part 3: Short Fill-ins.

_____ 18. That branch of theology that studies the meaning of the person of Christ is ___?___ .

_____ 19. A name for the Holy Spirit, an advocate, a helper, promised by Jesus in John 14:6 ___?___ .

_____ 20. Finish this quote: "God so loved the world that he gave his only Son so that everyone who believes in him ___?___ ."

Part 4: Short Response

Please list three facts about the resurrection narrative on which _all_ the gospels agree:

21. _____

_____

22. _____

_____

23. _____

Briefly discuss two major consequences for us because Jesus rose from the dead:

24. _____

_____

_____

25. _____

_____

_____

_____

Name ....

Passage Commentary Paper—Paul's Letters

Directions: Write a 750-word commentary paper on a selected passage in one of Paul's letters. Suggested passages include:

1 Thessalonians
Mission of Timothy (3:1-8)
Chastity and Charity (4:1-12)

1 Corinthians
Body of Christ (12:12-31)
Love (13)

Philemon
Dignity of All (entire letter)

Galatians
Called by Christ (1:10-24)
Justification Through Faith
(3:1-14)

2 Corinthians
False Apostles (11:1-15)

Romans
Faith, Hope, and Love (5:1-15)
Love and Law (13:8-10)

Use the following outline to help you organize your paper:
I. Text of the Passage
What does the passage say?

II. Content of the Passage
What do biblical commentaries and scholars say about the passage?
Analyze based on historical criticism, source criticism, form criticism, and redaction criticism.

III. Interpret the Passage
What does the passage mean for our world?
What does this passage mean for me?

Name ....

Chapter 8 Test

▶ Questions 1 to 22 are worth 4 points each.

Part 1: Multiple Choice. Write the letter of the best choice in the space provided.

_____ 1. Which is *not* true of St. Paul?
   A. tent-maker by profession
   B. Sadducee
   C. born in Tarsus
   D. Roman citizen

_____ 2. St. Paul was baptized by:
   A. Peter
   B. Philip
   C. Barnabas
   D. Ananias

_____ 3. All of these are one of Paul's "great letters" *except*:
   A. Galatians
   B. Romans
   C. Ephesians
   D. 1 Corinthians

_____ 4. Most scholars consider all of these as deuteropauline writings *except*:
   A. Titus
   B. 1 Timothy
   C. Philippians
   D. 2 Thessalonians

_____ 5. Paul's first epistle, acknowledged to be the earliest book in the New Testament:
   A. 1 Thessalonians
   B. 1 Corinthians
   C. Philemon
   D. Romans

_____ 6. Which of the following is a theological theme stressed by St. Paul?
   A. Jesus is Lord of the universe.
   B. Salvation is God's free gift.
   C. The Holy Spirit enables us to call God Abba.
   D. Christians are members of Christ's body, the Church.
   E. All of the above.

_____ 7. Which of the following is *not* a theme of Paul's preaching?
   A. Being a Christian means willingness to suffer for the Lord.
   B. Good works are necessary to earn God's gift of salvation.
   C. Christians will participate in Christ's resurrection.
   D. The brothers and sisters of Jesus are required to love.
   E. None of the above.

Name ....

_____ 8. Paul's theme of "justification" primarily means:
   A. salvation
   B. repentance
   C. redemption
   D. right relationship with God

_____ 9. Paul's companion at the time of his writing Philippians was:
   A. Timothy
   B. Peter
   C. Ananias
   D. Lydia

_____ 10. This, Paul's longest letter, is acknowledged to be his masterpiece:
   A. 1 Corinthians
   B. Colossians
   C. Galatians
   D. Romans

Part 2: True or False. Mark **+** if the statement is true and **0** if the statement is false.

_____ 11. Paul required his converts to accept the customs and laws of Judaism before receiving Christian baptism.

_____ 12. "Judaizers" were strong supporters of St. Paul in his ministry.

_____ 13. In his joyful letter to the Philippians, Paul teaches that we must conform ourselves to Christ's Paschal mystery as the key to living a holy life.

_____ 14. Paul teaches that God's rejection of the Jewish people is final, thus paving the way for the conversion of Gentiles.

_____ 15. Pseudonymous authorship was common and accepted in the ancient world.

_____ 16. St. Paul teaches that Christians are obligated to feed their fellow believers, even if these believers refuse to work.

_____ 17. Gnostics had a high regard for the human body.

_____ 18. The Pastoral Epistles reveal that overseers of early Christian communities had to remain unmarried or they could not be leaders.

Part 3: Short Fill-ins.

_____ 19. According to St. Paul's letter to Corinthians, the greatest spiritual gift is ___?___ .

_____ 20. For St. Paul, ___?___ is the fulfillment of the Law.

_____ 21. Finish this quote: "If God is for us, who___?___ ."

_____ 22. Who is the image of the invisible God?

Part 4: Brief Essay (worth 12 points)

Pretend that you are St. Paul writing to one of his churches in Asia Minor. A conflict has come to your attention concerning Christians who are arguing about money. Write a paragraph to instruct them how they should act. Discuss at least three points that draw on the theological insights of St. Paul.

Name ....

Your Knowledge About Jesus

This chapter will summarize some of the Church's major dogmatic statements about Jesus that developed in the early Church. (A *dogma* is a central doctrine or teaching of the Church taught with the highest authority and solemnity by the Pope and bishops.) Test what you know about Jesus by answering these questions **true (+)** or **false (0)**.

_____ 1. There was a time when Jesus was not God.

_____ 2. As light is identical to the light from which it comes, Jesus Christ is true God.

_____ 3. The Father made the Son.

_____ 4. The Son of God shared in the creation of the world.

_____ 5. There are two "persons" in Christ.

_____ 6. It is wrong to call Mary "the Mother of God."

_____ 7. Christ has two natures.

_____ 8. Jesus' divine nature swallows up his human nature.

_____ 9. Jesus shows us God in a human way.

_____ 10. Because he was God, Jesus did not have a human intellect.

Name ....

The Nicene Creed

Review the statements of the Nicene Creed. Then rate your own beliefs on major points of Christian teaching which stem from this creed according to this scale:

1—firm belief   **2**—good belief   **3**—a little shaky   **4**—not sure

_____ I believe in God the Father, Creator of all that is seen and unseen.

_____ I believe that Jesus Christ is God and human.

_____ I believe that Jesus died and rose again.

_____ I believe Jesus is my friend.

_____ I believe in the power of the Holy Spirit.

_____ I believe in the Ten Commandments.

_____ I believe that each person is God's child and my brother or sister.

_____ I believe that I must love everyone, especially "the least of these" in our midst.

_____ I believe in the power of the sacraments, especially the Eucharist and reconciliation.

_____ I believe that the pope is the successor to Peter, the vicar of Christ.

_____ I believe in the Trinity, three persons in one God.

_____ I believe in the power of prayer.

_____ I believe that the Lord will judge me at the end of time.

_____ I believe that I must love God above everything and my neighbor as myself.

_____ I believe in the Catholic Church.

_____ I believe that I am destined for an eternal life of glory with the Lord.

▶ Choose two statements. Write one paragraph for each that explains your response.

Name ....

Chapter 9   Test

▶   All items are worth 4 points each.

Part 1: Multiple Choice. Write the letter of the best choice in the space provided.

_____ 1. The central theological point of the epistle of the Hebrews is that:

        A. Jesus will soon come in glory.

        B. Jesus is the High Priest, our model of faith.

        C. Jesus is the Suffering Servant.

        D. Jesus is the Son of God.

_____ 2. Which of the following is _not_ a "Catholic" epistle?

        A. 1 Peter

        B. 3 John

        C. Titus

        D. James

_____ 3. The Catholic Epistles are so named because:

        A. They give general advice for all the churches.

        B. They were eventually accepted by Eastern and Western churches.

        C. They help reveal how the universal church grew.

        D. All of these.

        E. None of these.

_____ 4. Which epistle stresses social justice themes that are widely admired today?

        A. James

        B. 2 Peter

        C. 1 John

        D. Hebrews

_____ 5. The first letter of Peter teaches all of the following about suffering _except_:

        A. Christians should bless their persecutors.

        B. Christians should persist in doing good despite hardships.

        C. Christians should see suffering as a share in Christ's cross.

        D. Christians should interpret personal suffering as a punishment from God.

_____ 6. The latest New Testament writing is generally believed to be:

        A. 2 Peter

        B. Revelation

        C. 3 John

        D. Jude

_____ 7. The number 7 in the Book of Revelation signifies:

        A. imperfection

        B. the Church

        C. the world

        D. wholeness

_____ 8. Babylon in Revelation is a symbol for:

        A. Rome

        B. Antioch

        C. Jerusalem

        D. Damascus

Name ....

_____ 9. The greatest Father of the church was:
- A. St. Cyril
- B. St. Jerome
- C. St. Augustine of Hippo
- D. St. Athanasius

_____ 10. Which heresy claimed that Jesus, God's Son, was the Father's greatest creature, but not divine?
- A. Monophysitism
- B. Arianism
- C. Docetism
- D. Nestorianism

Part 2: True or False. Mark **+** if the statement is true and **0** if the statement is false.

_____ 11. The letter of Jude teaches that we need an objective standard of Christian faith and morality, namely, the teaching of the apostles.

_____ 12. The Catholic Church teaches that we should not use the symbols of the book of Revelation to identify *specific* political leaders living today.

_____ 13. The Revelation to John teaches that we must at all times worship the one true God and him alone.

_____ 14. *Apologists* were defenders of the faith.

_____ 15. *Docetism* taught that Jesus only seemed to be God.

_____ 16. God the Father *created* God the Son.

_____ 17. When we call Mary *Theotokos* we are affirming that she is the "Mother of God."

Part 3: Fill-ins.

_____ 18. According to the letter of James, faith without ___?___ is dead.

_____ 19. The number 666 in the Book of Revelation refers to ___?___ .

_____ 20. The Council of Chalcedon taught that Jesus is one divine person with ___?___ .

Part 4: Brief Essay

List and briefly discuss the meaning of five of your favorite titles of Jesus. Mention why you like each of your choices.

21. _____

22. _____

23. _____

24. _____

25. _____

Name ....

Recognizing Christ

As a review, name some of the people from the New Testament who met and recognized Jesus. Check the references to see how many you got right.

_____ 1.   This person said, "Come see a man who told me everything I have done. Could he possibly be the Messiah?" (Jn 4:29)

_____ 2.   This man said, "Who are you, sir?" After Jesus revealed himself to the man, he found out that he was blinded. (Acts 9:5-9)

_____ 3.   They traveled with Jesus for seven miles without knowing who he was, but came to realize who he was when they had dinner with him. (Lk 24:13-31)

_____ 4.   He said, "You are the Messiah, the Son of the living God." (Mt 16:16)

_____ 5.   This man thought Jesus was the Son of God because Jesus told him, "I saw you under the fig tree." (Jn 1:48-50)

_____ 6.   They recognized Jesus as a king when they gave him gifts of gold, frankincense, and myrrh. (Mt 2:1-11)

_____ 7.   Some thought this man was the Messiah but he said, "One mightier than I is coming. I am not worthy to loosen the thongs of his sandals." (Lk 3:16)

_____ 8.   This person said, "My Lord and my God!" Jesus answered him, "Blessed are those who have not seen and have believed." (Jn 20:28-29)

_____ 9.   When he saw Jesus, he cried out and fell down before him; in a loud voice he shouted, "What have you to do with me, Jesus, son of the Most High God? I beg you, do not torment me!" (Lk 8:28-30)

_____ 10. Jesus refused to perform miracles for this person. In talking with him, Jesus quoted some passages from the Old Testament including, "Again it is written, 'You shall not put the Lord, your God, to the test'" (Mt 4:1-11)

You (What would you say to Jesus?):

_____

_____

_____

_____

Name ....

Chapter 10 Test

• • • • • • • • • • •

▶ All questions are worth 4 points each.

Part 1: Matching. Please match the sacrament in Column B with its description in Column A.

Column A

———	1.	Strength to endure sufferings of old age
———	2.	Creates and celebrates Christian community
———	3.	Forgives original sin
———	4.	Renewal and healing of friendship with God the Christian community
———	5.	Strengthens faith commitment by showering the gifts of the Holy Spirit

Column B

A. Holy Orders

B. Confirmation

C. Matrimony

D. Reconciliation

E. Anointing of the Sick

F. Eucharist

G. Baptism

Part 2: True or False. Mark **+** if the statement is true and **0** if the statement is false.

——— 6. A concordance will help you locate where a particular word appears in your Bible.

——— 7. *Affective* prayer involves one's feelings and imagination.

——— 8. In *meditative* prayer, we empty our minds of thoughts about everything and just sit in God's presence.

——— 9. We should always trust contemporary television documentaries to be objective when they portray Jesus' life.

——— 10. We cannot say we love Jesus if we do not find him in the hurting, lonely, poor, and suffering people in our world.

Part 3: Fill-ins.

_____ 11. This virtue enables us to see the reality of who Jesus Christ truly is.

_____ 12. The word Eucharist means ___?___.

_____ 13. The Church is like a ___?___, that is, a visible sign and instrument of the hidden mystery and reality of salvation in Jesus Christ.

_____ 14. Which saint said that we are the hands, feet, eyes, and voice of Christ responding to the needy in our midst?

_____ 15. The church is the Body of Christ and the Temple of the ___?___.

Part 4: Essay

Suppose an extremely wealthy producer came to you to write a movie script on the life of Jesus. Based on your knowledge of Jesus and the New Testament, list ten events or specific teachings of Jesus that you absolutely want to include in your film. Then give a reason why you picked each particular event or teaching.

Key event/teaching	Reason for Choice
16.	
17.	
18.	
19.	
20.	
21.	
22.	
23.	
24.	
25.	

Notes

1   All quotes taken from *General Directory for Catechesis* (Washington, D.C.: United States Catholic Conference, 1997), #98-99, pp. 92-94.

2   Pope John Paul II, *Apostolic Exhortation* Catechesi Tradendae (Washington, DC: United States Catholic Conference, n.d.), pp. 9-10.

3   As of this writing, the National Catechetical Directory, *Sharing the Light of Faith*, is undergoing revision. The quote cited is from the first edition copyright date 1979, United States Conference of Bishops, p. 126.

4   *Guidelines on Doctrine for Catechetical Materials* (Washington, D.C.: United States Catholic Conference, 1990), p. 5-6.

5   "Churches must use outreach to combat 'biblical illiteracy'" at http://www.wfn.org/1999/01/msg00063.html